Other People's Dreams

Other People's Dreams

Myra Love

Long Beak
Productions

Long Beak
Productions

ISBN 978-1-105-75017-5

Cover design by Martha Merson
with gratitude to B.H. Bentzman, Laura DeSantis, and Valerie Martin
for their assistance with layout and design,
and to Martha for her relentless editing.

Table of Contents

PROLOGUE
1965
❖

"Lettie, someone is at the door."

Leticia sighed, wishing that for once her mother would answer the door without being asked. "Would you please..." she called out, but Lucille interrupted, "I'm in the bathroom."

Leticia moved quickly as usual, though her body felt heavy. When she opened the door, she was surprised to see Susan Russell, Lieutenant Colonel Susan Russell, her late husband's closest friend and colleague. The familiar scent of Susan's cologne was reassuring. Leticia realized that she and Susan had not been alone together since Paul's funeral.

Leticia felt proud of herself for getting through the awkward conversation that followed without tears. The two women exchanged addresses and promised to keep in touch. Then Lieutenant Colonel Russell handed Leticia a large manila envelope. "Memorabilia," she said with an off-center smile. "Be sure to take a look before you decide to let the matter go." Then she was gone, and Leticia added the envelope to the pile on the second shelf of the bookcase. She knew Susan wanted her to keep pressing for a fuller investigation, but she felt that she just didn't have the strength. Susan had her suspicions, as indeed Leticia did. But neither woman had any real evidence. The envelopes Susan kept sending her contained pictures and copies of documents, but nothing of substance that pertained to what Susan persisted in calling "the matter." Leticia was positive this envelope would be the same. With a soft sigh she went looking for Lucille.

"Mother, what are you doing?" she called out. She heard a muffled response and made her way through the tiny house to the far bathroom that Paul had claimed for his own.

"I'm cleaning the bathroom," Lucille replied. When Leticia walked in, she saw her mother's fashionably dressed figure reflected eight times in the double mirror. The sight made her dizzy, so she grabbed onto the counter. Lucille was frowning intently at the armful of toiletries she was poised to unload into a large, black, trash bag.

"You don't need to do that right now," Leticia protested. She walked briskly over to Lucille and tried to move the items back onto the counter. "I have a system for sorting. Anyway, let's have a cup of tea before we tackle this room."

3

"Nonsense," Lucille retorted, easily keeping the toiletries within her control. She deposited them into the bag. "Not even a beggar wants a used razor or deodorant."

"You're dumping the razor? Paul loved that!" Leticia objected.

"Exactly my point, Lettie. Who else would use a straight razor with a big nick in the blade? Paul is gone. You need to let him go. After tea, I'll make a run to the dump for you." She brushed past her daughter, trash bag in hand. "You're not very practical, Lettie. You never were," she announced heartily. "It's a good thing I'm here."

Leticia sighed for what felt like the hundredth time that day and followed her mother out of the bathroom.

CHAPTER 1
LET'S RENT A JEEP
1980
❖

Virginia Carr, M.D., closed the office door behind her and walked down the hospital corridor. Her day was finally over, and she looked forward to nothing so much as a long, hot shower.

"Good-bye, Dr. Carr," one of the older nurses said as Virginia passed her. Virginia waved. "Have a good evening, Mrs. Haverhill," she replied, as she pushed the door and emerged into the cool, humid San Francisco evening. She walked purposefully towards the parking lot, looking neither right nor left until she heard a voice very near her ear.

"My, my, you are preoccupied, Doctor. Some stranger could snatch you away and you would hardly even notice."

Virginia grinned but didn't look up. "Need a ride home, Dr. Matthews, or are you planning to walk?" she teased.

The tall woman with brown eyes who'd spoken to her reached out and took her arm. "I'd love a ride. How kind of you to offer! And I'd love to jump in the shower as soon as I get in the door of our home sweet home."

"If you want a ride, you're going to have to let me have the first shower, Carrie." Virginia squeezed the hand that clasped her arm.

"Agreed! Unless you'd rather shower together."

Virginia lifted an eyebrow, and the two women let go of each other and got into Virginia's black Volvo.

"Good God, Virginia," Carolyn complained as she always did, "when are you going to get something a little less flashy than this traveling church pew?"

Virginia put the car in gear and ignored the complaint. Her car was a joke to her flamboyant lover, who could not understand why a successful, young endocrinologist would drive a four year-old, black Volvo instead of something more fashionable. Carolyn adored her own car, a bright purple Alfa Romeo, which broke down constantly. Virginia preferred the black Volvo because it was reliable, safe, and understated, just as she imagined she was herself. She drove towards the ocean, enjoying the breeze that dispelled the close, pervasive dampness of the spring evening.

"Don't forget to pick up your car at the shop tomorrow morning," she reminded Carolyn, who frowned and shook her head.

"Why, oh why, my dearest Virginia, do you always pick the most unlikely times to remind me of what I have to do?" she queried. "Do you really believe that telling me now will help me remember tomorrow?"

"I remind you when I remember," Virginia said simply. "Anyway, you're the one who got me thinking about cars when you started in on this one."

"Well," Carolyn suggested, "instead of cars, you could think about going to Tahiti with me in July. I'd like to book our flights this week."

***

Virginia wandered around the house straightening up after the cleaning woman. She opened the blinds, rearranged the crystal cat and mouse, and turned her rocking chair toward the window so she could watch the streetlights flicker across the bay. Twenty-four hours earlier she had, much to Carolyn's amusement, straightened up in anticipation of the cleaning woman's arrival. Carolyn's amusement had made Virginia laugh then. Now, however, her mood was serious. She had made her weekly call to her father at noon, but hadn't reached him. Instead Toni, his office manager, had spoken with her. Toni was upset because two of her best staffers had quit after receiving a severe tongue-lashing from Dr. Henry Carr for relatively minor mistakes. "I don't like to go bearing tales," Toni had told Virginia, "but I can't be held accountable if Dr. Carr upsets my best people so they up and quit on me. He never used to be a screamer when your mother, God rest her dear soul, was alive, but in the last few years, he's changed. I don't know if you've noticed."

Virginia had indeed noticed. In fact, she and Carolyn had discussed Henry's irascible behavior after his last visit with them in San Francisco four months earlier. He'd almost gotten them thrown out of their favorite restaurant when he'd picked a fight with the waiter. He'd been irritable in the past, though not to quite the same degree. Maybe Toni was right.

The overpowering smell of Windex was giving her a headache, so Virginia waited for Carolyn to pour her some wine before broaching the subject of their summer plans. She knew Carolyn wasn't going to be thrilled with what she had to say, so she braced herself before speaking.

"You want to do what?" Carolyn howled. She corked the wine and sat down on a bar stool looking devastated.

6

"I want to stay in the continental United States," Virginia explained patiently. "Henry isn't getting any younger, and I spoke with Toni today, who said his behavior in the office is becoming erratic. I want to be easily reachable in case I'm needed."

"Jesus H. Christ, Virginia!" Carolyn exclaimed. "Your father isn't ninety years old, you know. He's been coping pretty well since your mother's death."

"Come on, Carrie! He's gotten more irritable each time he's visited."

Carolyn sighed. "Maybe he doesn't do well away from home. Or maybe he's just acting out to get you to move back to Hicksville. You know that's what he really wants."

"Still," Virginia persisted, "it's better if I'm not too far away."

Carolyn shook her head. "Hello-o!" she exclaimed. "Ever heard of long distance telephone? There is even such a thing as international calling!"

Virginia sat unmoved, and Carolyn jumped up and paced the room before sitting down again with a thump. "I just don't know what your problem is," she murmured plaintively. "I really don't know."

"Oh, yes you do," Virginia teased. "I just need a good psychiatrist, preferably one with a background in neurophysiology and a particular interest in diseases of the brain." She walked over to Carolyn and began rubbing her shoulders.

"You have a good psychiatrist," Carolyn grumbled, still annoyed. "You just don't listen to her, that's all."

"How about Yosemite?" Virginia suggested tentatively.

"Yosemite!" Carolyn groaned. "Yosemite!"

"Okay, not Yosemite. How about, I don't know, Sun Valley or the Grand Canyon or Yellowstone?"

"I'm dreaming of sunning on volcanic islands and scuba diving in warm Pacific waters, and you offer me Yogi Bear country?" Carolyn gestured emphatically.

"Well, I don't want to go to Tahiti," Virginia said firmly, leaving Carolyn's side. She checked the tortellini, then ransacked the refrigerator for some salad dressing.

"How about Thailand?" Carolyn ventured. "It's the sex capital of Asia. At least that's what Jill said."

"The heterosex capital of Asia," Virginia corrected, "where a lot of young girls get forced into prostitution. Thanks, but no thanks."

"Hmph, shows how much you know!" Carolyn grumbled.

7

Virginia grinned at her. "Anyway Jill is a sex maniac and I'm not."

"Tell me about it!" Carolyn affected a complaining tone of voice. "I ought to go and sleep with Jill."

"And get an STD you probably never even heard of," Virginia said dryly. "I didn't know you were interested in straight women."

"I'm not," Carolyn admitted, "and your sex drive is just fine. I was just trying to make you mad."

"Because I don't want to go to Tahiti?"

Carolyn shrugged. "Yeah, but that's not all. I think you want to go to Grant's Hill."

"So you know the name of the place isn't Hicksville. I'm impressed," Virginia laughed, swinging Carolyn's bar stool around to face her. "I'm not going to Grant's Hill this summer because you don't want to, Carrie, and I want us to take a vacation together. But someday soon Henry is going to be too old to work there, and he and I planned many years ago that I would take over his practice when that happened. I'm not about to do that, but we both need to understand that he'll be disappointed." Virginia put her face against Carolyn's neck. "Umm, you smell good."

"Don't change the subject!" Carolyn ordered, running her hand down Virginia's side. "Now tell me again where you want to go this summer? Besides Grant's Hill, I mean."

"The Rockies," Virginia whispered into Carolyn's ear. "You pick the precise place, okay? You're better at that."

"I'll look into it," Carolyn agreed. "Sun Valley could be nice, if it's not overrun with tourists."

***

Later in the evening over coffee, Carolyn returned to the subject of their vacation. Hoping Virginia was in a conciliatory mood, she asked, "Hey, can we drive my car?"

"If you're sure it won't break down," Virginia agreed graciously.

"Hell, I never think it's going to break down," Carolyn retorted.

"But it always does, doesn't it?" Virginia replied before she was able to stop herself. "Maybe we should take the Volvo. That way we'll be sure to get where we're going."

Carolyn moaned as if her stomach hurt, "Oooh no! Not the Volvo! That car makes me feel like an undertaker."

That's really lame, Carrie!" Virginia retorted, laughing.

8

"Hey, why not a compromise?" Carolyn suggested. "Let's rent a Jeep!"

It was Virginia's turn to groan. "Those things turn over way too easily, Carrie. They're not safe, they're not comfortable, and they don't carry as much luggage as my Volvo."

"Aw, come on and live a little, Virginia. They're not unsafe unless you take turns at seventy-five or eighty."

"Which is exactly what you do, Carrie. Admit it!"

Carolyn refused to answer, choosing instead to swear about the fact that neither of them had remembered to pick up cat food.

***

In the third week of July Virginia and Carolyn left for Jackson Hole, gateway to the Grand Teton mountain range. Carolyn had looked into and suggested a number of places, but in the end it was Virginia who had chosen. Carolyn got her way about the Jeep, though it wasn't the bright red vehicle she had wished for, but a more sedate white one, much to Virginia's relief. "I read that bright red cars get more speeding tickets," she'd observed, causing Carolyn to roll her eyes. "A nice burgundy Jeep would be all right though."

"Burgundy?" Carolyn repeated in mock outrage. "The only thing to do with burgundy..."

"I know, I know," Virginia completed her sentence, "is to drink it. But a burgundy-colored car would be a good compromise. You could pretend it was bright red, and I could escape terminal embarrassment."

"What's embarrassing about a red Jeep?" Carolyn demanded.

"It's too loud, Carrie. I prefer something more subtle."

Carolyn shook her head in astonishment. "How did you end up with me then?" she asked, sounding truly perplexed.

"As I remember, I didn't really have all that much of a choice," Virginia replied archly.

Ultimately neither of them had a choice about the Jeep. White was what was available, so white was what they drove off the rental lot. Carolyn complained that it was colorless, giving Virginia a chance to disagree and hold forth on the nature of color and the physics of light. Impatient with what she thought of as the Carr family tendency to deliver science lectures at the drop of a hat, Carolyn turned up the radio.

***

It was late morning, when they finally sat down to breakfast at the Bear Creek Lodge.

"I'm starving," Carolyn announced. Virginia, who never slept well during her first night away from home, just grunted.

Over her breakfast menu Carolyn mouthed something at Virginia, who was in no mood to lip-read. Virginia groaned. "What did you say?"

"Shh!" Carolyn whispered. "I said, I think you have a secret admirer. There's a man across the room who's been staring at you ever since we sat down."

"That's ridiculous," Virginia replied in her usual conversational tone. "You're the one men stare at." She picked up her menu.

Carolyn, with her long brown hair, long legs, and brightly colored leathers and silks, was usually the one men stared at, as she was the first to admit. But there was no doubt in her mind that this particular man had his eye on Virginia.

"Damn it, Sweetpea, I know when men are staring at me, and this guy isn't. He's not the type who's interested in me anyway. Too stern-looking and middle-aged."

Virginia started to turn her head, but Carolyn kicked her under the table. "Ignore him and he'll go away! He's giving me the creeps."

Virginia sighed. "So if you want me to ignore him, why did you tell me about him?" She shook her head but managed to resist looking behind her. The middle-aged man, however, continued to stare for another five minutes. Then he got up and approached their table.

"Excuse me," he said, clearing his throat nervously, "but aren't you Miss Carr, Dr. Henry Carr's daughter?"

"That's Dr. Carr," Carolyn replied quickly and haughtily, but Virginia stopped her with a look before she could say anything else.

"Sorry," the man said, his eyes crinkling in what could almost pass for a smile. "It would be Dr. Carr by now, wouldn't it? You probably don't remember me since you were about fourteen the last time we saw each other."

Virginia looked at him appraisingly for a moment then said, "Your face is familiar, but I expect to see the body it's attached to in a police uniform." She smiled. "You're Officer Johnson. Did you ever make it to law school?"

10

A slight shadow passed over the man's face. "No, Ma'am, I didn't. But I did get a promotion. Now I'm Captain Johnson of the Wyoming State Police."

"It's good to see you again, Captain Johnson," Virginia replied, extending her hand. "This is my friend, Dr. Matthews."

Carolyn's greeting was a smirk, and her eyes implored Virginia not to do what she knew Virginia was about to do. Virginia ignored her. "Would you care to join us, Captain Johnson?" she offered, indicating the empty chair next to Carolyn, who rolled her eyes upwards until only the whites were showing.

"No, thank you, Ma'am, I don't want to interrupt your meal. But if you have a little time, why don't you drop by the state police barracks right outside the town limits. Anyone local can give you directions. I'd love to talk a bit about old times."

Virginia's smile faded and her face took on a vacant look. "I don't reminisce much, Officer, I mean, Captain Johnson. I haven't kept in touch with the people I used to know in Grant's Hill. So if you want an update, I'm the wrong person to ask, I'm afraid."

The policeman smiled grimly. "I might be able to update you a bit. You'd be surprised how much a policeman gets to hear, even clear on the other side of the country. I'm on duty from eight in the morning to six these days. Be seeing you."

He walked stiffly to the exit. Virginia chewed her lip as she watched him leave, while Carolyn regarded her with equal parts consternation and concern. Finally Carolyn broke the silence. "I guess," she said, exhaling, "that I'm fated to be immersed in Grant's Hill this summer. Maybe it's my punishment for not letting you honor your father and all that." Virginia smiled vaguely and looked at the menu again. "Are you really going to go talk to him?" Carolyn asked.

"I don't know," Virginia answered. "Maybe. Maybe not. It all depends. I have to think about it. In the meantime, let's order."

But Carolyn was, for once, not to be distracted by the promise of food. "Depends on what?" she persisted.

Virginia shrugged her shoulders. "Didn't you say you were starving? Let's just order and eat, okay?" She waved at a waitress, who delivered more coffee and recommended the flapjacks with huckleberry syrup.

11

CHAPTER 2
CAPTAIN JOHNSON'S CASE
1980
❖

Virginia and Carolyn slid easily into a vacation routine. Aside from collecting wildflowers, Virginia was content to sit on their porch in the rustic swing and read. She was glad Carolyn had insisted that they not spend their vacation with her father, though she still felt a little guilty. She felt a bit less guilty when she remembered that she had insisted they stay in the country, just in case he needed her. She hoped he wouldn't need her or claim that he did.

Carolyn offered Virginia massages with scented oils and soothing lotions during their daily siestas. No matter how much she pressed and rubbed, working her way from freckled shoulders to milky thighs, Virginia's muscles remained tense. "Hey, Sweetpea," Carolyn whispered one sunny afternoon, "I'm the one who's been climbing hills and hiking all over the place. Why are you the one with the tight muscles?"

Virginia didn't answer, but the truth was that she was becoming increasingly anxious as their time away progressed. Eric Johnson's unexpected appearance had not only brought back memories of her summers with Leticia, but it had also sparked a nagging worry about his intentions. Although she doubted that he had anything sinister in mind since he had, she believed, come upon her by sheer coincidence, still she worried that he might spring something on her, perhaps some incriminating photos from her teen years.

She shuddered at the idea that someone might have spied on her and Leticia, but how damaging could anything from seventeen years ago really be? She knew that he had no recent dirt on her. Between her carefree summers with Leticia and her settled life with Carolyn she could remember no indiscretions whatsoever. During her undergraduate years she had kept to herself. There were no gay or lesbian student organizations back then, and even if there had been, it was unlikely that she'd have joined them. She was too busy studying. After graduating first in her class with a major in biology and a minor in chemistry, she'd gone on to medical school in Washington, D.C., where she persisted in her solitary ways. She ignored marches and meetings and declined invitations of all sorts. Eventually a young man in her cohort took her to a gay bar where she met some women. But even then she remained alone.

During the last month of her endocrinology residency, Virginia received the offer of a position with a medical group based at the hospital of the University of California in San Francisco. She had had offers in the Midwest, the Southwest, and in Seattle, but she turned them down. The idea of living in San Francisco appealed to her, and she liked the other doctors she met on her interview trip. A young, brash neurologist named Carolyn Matthews was particularly intriguing. She was a rising star at the hospital, having recently completed a second residency in psychiatry while working full-time as a consulting neurologist. Virginia went back to San Francisco once more before officially accepting the position. She spent most of her time with Carolyn, who teased, entertained and occasionally outraged her. At first she'd reminded Virginia of Leticia, but it soon became clear that Carolyn was steady and capable of great commitment. She made it obvious that she had every intention of becoming Virginia's life partner, if Virginia was willing to take the chance of a move across the country.

Much to her parents' initial chagrin, Virginia moved to San Francisco and set up a household with Dr. Carolyn Matthews, her cat Krishna, and a tank full of tropical fish that Carolyn called "cat TV." Exactly eleven years had passed to the day since Virginia's last encounter with Leticia Barnes.

***

Virginia had no idea how much Eric Johnson had learned about her life since he'd left Grant's Hill, but she realized that wondering and worrying were ruining her vacation. So after three days of indecision she decided to accept his invitation. She and Carolyn were canoeing down a small river when Virginia broke the news. "I'm thinking about going to see that state policeman," she began hesitantly. "He and my father got along really well when they both worked in Grant's Hill. I'm sure Henry would be tickled to hear how he's been all these years."

"Sounds good to me," Carolyn responded reasonably enough.

Virginia shrugged. "I don't know though. I'm worried that he'll want to reminisce and fill me in on the lives and whereabouts of everyone we used to know. I just don't want to hear about them."

"About her, you mean," Carolyn interjected. "You don't want to hear about old what's-her-name."

13

Sometimes Virginia regretted having told Carolyn about Leticia, but what was done was done. "It's not just her, honey," she insisted.

"Sure it is," Carolyn contradicted her. "I know you, Virginia Carr, and when something is unresolved, it makes you mad. You're still madder than hell at that woman, so you try not to think about her. That's okay, but don't lie to yourself about it."

Virginia snorted. "Oh, everything about my relationship with Leticia got resolved all right."

Carolyn dipped her paddle in the water and watched the ripples. "If you're afraid to talk with the cop, don't!"

"I'm not afraid," Virginia insisted. Carolyn grunted and paddled on.

***

Virginia hesitated for another couple of days. Then Carolyn decided that she absolutely had to climb to the top of one of the higher foothills to take photos because the morning mist had burned off early. "Do you want to come, Sweetpea?" she asked, already knowing the answer. Virginia declined but offered to drive her to the base of the hill. "I can walk from here," Carolyn replied.

"But I'd like to drive you," Virginia insisted.

Carolyn knew something was up. "Okay," she agreed, "just let me get that extra roll of film."

After dropping Carolyn off, Virginia turned onto the main road. The state police barracks were only a mile and a half away, but after three-quarters of a mile, she turned off and drove back into the center of town. She parked in front of a pancake house with a red awning. She paused and then entered, determined to relax and enjoy a cup of coffee. Eric Johnson sat in a booth by himself. A half-empty coffeepot stood on the table to his left. He was avidly reading through an official-looking file. At first Virginia thought he hadn't seen her and she considered backing out of the restaurant and returning to their cabin. She thought better of it, however, and seated herself at a table near the window.

Johnson looked up, smiled faintly, and gathered his papers. "Do you mind if I join you?" he asked rhetorically. By the time Virginia answered, he'd already seated himself across from her. "I was wondering if you were ever going to take me up on my offer," he said calmly.

"I thought about going out to your headquarters today," Virginia replied just as calmly, "but I suppose it's a good thing I didn't since you wouldn't have been there. Aren't you supposed to be on duty?"

Johnson chuckled, but his eyes looked wary. "I have the morning off today," he replied. "One of my sergeants needs the night off, so I'm switching with him."

"Nice of you to help him out," Virginia said.

Johnson shrugged. His right hand drummed on the file he'd set before him on the table, but he said nothing.

"There is something specific you want from me," Virginia announced. "You might as well just spit it out." Her assertiveness surprised her, but not nearly so much as it took Johnson aback. "Well,' he harrumphed. "If you put it that way, yes, there is something. I want to talk with you about a case that has stymied me."

It was Virginia's turn to be astonished. "What?"

He pushed his folder across the table at her. "Be my guest!"

She looked down at the label on the outside of the folder and read "Runcible, Perceval Paul." When she looked up again, Johnson was staring at her with an expression of inordinate interest.

She smiled neutrally to hide her discomfort. "I didn't know the man."

Johnson just kept looking at her, and Virginia wished she'd worn jeans or long pants since the backs of her legs were sticking to her chair. After a few moments of silence, Johnson spoke up, "But you knew his wife quite well at one time."

Virginia looked at him sharply, but his expression was bland. Only his eyes were focused intently on her face. She pushed the folder back across the table at him. "I believe I told you that I'm not interested in the past."

Johnson left the folder where she'd pushed it. "Don't you want to know what happened to him?"

Virginia shrugged. "Why? I never even met him."

"Well, he's dead," Johnson replied, "and I'd give you odds of a thousand to one that his wife killed him."

Virginia started to laugh and had a hard time stopping. Johnson waited patiently. When she finally regained a measure of equanimity, he pushed the folder back to her side of the table. "Read it, please."

She didn't at first. "Have you arrested her?" she asked.

The policeman drummed his fingers on the table before answering. "Nope. No proof. The murder was brilliant. She made it look like heart and respiratory failure."

Virginia sighed and opened the folder. "Captain Johnson!" she exclaimed as soon as she'd glanced at the first page. "This man has been dead for fifteen years!" She started to laugh all over again.

"Get hold of yourself, Miss...I mean, Doctor Carr," the policeman snapped at her. "There's no statute of limitations for murder."

Virginia, who'd collected herself, squinted at Johnson. "Why now?" she demanded. "They'd only been married two years when he died. Why are you only starting to investigate now?" She felt angry but tried not to show it.

"I just found out six months ago," Johnson replied. "I wasn't here when it happened."

"Where were you?" Virginia asked. "I thought you'd been here all along."

"Quantico," Johnson replied. "The department sent me to the FBI to learn a few things."

"And did you?" Virginia inquired, aware that she was playing for time, hoping to think of a way to get away from the policeman and his stupid file.

He shrugged. "You didn't finish with that file," he reminded her.

"There's no reason for me to read it. There's no proof; you said so yourself."

"The proof exists," Johnson insisted. "And you're going to help me find it."

Virginia shook her head vehemently. "No, Captain, I won't help you railroad an old friend."

"The way I heard it, you weren't such good friends at the end there," Johnson replied, and Virginia wondered exactly how much he knew.

"I don't care what you heard," Virginia said, hardly recognizing her own voice, "I'm not about to frame an innocent woman."

"Innocent? Come on, Doctor. That one was never innocent. If she were innocent, I wouldn't be going after her."

"You're still bearing a grudge, Captain," Virginia said firmly, finally feeling again that she was on solid ground.

The policeman balked. "No, I'm just trying to see justice done."

Virginia hissed in exasperation. "Why don't you tell me the facts of your so-called case, Captain? In your own words, please. I don't want to read your file."

Johnson smiled triumphantly. "Fine! That's exactly what I'll do."

CHAPTER 3
WHAT DO YOU DO FOR FUN?
1961
❖

"Lettie, where are you, dear?" Leticia heard her mother call but did not respond. She was hiding in the apple tree where she always went to think in private. "Leticia Fredericks Barnes, you get in here this minute, do you hear me?" Leticia sighed softly to herself and climbed down from her special tree as slowly as she could. Then she headed into the house, only to be greeted by scolding. "You are the most unruly girl. I swear, if I didn't know better, I'd think someone had switched you at birth. I never imagined that any daughter of mine could turn out so wild and tomboyish. Now you know we're having guests for dinner, so please go upstairs and get dressed immediately. And don't forget to wash first. You look as if you'd been playing with pigs."

Leticia trudged up the stairs and finally released her pent up annoyance at her mother by rolling her eyes and muttering. "Leticia, you are the most unruly pig. You look as if you'd been playing with girls." Her mockery was not quite as satisfying as she'd hoped, so she topped it off with several deep snorts and an evil laugh. She'd been practicing her evil laugh for weeks, and it was coming along quite nicely, she thought. She heard her mother's voice behind her as she reached the top of the stairs and raced into her room, slamming the door. She couldn't quite make out the content of her mother's complaint from what she heard, but she knew it by heart anyway. "Don't snort and cackle so, Lettie, it's unbecoming to a young lady. And don't slam the door."

Leticia hated her bedroom almost as much as she hated her name. Leticia Fredericks Barnes: it sounded like the name of a character from some awful Gothic novel. She shook her untidy hair and pulled off her shorts and polo shirt. Her underwear followed, and she stared at the pile of clothes on the pink carpet. "Pink," she snarled. "Everything is so pink in this room. I hate pink." She left the pile where it had fallen instead of gathering the clothing for the laundry hamper. Turning briefly to the mirror, she pulled her cheeks out and crossed her eyes. In one motion, she twisted and pulled the doorknob, looked out quickly to see if anyone was in the hall, and then made a mad dash, naked as the day she was born, for the bathroom. Once inside, she shut and locked the door, and turned on the water for a shower. She let it run for a couple of minutes before entering, but once inside she washed thoroughly, shampooed her hair, and let the water pour over her as she thought more of the thoughts she'd been thinking in her tree. About fifteen minutes passed in this fashion before she heard the expected knocking and rattling and her mother's voice demanding that she turn off the water and get dried and dressed. She considered practicing her evil laugh again but thought better of it. She knew that she would have ample opportunity to annoy her mother before the dinner guests arrived, so she complied.

When Leticia emerged from the bathroom wrapped in a large navy blue towel, her mother was waiting in the hall. "Lettie, how many times do I have to tell you not to use your father's towel? You have your own towel," Lucille Barnes whined. Leticia walked right past her mother into her room and shut the door behind her. She quickly ran a comb through her hair and pulled a button-down magenta and white striped shirt and black trousers from the closet. By the time her mother realized that Leticia had only shut and not locked the bedroom door, Leticia was pulling on magenta socks. "Lettie," her mother almost squealed in horror, "you cannot dress like that for dinner. We are having guests!" Her daughter's choice of attire so outraged Lucille that she hardly seemed to notice the pile of dirty clothes on the floor. Leticia smiled and pulled on black oxfords. "Leticia, what am I going to do with you?" her mother wailed. "You look just like a boy in those clothes."

"Don't be ridiculous, Mother," Leticia bit off the words. "Boys don't have hair down to their waists. And I've never seen a boy wear magenta either." She pushed past her mother once again and headed for the door.

"That's it, Lettie. I'm not going to put up with this any longer. I'll have your father deal with you. After all, our guests are his business colleagues." Mrs. Barnes stalked out of the room after her daughter.

***

Leticia Barnes sat in bed eating from a dinner tray, exactly as she had planned. A small smile flickered over her face and dimmed as she finished her meal and deposited the tray on a bedside table. She rested her face in her hands and returned to her earlier thoughts. She had had a most unusual experience that morning and was having difficulty coming to terms with it.

At ten o'clock, she rode her bicycle into town to pick up the family's mail, one of her favorite summertime chores. After stopping at the post office, she wandered over to the small park near the town hall to look at the ducks wading in the pond. Usually she was alone in the park, for most of the summer population of Grant's Hill spent their days at the luxurious resorts in the surrounding countryside. That morning, however, when Leticia approached the duck pond, she noticed a thin figure squatting by its edge. She slowed down and watched as the person tossed pieces of bread into the water for the ducks.

At first, Leticia felt a brief upsurge of annoyance, for the park and pond were another of the few places where she could think without interruption. Curious, though, she moved a little closer and cleared her throat loudly. The figure stood up instantaneously and turned to face her. Leticia started in surprise, for facing her was a girl her own age with bright orange eyes set in the most humorous face she had ever seen. She stepped back to gain her composure, but the girl advanced.

"Hi," she said and smiled a big, goofy smile. "My name is Virginia Carr, and we're here for the summer. My father runs the pediatric unit in the clinic here in town, and I'm helping him. I want to be a doctor."

Leticia didn't know whether to laugh or not. Her upbringing prepared her to look down on others, even doctors and lawyers, and she was briefly tempted to treat Virginia as she would the hired help. However, the girl's friendliness disarmed her, and she was lonely for a playmate, even one who was an orange-eyed goofball.

"My name is Fred," she said, "and I live in the big house on the dirt road that leads to the highway north of town. My father owns most of the stock in Eastern Electric and is the chairman of the board of United Utilities. We come here every summer." She examined Virginia's face carefully to evaluate the effect of this announcement. Virginia looked blank for a second, then said: "Cool. So what do you do for fun?"

Leticia breathed a sigh of relief. "I bike, climb trees, think, and fight with my mother, who wants me to be more ladylike and wear dumb clothes and not get dirty. You know." She stared intently at Virginia to see if she really did know.

"Yeah," Virginia exhaled. "I know. My mother is a little like that too, but I guess that's how they're supposed to be. To prepare us for life as married women and stuff." She snickered, and Leticia grinned at her. "I don't ever want to get married," Virginia proclaimed. "I want to be a

19

great doctor and humanitarian, like Albert Schweitzer. But without the mustache, of course." She snickered some more.

"Well, I plan to get married," Leticia declared. "To a very, very wealthy man who can support me in the way I want to live. And to someone whose life is wildly exciting. I want to travel in style and see the world. Of course, I'll be independently wealthy when I get older, but I still think a rich husband would be best for me. Don't you agree?"

Leticia stared at Virginia, who just looked back at her in amazement. "For you, maybe," she replied. "But not for me." A short silence followed her announcement, and the two girls just kept looking at each other. The longer Leticia looked at Virginia the more she liked her.

"I've never met anyone with orange eyes before," she blurted out. "I mean, they're really orange, not hazel or even yellow like a cat's."

"Yeah," Virginia smiled at her. "Sometimes I think that I must really be an alien, you know, from a different planet, where orange eyes are as normal as blue or brown ones are here. I like having orange eyes, even though some people tease me about them." She opened her eyes wide and fixed them on Leticia's face. "What do you think, Frank?"

Leticia groaned. "Fred," she said, "my name is Fred, not Frank. And I think they're weird. But neat. Definitely neat." And she smiled at Virginia, showing all her teeth.

"Nice teeth," Virginia said, grinning. "So how did you get the name of Frank, I mean, Fred anyway? Are your parents strange or what?"

Leticia blushed a deep red. "Uh, well, it's my middle name actually, but my first one is so awful that I use it instead."

"So what is it? Your first name, I mean?" Virginia jutted her chin out in an aggressive way, as if daring Leticia not to tell her.

"Um, I'd rather not say," Leticia mumbled. "It's a good name for a cow."

"Don't tell me," Virginia laughed. "Your parents named you Bossy."

"No, not Bossy, but it's almost as bad." Leticia took a deep breath and decided to trust Virginia. "I'll tell you if you promise not to laugh."

"Okay," Virginia promised laconically. "Out with it."

Leticia cleared her throat noisily. "Leticia. My name is Leticia Fredericks Barnes, and that's why I call myself Fred." She waited for Virginia's reaction.

Virginia just looked at her for a moment quietly. "It's pretty bad all right, but it could be worse. Actually, I think Bossy Barnes has a nice ring to it. I could call you that."

20

Leticia felt called upon to defend her family name. "I'll have you know that the Barneses are a very old, respectable, and reputable New England family. My father's ancestors came over on the Mayflower. Besides, since when is Barnes funnier than Carr? What did your family do, shorten their name from Cartoon to Carr?"

At that Virginia let out a howl of fury and jumped on Leticia, pushing her into the duck pond. Leticia got a hand on Virginia's shirt and pulled her in as well. They struggled in the water for a few minutes, driving all the ducks to the other side, before scrambling up onto dry land. There they started wrestling again, and Leticia, who was larger but less agile than Virginia, found herself on the ground under the other girl's wiry body. They fought for a few minutes more and then started to laugh. Leticia felt lightheaded and elated. She didn't understand why. Instead of fighting, she wanted to roll in the grass with Virginia. She reached up and grabbed her by the head, pulled her face down, and kissed her full on the mouth. Virginia didn't resist or say anything. She just kissed her back and then extricated herself from Leticia's grasp. "Gotta go, Fred," she whispered. "I'm supposed to help my father in fifteen minutes, and I have to get out of these wet clothes." Then she was gone.

Leticia wandered around in the park for another half hour, hoping her clothing would dry enough so as not to be noticeably wet when she got home. She didn't want her mother asking any more questions than necessary. She couldn't quite fathom her feelings. "Virginia," she snarled. "That's as dumb a name as Leticia. I wonder what her parents were thinking of!" When she thought of Virginia's orange eyes, however, and the way it felt to be trapped on the ground under her slight but strong frame, she started to hear a pleasant buzzing noise in her head and felt her neck get hot.

And that is what Leticia Barnes was busily thinking about in her bedroom while her parents were entertaining dinner guests downstairs. She wondered what it all meant and whom she could ask and when she would see Virginia again. After an hour of these and related thoughts, she fell asleep, still dressed in her black pants and striped magenta shirt.

CHAPTER 4
ENCOUNTER
1961
❖

Leticia knew better than to ask her mother or father about her unexpected encounter with Virginia, so when she awoke early the next morning, she changed into the clothes she'd worn to the park the day before and set off on her bike again. Her clothes were still damp and had a stiff and sticky feel to them, but she didn't care. Her mind felt overly active and her emotions were in turmoil.

At fourteen and a half, Leticia was old enough to know that she was not feeling what she was expected to feel, but at the moment she didn't really care. One advantage of her birth and upbringing was the sense it gave her of her right to do and have whatever it was she desired. However, she wanted to be sure that Virginia felt the way she did, and of that she couldn't be certain yet. So she headed for the park, half expecting to find Virginia there, feeding the ducks again. She was disappointed. The park was deserted.

Leticia decided to give Virginia fifteen minutes to show up before taking off to search for her. She glanced at her watch every thirty seconds to see if it was time yet. By the time fifteen minutes had passed, Leticia had decided on a plan of sorts. She mounted her bicycle and started pedaling toward the town's tiny business district. When she reached the intersection with the main street, she turned onto it, let go of the handlebars and stood up. As the bike hit the old train tracks running down the center of the street, she was thrown to the ground, which was covered by a layer of gravel. As she had anticipated, the gravel got into several of the scrapes she acquired as a result of her fall, and she waited for someone to notice her, come to her rescue, and take her to the local medical clinic, wherever that was.

What Leticia had not counted on was that the first person to come to her rescue would be a man with little patience for what he considered childish pranks. The police officer had seen her racing down the street and was determined to teach her a lesson. Instead of offering her sympathy and a trip to the doctor, he hauled her into the station, confiscated her bike, and called her parents. When she demanded that he have something done about her injuries, he ran hot water into the sink, dragged her over and washed the scrapes. Most of the gravel came out. Then he put some antiseptic on her wounds and told her to sit over by the window until her father or mother came to get her.

Leticia was not used to being treated in so cavalier a fashion. The young officer ignored her, and she decided to teach him a lesson. She slumped over in her chair as if she'd passed out, but he paid no attention. Then she noisily fell to the floor, keeping her eyes tightly shut so as to seem unconscious.

She waited for what felt like an eternity. Then she heard her mother's voice. "Lettie, what are you doing on the floor?" She groaned as convincingly as she could and sat up, holding her head. "Uhhh, I fell off my bike. I need a doctor," she moaned, opening one eye. She didn't like what she saw through that eye.

Her mother was standing quite close to the young policeman, looking up at him with a stupid grin. The officer looked down at Mrs. Barnes with a self-important expression on his face. "Ma'am, your daughter did not fall off her bike accidentally. She was riding recklessly down Eagle Drive right here, standing up on the pedals, no hands on the handlebars, just as if she wanted to fall. I took her off the train track, brought her in here, and cleaned up her scrapes. She pulled quite a fake faint on me, but I know a spoiled brat when I see one. No disrespect intended, Mrs. Barnes, but what your daughter needs isn't a doctor, just a good spanking."

Leticia stood up. "Mother, will you have this boor return my bike, please? I have to see someone on the other side of town."

"I'm sorry, Ma'am," the policeman said sternly, turning his back to Leticia and addressing Mrs. Barnes, "I can't in good conscience give her back the bike until I have reason to believe she'll ride it less recklessly in the future." Mrs. Barnes' face looked rather blank for a moment, as if she couldn't decide whether to defend her daughter and her class privilege or defer to the policeman. Leticia held her breath and tried to look as injured and innocent as possible. Finally Mrs. Barnes looked away again.

"You're quite right, Officer, on every count," she said, a little pompously, Leticia thought. "However, I hope you'll entrust the bicycle to me. I'll lock it away at home until my husband gets a chance to deal with my daughter's behavior. I hope that is satisfactory."

The policeman looked skeptical, but he allowed Mrs. Barnes to wheel the bicycle out to her car. Leticia followed with her head held as high as she could hold it. Before she got to the door, however, the policeman's voice stopped her.

"Just a minute, young lady," he said. "If I ever see you riding that bike recklessly again, I'll confiscate it for good, and I won't call your mama, I'll spank you myself. Do I make myself clear?"

Leticia gave him what she hoped was a withering look and walked out the door without answering. Her mother was already waiting in the car, and Leticia got in without saying a word. As her mother turned the corner off the main street, Leticia told her to stop. "I want you to drop me here, and I'll bike home a little later. I really do have someone to see in town."

"Lettie, you can't bike back into town. Didn't you pay any attention to what that officer said? Now sit still. We'll be home in five minutes."

Leticia sat back and fumed until they turned into the enormous drive leading to the house. Her mother pulled the car up to the front entrance and got out. Leticia followed her to the trunk and grabbed at her bike as her mother lifted it out. "Oh no you don't," her mother said and pulled the bike away from her. "This is going inside until your father comes home this afternoon."

"Okay, okay," Leticia soothed her and backed away from the bike. "When is he supposed to be home?'

"At four," her mother replied, "after his golf game with Jeff."

"Keee-rist," Leticia swore under her breath. "And what," she demanded in an injured tone, "am I supposed to do until then?"

"Well, you might do any number of things, including your laundry. Those clothes you are wearing positively reek. And you look like you fell into a swamp," her mother replied.

"Well, thanks for nothing," Leticia mumbled again and stalked off in the direction of her tree.

***

Once she was comfortably settled on her regular perch, a large branch about midway up the tree, Leticia relaxed and considered her options. She knew that her father would hear her out and return her bike to her. He always did what she wanted him to do. It occurred to her that she might even be able to persuade him to take some action against the policeman who had treated her so abominably, but she wasn't sure that she wanted to put out the effort, much as he deserved a comeuppance. The certainty that her father would understand and side with her did not, however, offer her the least bit of help with her uncertainty about

24

Virginia. Perhaps she could convince her father to locate Dr. Carr for her, she thought, but she wondered how she would go about it. It was almost one by the time Leticia came out of her tree and trotted into the house for lunch. She washed her hands at the kitchen sink and examined the contents of the refrigerator with considerable disdain. Leticia hated leftovers, and for all that she enjoyed her family's summer vacations in Grant's Hill, the lack of household help truly appalled her. Having to clean her own room, which she did about twice a month, and to do her own laundry, which she only did when she had no clean underwear left, seemed to her a tedious waste of her time. "When I marry, I shall always have servants everywhere I go," she said aloud, removing some cold chicken, half a head of lettuce, and a tomato from the refrigerator.

"And who will supervise the servants if you don't know how to do what they must do?" she heard her mother's voice ask.

Leticia turned in the direction of the voice and acknowledged her mother's presence. "Mother, I didn't hear you come in. Would you like a chicken sandwich?"

Lucille Barnes examined her daughter carefully. "Thank you, no, my dear," she replied, after clearing her throat. "I see that you haven't yet changed your clothes, Lettie, and I suggest that you do so immediately after lunch. What you are wearing belongs in the trash can."

"Whatsa matter with my clothes?" Leticia mumbled with her mouth full of food.

"Don't speak with your mouth full, dear," her mother answered absentmindedly. "It's ignorant."

"Well, I'm not tossing them out. There's nothing wrong with them that a bout with laundry soap and water won't fix."

"Fine," Mrs. Barnes said pointedly. "Please see to it right after lunch."

Leticia just rolled her eyes as her mother left the kitchen. She stuffed the rest of her sandwich in her mouth and drank some iced tea out of the pitcher. She'd been waiting for her mother to leave so she could drink the tea that way. It saved washing a glass. She brushed the crumbs off her plate into the garbage and rinsed the plate under running water. The dish rack was full, but she did not want to empty it, so she wedged the plate in between a saucer and a bowl and raced outside again, forgetting all about her laundry.

The day was unusually breezy, so Leticia decided to go through the boxes of old toys in the cellar to see if she could find the kite her father had flown with her the second summer the family had vacationed in Grant's Hill. She searched until two-thirty and then gave up. Her restlessness increased, but she managed to hold out until her father got home.

Just before four, Leticia went up to her room, showered, and changed her clothes. She dumped her shirt and shorts, which smelled faintly of pond scum, into the laundry hamper. Then she went downstairs to await her father.

When he got into the house, Leticia's mother immediately took him aside to report on the day's happenings, but it only took Leticia ten minutes to persuade him that she had been treated unjustly by the police officer. He gave her permission to ride her bike. "Just be careful not to get caught doing anything fancy on the bike in town, that's all," he told her with a wink. "We don't want you getting spanked by some cop, do we? What was his name anyway, honey? Maybe I can find out what sort of reputation he has."

Leticia knew what that meant. She didn't have to persuade her father to make things difficult for the rude cop. He would do that on his own. She nearly burst with satisfaction as she closed her eyes and visualized the nametag the young policeman had worn. "Let me see. His name was Johnson, I think. Yes, I can see the nametag in my mind's eye. Eric Johnson, Jr."

Mr. Barnes smiled proudly. "See, I told you all that practice with visual recall would be good for something someday, didn't I? Now that I have the name, I'll see what I can do about Junior."

Leticia smiled at him and gave him a hug. "You were right, Daddy," she said, squeezing his upper arm. "You always are."

CHAPTER 5
UNEXPECTED
1961
❖

Leticia had already learned as a toddler how easy it was to manipulate her father, and she'd become quite expert at it over the years. She knew that her father doted on her and she used that knowledge shamelessly. Calvin Barnes was a tough-minded and successful businessman who'd made a proper marriage to further his career. In the early years of his marriage he'd been quite courtly and generous towards his wife, but he'd rapidly tired of her. Had it not been for his daughter, he would probably have left his wife. His daughter, however, captivated him as his wife had never done, and his adoration of her kept him close to home.

Calvin spent time teaching his daughter many of the things he would have taught a son, had he had one. He was impressed by her quickness and enormous capacity to argue well for whatever she wanted. "The world has lost a great lawyer in you, Lettie," he would say whenever she'd convinced him to allow her something he'd had no intention of allowing her. They would laugh heartily together and plan ways to deceive poor Lucille, whose insistence had been the basis for Calvin's original refusal.

Leticia enjoyed her father's company and depended upon his indulgence. She didn't even mind his calling her Lettie, though it made her skin crawl when her mother did. She had briefly considered asking him to call her Fred, but she'd thought better of it. Although her father tolerated what her mother decried as her outrageously tomboyish ways, she doubted very much that he would approve of her calling herself Fred.

"No," she said softly to herself in her room after dinner, "he wouldn't like me to be Fred, and he wouldn't like me to kiss Virginia again."

Leticia mashed her pillow in frustration. "I'm left with the same problem as I started the day with, namely, how to find Virginia if she doesn't show up at the duck pond tomorrow." And then she remembered one of her father's favorite sayings: "Expect the best, prepare for the worst, and take whatever comes with thankfulness." She knew it was a quote from someone famous. Emerson or Thoreau or Longfellow. She snorted as she flattened out her pillow again and decided, for want of anything better, to practice her evil laugh for a while. After ten minutes of practice she felt much better and settled down to read until she fell asleep.

***

The next morning was gray and rainy, and Leticia woke up much later than she'd expected. She looked out her bedroom window and decided that the likelihood of finding Virginia at the duck pond was almost nil. She took her time putting on jeans and a short-sleeved sweatshirt and finally loaded her dirty laundry into the washer and started it. By the time she went into the kitchen for breakfast, it was almost ten o'clock. She found a note from her mother saying that she and her father had driven into town and would be back after lunch. So Leticia was on her own.

She spent most of the morning hanging around the house, reading and waiting for her laundry. When it was finally dry, she rescued her magenta shirt and black pants, smoothed them, and put them away. Then she pulled out the shorts and shirt that her mother had tried to relegate to the trash, put them on, and went to inspect her bike. She added a little air to the tires and greased the chain. Then she was ready for a trip to the park and a meeting with Virginia, if only the rain would stop.

Finally at two, her parents returned, laden down with parcels and ready for lunch. Leticia helped her father fix himself a drink. "Ah Lettie," he said, "the world has lost a great bartender in you." She giggled and messed his hair. "Now, now, don't rumple the old wig," he said, sending her into another giggle fit.

By three-thirty the rain had eased enough to make a trip to the park possible, and Leticia was off. She got to the duck pond in record time and looked around. Virginia was nowhere to be seen.

Leticia felt something she'd never felt before in her fourteen and a half years. It was heavy and sad and made it hard for her to breathe. She sat down on the wet ground and put her head between her knees. "I wonder if I'm catching something," she muttered, breathing as deeply as she could, which was not very deep because her chest hurt.

She was so taken aback by her unexpected symptoms that she didn't hear Virginia's footsteps. "Hey, what's with you, Fred? Are you sick or something?" Virginia's voice sounded concerned, and the nearness of her body as she knelt by Leticia was reassuring. She put her arm around Leticia's shoulders. "Just lean back against me, sweetie," she said. "Everything is going to be okay."

28

Leticia had always hated being sick, even though she was not above pretending to faint from time to time just to make a point. Suddenly, however, the advantages of being taken care of burst like a meteor shower in her mind. "Oh, I'm all right," she said as unconvincingly as she could and started to stand up.

"Oh no you don't," Virginia tightened her arm across Leticia's body. "You just stay still until you look less pale."

"But I'm cold, and it's wet here," Leticia whined, astonished at how much she sounded like her mother. She snuggled into Virginia's arms, and Virginia wrapped as much of her body around her as she could.

They sat like that for a few minutes until Virginia was satisfied that Leticia was well enough to stand up. Then they both stood up, still hugging. "Hey, Fred," Virginia whispered, "you can let go now. I'm not going anywhere."

"Okay," Leticia whispered back. Their bodies separated, and Virginia reached into the pocket of her cape. "I want to feed the ducks." She pulled out two slices of bread and crumbled them into bits. Leticia experienced a brief flash of jealousy. "So you came here just to feed the ducks," she said before she could stop herself.

The goofy smile that she remembered from her first encounter with Virginia appeared. "Yeah, sure, Fred. Hey, you wanna feed them too?" Virginia offered.

There was something about the way Virginia answered her that put Leticia at ease. "Yeah, sure, gimme some of that bread."

They stood companionably feeding the ducks until the bread was gone. "Well, that's that," Virginia announced with finality. "I gotta go."

Leticia grabbed onto her cape. "Just wait a minute. We need to talk."

Virginia took the hand from her cape and held it. "You need to talk. I need to go. Bye, Fred." And she was gone.

"Wait a minute," Leticia yelled after her. "When will I see you again?"

Virginia turned and waved. "Here every morning at eleven unless it's pouring." And then she disappeared from view.

Leticia couldn't decide if she was more happy or more frustrated. Her ears buzzed as she absentmindedly picked up her bike which had fallen over on the path leading to the pond. She walked it to the edge of the park instead of riding because she felt a little dizzy. It was a good thing too, for as she came to the edge of the park, which was also the town's border, Officer Johnson drove by in his cruiser and waved. He shouted out the window at her, and she tried to ignore him but couldn't. "Glad to see you're on foot, girl. You'll keep out of trouble that way." He drove off, and she was tempted to give him the finger, but her mother's training caught up with her, and she just made a face and laughed her evil laugh after him. "I'll get you, my ugly," she whispered to herself and laughed even louder. Then she hopped up onto her bike and pedaled home.

***

The first sight to greet Leticia's eyes when she raced into the house was her father's head buried in the *Wall Street Journal*. "Hi Daddy," she yelled as she raced up the stairs. I'll be down in a minute soon as I change." She hastily stripped down to her underwear and tossed her clothes on the floor. "Okay, okay, clean pants and shirt and dry socks," she mumbled, as she dressed. She took a quick look at herself in the mirror and ran her fingers through her unruly hair. Then she took off down the stairs again.

Her father was still reading the paper but he put it aside as soon as she entered the room. "Did you have a good day, Lettie?" he inquired, although they'd seen each other only a few hours earlier. It was a ritual, and both of them were attached to their shared rituals. "Yep," she said. "Once the rain quit, I took a ride to the park and hung out with ducks for a while. Before that I did some laundry to keep Mom happy."

Her father wrinkled his nose at that. "I suppose I really should get us some help up here. This is supposed to be your vacation."

Leticia sat down on the love seat across from her father's armchair. "Hell, I don't mind that much. As long as Mom doesn't drive me nuts with her ladylike kick, a little laundry won't kill me. If anything will drive me nuts around here, it's the abominable pinkness of my room. Kee-rist!"

Calvin Barnes tried not to laugh when his daughter swore, but he couldn't resist. "I just love the way you do that, Lettie. The world has lost…"

"Yeah, I know," Leticia interrupted with a grin, "a great longshoreman in me." They both laughed at that. "I guess I do repeat myself a little, but it is a good line," her father beamed at her. Leticia just sat quietly for a minute and looked at him. She really enjoyed her father. He was so much more easygoing than her mother and so worldly.

"Was there something you wanted to talk with me about, Lettie?" Mr. Barnes asked. "If not, I'll just finish up this section and then you can fix me a drink."

"No, nothing special," Leticia answered. "I just thought you might want to know that the obnoxious cop was bugging me again today. Nothing serious since I wasn't even riding my bike, just walking it. He kind of let me know that I'd be in trouble if he caught me riding it in town. I guess there's nothing you can do about it, but it is awfully annoying to have him on my tail."

"There most certainly is something I can do about it, Lettie. Don't ever underestimate your dad. I can talk to the town mayor and selectmen about his behavior. There are regulations governing police conduct, you know. He's not authorized to harass you. We summer folk are the mainstays of this town's piddling economy, and they'd better not forget it. Why, without us they wouldn't be able to afford to keep that new clinic open. And they certainly wouldn't have been able to lure that doctor here to look after the children. He's quite a name in his field, so I hear. I can't remember exactly what field that is or why he's here looking after children instead of practicing whatever it is in Baltimore. But it's not important, is it?"

"You mean Dr. Carr?" Leticia asked without thinking.

"Yes, I do believe that's his name," her father replied. "How do you know him? You haven't been sick, have you? No, of course not. I'd have known if you'd been sick. Anyway, you're too old for a children's doctor now."

"Um," Leticia considered lying but thought better of it. "I ran into his daughter in the park the other day. She seemed pretty friendly. And smart too. But kind of funny-looking. She has orange eyes." Leticia always offered a critical comment or two when she described someone to her father. She knew he approved of keeping a cool head and not going overboard in enthusiasm about anyone. She felt a little uneasy though, as if she might have been disloyal to Virginia.

Mr. Barnes didn't seem to notice his daughter's discomfort. "Well, well, I didn't know he even had a daughter. I hope she doesn't take up too much of his time. He should be working this summer, not vacationing with his family. We're paying him pretty well."

Leticia was tempted to tell her father that Virginia was helping in the clinic, but she knew somehow that it was better not to do so. For the first time in a long while, she wasn't quite sure about her father.

Usually his siding with her in all arguments with her mother cast him in a shining light, but his comments about Virginia and her father made Leticia feel a tiny bit ambivalent.

"Gotta go now, Daddy. I promised Mom I'd go to the caterer with her. She wasn't happy with the last meal we served your guests."

"All right. I'll fix my own drink, even though it won't be as good as the ones you make me. Go give your mother moral support."

Leticia went up the stairs and knocked on her mother's door. "Mother, are you napping?" There was no answer for a few seconds and then she heard the sound of a glass hitting the floor. "Shit," she mumbled to herself, "not again." She tried the door and found it unlocked, so she walked in. Mrs. Barnes was lying in bed, reaching groggily for the pill bottle on her night table. "Mother," Leticia said gently, "you don't need another Valium. You need to wake up." She took the pill bottle and put it in the drawer. Then she sat down on the bed next to her mother and helped her sit up.

"I've got a terrible headache, Lettie," her mother complained. "I need something for it."

"You've been cooped up inside all afternoon. Let's go out, okay? We need to talk to the caterer, don't we?"

Mrs. Barnes lowered her head. "He doesn't love me anymore, Lettie. Your father, he … he doesn't love me anymore."

Leticia put her arm around her mother's shoulders. It was not something she had ever done before, but it felt right. "Mom, forget about him right now. Look, we have an appointment in fifteen minutes. Why don't you go shower, and I'll clean up the broken glass, okay?"

Mrs. Barnes nodded groggily and dragged herself to the bathroom, while Leticia went downstairs for a broom and dustpan.

CHAPTER 6
ERIC JOHNSON DESCRIBES THE FACTS
1980
❖

Virginia looked at the man seated across from her. His face still looked boyish, but his eyes were tired. "Please go ahead, Captain Johnson," she said in a voice without warmth. The man shuffled through the papers before him at length, cleared his throat several times, then offered a summary.

Colonel Perceval Paul Runcible, USAF, and Leticia Fredericks Barnes were married on May 30, 1963 at the First Presbyterian Church in Palm Springs, California. After a brief honeymoon in Mexico, the colonel and his bride left for a United States Air Force base in Turkey, where he had been posted before his marriage.

Approximately two years later, after shorter stints at various bases in Asia, Colonel Runcible was abruptly ordered back home and stationed near Laramie, Wyoming. The Runcibles rented a small house near the base. As far as anyone could tell, they were a normal, young military couple. A few of their former neighbors reported that Mrs. Runcible had occasionally complained of the dullness of life as a military wife in Laramie, but her husband seemed devoted to her and she to him, the neighbors thought. They were sure her boredom would dissipate when the couple had their first child.

Colonel Runcible was in excellent health. He didn't smoke, drank only in moderation, and exercised regularly. He seemed content in his chosen profession and happy with his life.

On April 30, 1965, Mrs. Lucille Barnes, who had moved after her husband's death from Palm Springs, California to Palm Beach, Florida, came to visit her daughter and son-in-law. She spent two weeks with them before leaving to see old friends in California. She left the Runcible home on May 15. On May 18, Colonel Runcible suffered coronary failure in his bathroom. He'd been shaving when he apparently keeled over. By the time his wife discovered him and summoned an ambulance, he was already dead.

Since he was a military officer, the air force undertook an investigation of the circumstances of his death. However, because he died off the base, the local authorities also became involved. The medical examiner's office in Laramie performed the autopsy and verified that the cause of death was a cardiovascular episode that led to complete failure of the circulatory and respiratory systems. There was no suspicion of foul play, but Mrs. Runcible insisted on toxicology screenings. They all came back negative.

Lucille Barnes returned from California to stay with her daughter after the untimely death of her son-in-law. After a month in Wyoming she returned to Florida. Shortly thereafter, Leticia Runcible, née Barnes, left Laramie with two suitcases and ten boxes to move back to the Barnes family summer home in Grant's Hill, Delaware, where she still resides.

***

Having finished his summary Eric Johnson cleared his throat once more and looked intently at the woman sitting across from him. Virginia's face was blank, except for the touch of impatience that tightened her lips. "Hardly your own words, Captain Johnson," she said in the tone of voice she used to dress down incompetent interns. "But I suppose I need that information as background."

Johnson's lip curled, but he didn't reply. His eyes narrowed slightly, and Virginia found herself thinking that Leticia may well have been right about him all those years ago. "So, having given me the bare bones, Captain, please be so kind as to flesh them out. What makes you think that Colonel Runcible was murdered by Leticia?"

Johnson smiled unpleasantly. "I should think the answers to those questions would be obvious to a woman of your intelligence," he sneered. He put up his hand and started counting off on his fingers. "First, she was bored with military life, but he wouldn't quit. Second, he was in excellent health. Third, she knew all about poisons from that spooky South American woman who used to work for the Barnes family. Fourth, she is a one hundred percent, dyed in the wool, spoiled brat who wouldn't think twice about killing her husband if he crossed her. Fifth, she stood to gain control of a lot of money once her husband died, and you can never underestimate the importance of money as a motive in a crime like this one."

Virginia raised her eyebrows. "Captain, there was no crime, except in your head. Besides, as far as I know, Colonel Runcible did not have a lot of money."

"True enough," Johnson acknowledged, "but he had considerable control of his wife's money while he was alive. The late Mr. Barnes saw to that. He knew his daughter was impulsive."

"So the money reverted to Leticia upon her husband's death?" Virginia asked.

Johnson nodded.

"Why then did Leticia move back to Grant's Hill? As far as I could tell the Barnes' home there was hardly luxurious. If, as you claim, she was bored with military life, why didn't she take the money and go someplace glamorous?"

This time Johnson shrugged. "Maybe she felt guilty. Maybe she had an attachment to that place as the last place where she'd been happy. I don't know, but there are lots of possibilities."

Virginia sighed. "And what exactly do you want from me, Captain Johnson?"

Johnson smiled broadly. "Well, first of all, I wanted you to hear me out. Second…"

Please, no more counting," Virginia interrupted him.

"Fine," he replied, then added succinctly, "I'd like your help in finding out what really happened."

"And if what really happened was a perfectly natural failure of Colonel Runcible's respiratory and circulatory systems?"

"If that's what you come up with after an honest investigation, I'll accept it and let the matter drop."

Virginia chewed her lip. "Why me?"

"Who better, Dr. Carr? You knew her. You're trained to be an objective observer. And you'd have a much easier time getting access to Miss Barnes, I mean, Mrs. Runcible than anyone else I can think of." Johnson crossed his arms over his chest and looked at Virginia as if daring her to disagree.

"I think you're mistaken, Captain. Leticia and I haven't exchanged a word since we were seventeen."

Johnson's expression didn't change. "I know, Dr. Carr, but I stand by what I said."

Virginia wondered what else he knew, but she didn't ask, grateful that he didn't indicate any explicit knowledge that she and Leticia had been lovers. "I wasn't planning to go to Grant's Hill this summer, Captain Johnson. In fact, I promised Dr. Matthews specifically that I wouldn't."

Johnson frowned. "Even though your father asked you to," he said sternly. "I know that too. Your father and I are still in touch from time to time. He's very proud of you and knows that you really want to be a good daughter."

"I am a good daughter," Virginia snapped.

"I think that in your heart of hearts you know you could be better," Johnson said, as if stating an irrefutable fact. "After all, your father has gone above and beyond. He accepts your relationship with that Matthews woman, which isn't something every father would do."

"My father is very attached to Carolyn," Virginia snapped again, wondering why she was explaining herself to Johnson. "He likes her and trusts her."

Johnson looked dubious. "Be that as it may, if she cared at all about him, she'd be willing to have you go to see him. Circumstances change, Dr. Carr. A promise is a promise, I know, but surely she'll understand. After all, you made a promise to your father long before you met her."

Virginia laughed, but the laughter wasn't cheerful. "If that's what you think, you don't know Carolyn."

"I don't know her and I don't want to know her," Johnson replied heatedly. She reminds me of Miss Barnes, er, Mrs. Runcible. What I can't understand is why a woman like you would take up with women like that when you could get yourself a husband and raise a family."

"Women like what?" Virginia raised her voice. "Don't tell me you think that Carolyn has the potential to murder someone out of boredom, Captain?"

"No, ma'am," Johnson said softly. "Not out of boredom, but out of jealousy maybe. They're unpredictable, you see, Dr. Carr."

Virginia nearly tipped her chair over as she stood up to leave. "What you don't seem to understand, is that I am one of 'them', Captain. I am just as much a lesbian as Carolyn. And as for Leticia, she did exactly what you just suggested to me. She got herself a husband, and thankfully there were no children for her to raise on her own. As far as I can tell, all that marriage earned her was early widowhood and your suspicion. Now if you'll excuse me, I have to meet someone."

Johnson stood up. "You've misunderstood me, I think, Dr. Carr. I am as well aware of your relationship to Dr. Matthews as I was of your affair with Miss Barnes. But you're not one of them; you have a conscience. You're honest and fair, and you want to know the truth. And that's why you're going to help me. Good afternoon, ma'am."

Virginia stood silently, but as Johnson turned to go, she couldn't resist having the last word. "I will not help you, Captain, because I don't believe you really want to find the truth. You want to avenge yourself on Leticia for what happened back in Grant's Hill. However, you are right about one thing: I do want to know the truth. Always. Good afternoon, Captain."

They walked out of the restaurant and headed in opposite directions down the street. Virginia was frowning so intently that she almost walked past her car. Eric Johnson's face, however, wore a satisfied smile; he'd gotten what he came for.

CHAPTER 7
A SAFE PLACE
1980
❖

For as long as she could remember, Virginia Carr had wanted to become a doctor. Her earliest memories were of sitting in her high chair listening as her parents told each other of interesting cases and treatment strategies. She announced her intention to go to medical school when she was four and never deviated from her course. While her peers played tag and dressed their dolls, Virginia prepared to practice medicine. Although her parents were pleased by her desire to follow in their footsteps, her mother was disturbed by her daughter's single-mindedness.

"Let her be, Louise," Virginia's father said, trying to reassure his wife. "Playing with a chemistry set is no worse than making mud pies and it's certainly a hell of a lot more creative. As long as she doesn't stab anyone but her dolls with that fake hypodermic, there's no harm done."

If the truth were known, Virginia despised her dolls. They had no temperature, no pulse, and no orifices into which she could stick her toy medical instruments. She tried to give the family cat a physical examination, but her mother intervened and rescued the startled animal. So Virginia limited her ministrations to a neighbor's son. He was two years younger and neither quick-witted nor forceful enough to avoid being drawn into her medical games. Late one afternoon Louise Carr came upon them in the backyard and nearly fainted. Her daughter had cut all the hair off the boy's head. She was prepping him, so she explained to her appalled mother, for brain surgery with a solution of Mercurochrome and rubbing alcohol.

At that point Louise decided enough was enough and signed Virginia up for piano lessons and the local Brownie troop. Virginia took only three piano lessons before her teacher quit after Virginia diagnosed her with hemorrhoids from the way she sat. Brownies, Virginia complained to her mother, bored her. Exasperated, Louise Carr turned her daughter's upbringing over to her husband Henry. He started training Virginia to assist him in his practice.

Initially, Henry simply allowed his nine year-old to hang around the office after school and organize the medical texts in the examining rooms and the magazines that lay on the table in the waiting room. She also straightened up after particularly untidy patients. Whenever she had a spare moment, Virginia sat down and paged through the medical texts that were too difficult for her to read. She had better luck with the magazines, though she found them less interesting.

As Virginia grew older, she became more useful to her father, keeping his records in order and increasingly taking over other small tasks that required no professional qualifications. She was a quiet and idealistic child, whose vision of life had crystallized when she found a biography of Albert Schweitzer in the public library. She decided that she too wished to be a healer motivated by the desire to serve humanity. Her idealization of Albert Schweitzer allowed her to follow her natural bent toward solitude and to cope with what became an extraordinarily difficult school experience.

During the school year right before Henry accepted a summer job in Grant's Hill, Virginia noticed that she no longer liked playing with the boys in her class. They had started to treat her as the object of their new interest in female anatomy. After winning a few fistfights, Virginia had to accept that her days as one of the guys were over. Her disenchantment with her former playmates turned into aversion. So she tried to make friends with girls her own age, the ones she had previously scorned as shallow fluff-brains. Their interests had changed over time as well, but the new ones, boys, clothes, and hairstyles, had no more appeal for her than dolls. Had she not had the long afternoons at her father's office to distract her, Virginia would have been horribly lonely. Louise worried about her daughter's isolation from her peers, but Henry dismissed his wife's fears, comforting himself and her with reminders that all of their own lasting friendships had been formed in medical school.

Derided by her classmates as a science geek, possibly queer, and therefore someone to avoid, Virginia drifted socially and emotionally. The only people for whom she felt any affection, besides her parents and the handful of their adult friends who paid any attention to her, were a few older girls with serious commitments to science or the arts. She admired them from a distance, imagining in her spare time what it would be like to get to know them. Soon all of her fantasies focused on one particular girl, a talented pianist named Diana. By the end of the school year Virginia was totally infatuated with her. Yet they had never exchanged so much as a single word.

***

39

One cool October afternoon during Virginia's twelfth year, she was on her way from school to her father's office when she noticed an emaciated looking young woman carrying a sick child. The little boy was whining and twisting in his mother's arms, and when she shifted position to make him more comfortable, she dropped the plastic bag she was carrying.

"Here!" Virginia called out impetuously. "Let me!" She picked up the bag and handed it to the struggling mother.

"Gracias," the young woman mumbled. Then she corrected herself. "Thank you," she said with a thick accent. She looked around, and Virginia could tell she was lost.

"Are you looking for something?" Virginia asked gently.

The young woman sighed. "My son, he is sick. I need a clinic."

"My father is a doctor," Virginia exclaimed. "Come with me, please!"

The young woman looked at her suspiciously for a minute.

"My father really is a doctor," Virginia insisted. "My name is Virginia Carr, and he's Henry Carr. You'll see his name on the office door. I'm sure he can help."

The young woman's expression softened. "I am Maria Mendoza, and he is Pablo," she announced patting her still squirming child on the back. "He has big sores that do not heal."

***

Henry Carr took one look at the infected wounds on Pablo's torso, legs and arms and whistled. "These are deep slashes," he said to Maria.

She looked frightened. "Sí, a bad man cut my son many times. Can you help him?"

Henry sighed. "I'll try," he said. "This really is a matter for the police."

Maria shook her head very hard. "No police!" she cried in a frightened voice. She reached out to pick her son up from the examining table. "You call the police, and I will go away."

Shaking his head, Henry stopped her from picking up the injured child, and started to treat the boy's wounds. He told her he couldn't promise that Pablo would survive. "He's lost a lot of blood and all the slashes are infected. He'll be a very lucky boy if gangrene doesn't set in. He really needs to be hospitalized."

"No hospital!" Maria called out.

Henry snorted and grumbled under his breath, but he finished working on the child. "All right," he growled at Maria. "You need to

40

keep him still and watch out for spikes in his temperature. I'll give him a penicillin shot and write you a prescription for antibiotics."

Virginia, who'd been standing by during Henry's entire interaction with Maria and Pablo, finally spoke up. "Do you have a place to stay, Maria?"

The young woman looked down at the floor and shook her head. "No place and only little money," she said softly.

Henry sighed again and glanced at his daughter, only to find her looking at him beseechingly. "Oh, very well," he said, turning back to Maria. "Never mind the prescription. I'll give you some samples." He reached into a cabinet beside the examining table. "This is an antibiotic salve and this liquid is something he has to swallow eight times a day. That's every three hours, even during the night. Give him a tablespoonful each time."

When Henry looked up, Virginia was still gazing at him with an imploring look on her face. "What?" he asked, feeling slightly impatient. Virginia's eyes mirrored his impatience. "They really need someplace safe to stay, and we have a guest room."

Henry cut off his daughter's plea: "Virginia, your mother put a lot of work into redecorating that room. We can't just let anyone stay there."

Virginia looked at him intently. "They're not just anyone. Pablo is your patient."

"Absolutely not!" Henry replied. Then he hesitated. "At least not without your mother's permission."

Virginia raced up to her father and hugged him. "Thank you, oh, thank you. You're a wonderful man. I'm so proud you're my father!"

Henry rolled his eyes. "Oh, all right. Now how are we going to get this past your mother?"

***

Virginia and Maria stayed up late that night. Pablo was feverish and needed fresh, cool cloths every hour. He didn't like the taste of the oral antibiotic either and spat it out the first time Maria spooned it into his mouth. "Wait," Virginia said. "I think we have an unused eyedropper somewhere." She disappeared for a few seconds and came back with an eyedropper. "I'll fill it and you hold him and get his mouth open," she ordered Maria. Maria did as Virginia suggested and they soon had Pablo dosed. The little boy was exhausted and fell asleep with Virginia's favorite blue washcloth draped over his forehead.

Maria shook her head and looked desperately at Virginia. "If he dies, I will kill myself," she said softly. "It is only to save him that I have come here to this land where I can barely understand what people say. It would be a bitter thing if trying to save him led to his death." Large tears rolled down her cheeks, but her weeping was silent.

"How did he get cut so badly?" Virginia inquired, partly out of curiosity and partly to get Maria's mind off the idea of killing herself.

"A bad man hurt him," Maria said shortly and looked down at the rug in the guest room.

"What man?" Virginia demanded, then caught herself. "Look, I understand if you don't trust me enough to tell me, but I'd really like to know how you and Pablo came to be in Baltimore."

Virginia almost staggered at the ferocity with which Maria grabbed her arm. "Not trust you?" Maria hissed, giving her arm a shake. "How can you say such a thing? If you had not rescued us, my Pablo would surely die. I will bless forever the moment that you came up to me on the street to help. Even Ana Mendoza Velasquez, who knows the secrets of the earth, could not have done what your father did for Pablito."

Once over the suddenness of Maria's response, Virginia realized she liked the way the young woman was holding her arm, running her hand along it as if in a caress. She felt warmth spread through her body and smiled gently at Maria. "Who," she asked, "is Ana Mendoza Velasquez?"

Maria's face softened. "My mother," she whispered, "who knows how to cure with plants and how to kill without leaving a mark on the body." Maria sighed and her face took on a melancholy expression. "You have asked for my story. It is a common one, too common among my people."

"Your people?" Virginia prompted her.

Maria nodded. "Yes, the Indios of what you call South America."

Maria, whose father had died when she was in her early teens, was working in the fields when a Latino overseer took a liking to her. Her uncle and brothers were working far away so there was no man to protect her from the overseer's advances, nor to pressure him to marry her once her pregnancy was discovered.

The overseer did not want a fieldworker for his wife, and he denied that the boy, who looked like a purebred Indian, was his son. So Maria raised her child with her mother's help but without his father. Then when the boy was a year old, he became ill with a wasting disease. Virginia recognized the symptoms: dysentery. But for his grandmother Ana, he would have died. Though her herbal know-how saved his life, he remained weak. Then Maria learned of a clinic that offered vitamins for babies and toddlers. At the clinic she met a North American who claimed to be hiring people to work in California. He promised papers that would make the workers legal residents and jobs with good salaries. "Your son would eat well and see doctors to make him strong," he told Maria.

Without consulting her mother Maria went with the recruiter, only to learn that his promises were lies. Far from home, with a young child to care for, Maria was easy to control. The recruiter sold Maria and Pablo to a pimp, who threatened to kill Pablo if she did not cooperate. So she did. For two years Maria worked as a prostitute. Then one evening a customer became violent. He sodomized her with a bottle, which he then broke on the cinderblock wall. He came towards her, aiming his bottle at her throat. Somewhere within herself Maria found the strength to kick him in the gut. He vomited and stumbled, and she raced out of the room into the kitchen were Pablo sat on the table playing with spoons. Grabbing a knife with one hand, she leaned over to scoop up the boy with the other, but the enraged customer had followed her into the kitchen. When he saw the knife in her hand, he turned the broken bottle against Pablo, slashing him repeatedly before Maria plunged the knife into the man's shoulder and he staggered away.

After he left, Maria bandaged the boy's wounds as best she could and decided to run away. She had no money, but she knew where the pimp hid some "for emergencies." he said, the main emergency being the need to pay off police. He'd just made a payment the day before, Maria knew, so there was only a handful of twenties left. Maria took the money, boarded a Greyhound bus with her son, and headed east as far as the bus would take them. She would have made it all the way to the ocean if Pablo's wounds hadn't become infected. The child began to scream in pain and Maria could not quiet him. So the bus driver threw them off in Baltimore.

Although some people might have regarded Maria differently once they'd learned the details of her past, Virginia's esteem for her only grew. Maria, to her way of thinking, was heroic. If she'd walked all the way from California to Baltimore Virginia couldn't have admired her more.

As Pablo recovered, Maria began to relax. Virginia's support and unabashed admiration gave her back a sense of herself that she hadn't felt since childhood. When she looked in the mirror, she no longer saw a beaten down, former prostitute. Instead she saw a younger version of her mother Ana, the woman of power.

By caring for Maria and Pablo, Virginia too started to come into her own. Instead of living in her fantasies, she found outlets for her energy and discovered the seductive pleasure of protecting those weaker than herself.

Louise observed the change in her daughter with pleasure. Virginia had gained a degree of emotional grounding that Louise hadn't even dared to hope for. But she and Henry remained chagrined at their daughter's ongoing isolation from her own age group. "After all," Louise reminded Henry unnecessarily, "Maria is twenty and a mother. And Pablo is a child of three. Hardly suitable friends for Virginia."

So both of Virginia's parents were relieved when she made a friend her own age in Grant's Hill. If Louise guessed that the friendship was more intense than was usual or, by her standards, normal, she never expressed her reservations to Virginia or to Henry. And Henry, in whom Virginia eventually confided the true nature of her relationship with Leticia, advised her to spare her mother the details she had just shared with him. Virginia did as he requested, happy to avoid a possible confrontation.

The summer morning was bright and warm, and Leticia got to the park well before eleven. She needed time to be alone and think. Despite her excitement about meeting with Virginia again, she felt deflated. Scenes with her mother always brought her down like that because she couldn't argue with her. Lucille was right; Calvin didn't love her. What her daughter suspected is that he never had. She had no idea what to do about this suspicion, and that troubled her. "I just wish she would have a little dignity about it all," Leticia muttered as she threw a stone in the water, scattering the ducks.

"Hey," Virginia's voice resounded clear, and cheerful, "don't chase my babies away. You're supposed to throw bread, not stones."

"Yeah," Leticia snapped, suddenly feeling sarcastic, "you would have babies with beaks and webbed feet." She was surprised when Virginia didn't take offense.

"What's wrong, Fred? You look depressed. Is something the matter at home?" Virginia's voice sounded concerned, but Leticia was too confused to change her behavior.

"No, nothing's wrong at home! Nothing's ever wrong at home. We're rich, and the rich never have any problems!" She felt as if she were going to cry.

"Oh, honey," Virginia reached out and hugged her. "Don't be sad. Whatever it is will change. Everything changes."

"Virginia, for God's sake, will you stop being trite?" Leticia demanded, as she tried to pull away. Virginia didn't release her and refused to take the bait. "Why should I? Didn't you know that trite is my middle name. Virginia Trite Carr. Sounds dreadful, doesn't it? Virginia Dreadfully Trite. There, that's much better, isn't it?" She squeezed Leticia and began to rub her left shoulder. "You're all tight, Fred. Let me give you a back rub."

Leticia didn't want a back rub. She wanted to brood, but it was obvious that Virginia wasn't going to let her. "Don't you have to feed your ducks first?" she inquired savagely, still trying to break loose from Virginia's hold.

"They'll live," Virginia said casually and led her over to a large tree about twenty yards from the pond. "Here, lie down on my cape. Face down, that's right. I'll just loosen up those muscles in your back and shoulders."

Leticia did as she was told, and soon she felt Virginia kneeling over her, kneading all the muscles that hurt. "That feels good," she grunted.

"Yep, nothing like a back rub for getting rid of tension," Virginia said. Leticia didn't respond so Virginia just kept on working away at her shoulders. After fifteen minutes she stopped and rolled over onto the cape next to Leticia. "Feel better?" she asked, resting her arm on Leticia's waist. "Yeah, thanks. And thanks for not getting into a fight when I was so grumpy before."

"It's okay, Fred. Do you want to talk about what's bothering you?" Virginia asked.

"Nah, I'd rather not. I do want to talk about us, though, Virginia."

"Whaddaya mean by 'us'?" Virginia replied very quickly.

"You know. Us. The way we act with each other?" Leticia insisted. "And the way we feel. The way I feel about you anyway."

"And what way is that?" Virginia probed.

"Well, excited and kind of always eager to see you." Leticia thought hard. "And then there's the feeling that I shouldn't tell anybody, you know, like my father. It's like I have to play it cool when I really want to tell everyone."

"But tell everyone what?" Virginia persisted. "That you go to the duck pond in the park to hang out with the doctor's kid? There really isn't anything to tell, is there?"

Leticia felt herself getting irritated with Virginia, but the irritation passed quickly as Virginia rolled over onto her back and pulled Leticia over on top of her. "Or is this what you're not supposed to tell?" she teased, pressing Leticia's body into hers and holding her tight.

Leticia tried to take a deep breath, but Virginia was holding her too tight. "Hey," she whispered, " let me breathe."

"Virginia released her a little. "Okay, breathe," she whispered back. "You have ten seconds."

Leticia giggled and drew a couple of deep breaths. Then Virginia squeezed her tight again and drew her head down.

"What…" Leticia started to ask, but she couldn't finish her question because Virginia covered her mouth with her own. Leticia's nose tickled, but she didn't even try to scratch it.

After what felt like a few seconds but was actually a very long kiss, Leticia pulled her head back and looked down at Virginia's face. Virginia smiled up at her. "Well?" she asked.

"Well what?"

"Is that what you're not supposed to tell?"

"Of course it is, silly," Leticia tried to sound annoyed but couldn't. "Don't you think my father might find it just a little odd?"

"Well why would you even want to tell him?" Virginia sounded genuinely perplexed.

"Don't you tell your father things?" Leticia inquired. "Or your mother?"

"Come on, Fred," Virginia sounded as if she wanted to laugh but was controlling herself, "there are some things I tell my parents, but not everything."

"Well," Leticia said smugly, "I guess you're just not as close to them as I am to my father. He understands everything and always takes my side."

Virginia looked at her dubiously. "I'm not so sure that's such a great arrangement," she said seriously. "How will you make your own decisions if you consult your father on everything?"

"Ha," Leticia came back. "You're a fine one to talk. I bet the only reason you want to be a doctor is because your father is one."

"My mother is one too," Virginia admitted, "but that's beside the point. I don't tell them everything. I decide for myself what I want them to know."

Leticia hated being criticized, so she rolled away from Virginia and stood up. "I gotta go, Virginia, but don't worry, I won't tell my father about you. He wouldn't think you're my type, and to tell you the truth, I'm not sure of that myself."

Virginia sat up and smirked at her. "No, your type is a very, very wealthy man who will support you in the style in which you want to live. I know all about it, Fred, you already told me. I don't know why I like you either. You're such a spoiled brat. But I do like you."

The idea that Virginia liked her despite her better judgment pleased Leticia since it made her feel irresistible. Usually she only felt that way with her father. However, Virginia's calling her a spoiled brat demanded a response, though she couldn't come up with something clever and devastating right at that instant.

47

"You sound like that pill of a cop. He's the only other person I know who thinks I'm a spoiled brat. You know who I mean, I'm sure," Leticia tried to sound as superior as she possibly could but only sounded like a bad imitation of a snooty butler. Virginia started to laugh.

"Fred, Eric Johnson is okay. He's studying to be a lawyer, did you know that?"

"Lawyer, cop, doctor, servant, what difference does it make? Boring people with boring lives," Leticia said, trying to sound sophisticated.

Virginia laughed even harder as she stood up and walked towards Leticia. "Oh Fred, Eric is right. You do need a spanking."

"Oh is that right?" Leticia growled as she stalked off towards her bike. "Well, you need a life, Virginia Carr, so what do you think of that?"

Leticia was furious. She just wasn't sure if she was more furious at that stupid cop or at Virginia. Imagine them talking about her behind her back like that. She reached her bike a second before Virginia got to her and pulled her off.

"Come on, Fred, don't be such a twit," she giggled, as she pulled Leticia to the ground and sat on her.

"You're a stupid slug, Virginia Carr, and I hope your eyes fall out," Leticia squealed struggling to throw Virginia off. Then she suddenly stopped struggling, took a deep breath, and started to laugh her evil laugh. She cackled and snorted for a couple of minutes while Virginia stared down at her with scientific curiosity. Leticia had hoped to startle Virginia and then to throw her off when she wasn't expecting it, but Virginia sat imperturbably observing Leticia's gyrations, holding her wrists at her sides with long, thin, but strong hands.

"Okay, okay, uncle, or whatever you want me to say," Leticia said at last. "Let me up, Virginia, I really do have to go home."

Virginia carefully raised herself, still holding Leticia's wrists down. Just as she had most of her weight on her knees and Leticia's wrists, however, Leticia twisted out from under her and rolled her over. She lay on Virginia's chest and grunted at her. "Okay, see how you like being pinned down, goofy."

Virginia didn't resist. She didn't say a word or make a move. She just looked up at Leticia with the same curious look on her face. After a few seconds, Leticia lost interest in her conquest. As soon as her mind started wandering, Virginia flipped her off and to the side. She turned towards Leticia, slipped her arm under her neck, and brought her face close again. She kissed her and let her mouth wander over Leticia's face, kissing and nipping and kissing again.

It didn't take Virginia long to get Leticia's attention that way, and as soon as she had it, she stopped. "Hey Fred, I didn't mean to hurt your feelings. Honest I didn't. You just act so...". She thought better of completing her sentence and just kissed Leticia's mouth again.

After a short while, they both sat up. Leticia looked at Virginia inquisitively. "If you like me, how come you talked about me behind my back with that cop?"

"I didn't," Virginia replied. "He came into the clinic to talk to my father while I was helping out. He had a little kid with him who'd fallen off his bike and broken his arm. He said it was a bad day for kids on bikes and told my father about you. I was listening. That's all."

"How did you know it was me?"

"How many other children do your parents have?"

Leticia didn't answer. She wasn't sure she believed Virginia, but she didn't want to fight. When she stood up to leave, Virginia did too, and they kissed again. Leticia hopped on her bike and took off down the path to the main road. When she looked back, Virginia was calmly kneeling by the pond feeding the ducks. She didn't look up, so Leticia didn't wave. She pedaled home and went directly to her tree to think.

CHAPTER 9
FLIRTATION
1961
❖

The next week passed without incident. Every morning Leticia biked to the duck pond and spent the hour before lunch with Virginia. They fed the ducks, kissed and caressed each other, and fought whenever they tried to talk about anything. Leticia didn't mind because she enjoyed arguing, and whenever their arguments threatened to get out of hand, that is, whenever it seemed that Virginia might win, Leticia turned the verbal battle into a physical encounter, which always ended with more kisses and fondling.

Occasionally Leticia worried that someone might discover them in what she could not help but consider a compromising position, but that possibility did not seem to disturb Virginia at all. Whenever Leticia tried to discuss it with her, Virginia just laughed and started to tickle and wrestle with her. "Let them come and find us, Fred. I'll tell them I'm engaged in a very important scientific experiment."

Leticia admired her friend's brashness and tried unsuccessfully to emulate it. Virginia realized that Leticia, despite her conviction of her right to do and have whatever she wanted, had a deep streak of insecurity that made her dependent on others' approval, particularly those she thought of as wealthy and powerful. She's just the tiniest bit conventional, Virginia often thought when she was alone, but she never held that against Leticia. It was useful information to be stored away in preparation for a time when she might need it.

It wasn't until the following week, two weeks before the end of the summer that something happened, and it didn't happen to them but to Officer Johnson. Virginia arrived at the park on Tuesday with the information that the town's selectmen had decided not to renew his contract for the following year.

"He came to the clinic early this morning with a woman and her kid. The little girl had a really bad case of ringworm, and while my dad worked on her, Eric told him that losing this job means he won't be able to go to law school next year the way he'd planned. You know, he has a winter job as a sheriff's deputy in some city out west, but they don't pay him nearly as much in two years as he makes in a summer here. I feel really awful for him. I think he'd make a really good lawyer."

"Well, I think it serves him right," Leticia gloated. "Anyway, the country has more than enough lawyers already, especially self-righteous ones like Johnson."

Virginia sighed. "Fred, you sure know how to hold a grudge, don't you?"

"Well, I didn't ask him to start a fight with me, did I? He started it, and now he got what's coming to him."

"Did your father..." Virginia started, then changed her mind.

"Did my father get him fired?" Leticia finished her thought. "I don't know, but I certainly hope so. I really don't like that man, Virginia, not just because he treated me badly either. There's something creepy about him."

"Oh come on, Fred, Eric is all right. He's just serious, that's all."

"Well, that's your opinion. I'm glad he won't be back next year."

A silence greeted that statement, and Leticia looked down at her feet. "Uh, Virginia, what about you? Will you be back next year?"

Virginia looked at her in surprise. "Of course I will. My father has a five year contract with the clinic."

Leticia suddenly felt very cheerful. She started to tickle Virginia, and soon they were rolling on the ground, tickling each other and kissing and nuzzling, and Officer Johnson's fate was forgotten. Afterwards, they fed the ducks as usual, and Virginia walked Leticia home. At the start of the Barnes' driveway, Leticia hopped onto her bike, waved good-bye to Virginia, and pedaled swiftly. Virginia turned back toward town, whistling to herself as she always did after spending time with Leticia.

***

The Barneses were having dinner guests that evening, and Leticia could not persuade her parents to let her have a tray in her room, as she so often did on formal occasions. Even her father was unmoved by her pleas.

"Listen, Lettie darling, I absolutely need you to be there tonight. Jeff is bringing some fellow with him who needs a job, and I want you to check him out and let me know what you think. You know how I value your opinion, love, don't you? Besides, we're not dressing for dinner tonight. We're going to barbecue, and that means you can wear pants if you like."

Leticia was only slightly mollified by her father's permission to wear pants. Mostly she found dinner guests boring, and Jeff was no exception. He was chairman of a company with which her father had business dealings, and the Barnes family entertained him at dinner at least three times a summer. He was a tall fat man, whose full name was Thomas Jefferson Alger, and all of his business colleagues who knew him well simply called him Jeff. Leticia particularly disliked him because, in addition to being boring, he condescended to her, paying her ridiculous compliments that made her uncomfortable. Her father got along well with him, though he often told Leticia in private that Jeff was a bore and that he only kept him on as a golf partner because he was so easy to beat.

Leticia could not imagine that anyone Jeff brought around could possibly be at all interesting to her, but she had no choice. Shortly before six in the evening, she went upstairs, showered, and dressed in her favorite magenta and white shirt and black pants. She was trying to run a comb through her hair when the doorbell rang.

Leticia's hair was long, curly, and thick. She rarely combed it but was usually satisfied with running her fingers through it to establish a semblance of neatness. Her mother, however, had insisted that she comb it for company, so she compromised, running a comb along her crown and a brush through the rest of it. Once. It was still a tangle, but a tangle that gave evidence of having been fussed with recently.

When she heard male voices drifting up the stairs, Leticia realized it was time to make her appearance. She raced down the first half of the stairs and then slowed to make a more dignified entrance. Her father was standing by the living room window talking with two tall men. One she recognized immediately as Jeff. The other was a lot younger, thinner, and ruggedly handsome. He wore a military uniform. Leticia had no idea which branch of the service he belonged to, but he looked too old to be attending military school or college.

None of the men had a drink in hand, so Leticia knew she would have the chance to play bartender. She enjoyed it, and it limited her required socializing with guests. She preferred to leave the socializing to her mother, who had not yet put in an appearance.

"Hello, Leticia," her father said warmly, as if he hadn't seen her in hours. He extended his arm and draped it lightly over her shoulder. I'd like you meet our guests. "Jeff, you know my daughter, I'm sure." Jeff nodded and smiled, and Leticia forced a smile to her lips. Her father continued. "Paul, this is my daughter Leticia. Leticia, please shake hands with Lt. Colonel Perceval P. Runcible. His middle name is Paul, and he prefers it to Perceval."

Leticia put out her hand, and the young man took it and shook it warmly. He had a big white-toothed smile that he turned on her as he inclined his head in her direction. "Glad to meet you, Miss Barnes," he said softly. "Your father was just telling us what an excellent bartender you are."

Leticia raised one eyebrow slightly. "Would you like a drink, Colonel Runcible?" she asked.

The young man laughed. "Paul, please. Colonel Runcible was my grandfather. He was in the army, while I'm in the air force, but I suppose I am trying to follow in his footsteps. And no, I really am not trying to get you to mix me a drink, just attempting in my feeble way to make conversation. I so rarely get to talk with young ladies."

Leticia wasn't sure if she liked him or not, but she had to admit he was better company than Jeff. And he was good-looking and dashing. She might have called him distinguished too, except for his youth and the small scrap of toilet paper that covered a spot on his chin. She found herself staring at it, wishing it weren't there marring his otherwise splendid appearance. She decided to distract herself from it.

"Excuse me for a moment, Paul," she said, turning to her father. "Daddy, do you know where Mother is?"

Her father smiled sweetly, and she realized that his smile resembled Paul's. "She's out by the grill, Lettie. The caterer sent over a man to start the fire, and she's supervising him in true lady of the house fashion." Calvin Barnes winked at his daughter, who realized that he'd already had quite a bit to drink. Generally he refrained from mocking his wife before people outside the family.

Leticia suddenly felt lightheaded. She turned back to the young airman and excused herself. She was halfway onto the grounds behind the house before she realized he was following her.

Lucille Barnes looked tired and cranky. She was waving her hands and obviously upset with the caterer's assistant. Leticia raced over only to hear her mother, who'd never attended, much less hosted a barbecue in her life, tell the man to turn down the flames. The assistant shrugged his shoulders helplessly and turned away. Leticia turned to her mother, who, she realized, had once again taken more Valium than was good for her.

"Lettie, I don't know a thing about this, but I am certain the meat will burn and the entire dinner will be a disaster. Your father will be most upset. I don't know what the caterer could have been thinking of when he sent me a boy who doesn't even know how to turn the flames down," Mrs. Barnes spoke contentiously in the tone of someone hard done by.

Leticia took her by the arm and led her away from the grill. "Mother," she said soothingly, "there is nothing to worry about, I'm sure. Just sit down here on this chair and rest. I'll see to the grill." Mrs. Barnes, delighted to have someone else assume responsibility for once, followed her daughter's instructions, and Leticia headed back to the grill.

Paul came up to her immediately. "I just spoke to the catering fellow," he said, "and everything is under control. The flames will die out in a while, and he'll put the meat over the hot coals. There's no problem really." He smiled his big smile again. "Is your mother all right? She looked a bit confused."

Leticia immediately came to her mother's defense. "She's been tired lately. She never sleeps well in the late summer. The heat has a bad effect on her."

Paul said nothing, but Leticia was glad he was standing nearby and decided to try to make conversation. "You are rather young to be a lieutenant colonel, aren't you?"

"Oh, I inherited the rank, so to speak. I went to the academy in Colorado Springs and came out a junior officer like everyone else. I rose in the ranks quickly after that, though, partly because of my name, I suspect. Not that I didn't deserve it. I worked hard and followed orders."

Leticia was not that interested in his rise through the ranks, but she feigned interest to be polite. "How old are you actually, Paul?"

Paul straightened his shoulders and beamed at her. "I'll be twenty-six on August 23," he answered. "I am the youngest lieutenant colonel in all the United States military services."

His pride amused Leticia, but she was careful not to show that she found him funny. "Well, I'll be fifteen in November, but I'm sure that I'll be nothing so grand as a lieutenant colonel by the time I'm twenty-five."

Paul laughed at that and offered her a mock salute. "Miss Barnes, if I am correct in my estimation of you, you have the makings of a six-star general," he said solemnly.

"I didn't know there was any such thing as a six-star general," Leticia protested.

"There isn't yet," he agreed, "but I'm sure you're more than capable of being the first."

"Why Paul," Leticia said sweetly and realized she was flirting, "I do believe you are making fun of me."

The young man looked at her with admiration, and she felt as if she were much older than her fourteen and a half years. Leticia was proud of herself. There's nothing to this, she thought. I don't have to be ladylike or even pretend to be very interested in this man. She smiled up at her uniformed companion, and when he offered her his arm to escort her back into the house, she accepted. Her mother followed, smiling wanly, and immediately headed upstairs to her room. She's probably going to take another Valium, Leticia thought. But there was little she could do, so she rejoined her father and Jeff, who had already mixed their own drinks. Paul followed her into the living room, and when she offered him a drink, he asked for a gin and tonic.

It was almost eight o'clock when dinner was ready. Her mother came down the stairs at just the right time. "Why she has it down to a science," her father told her in a stage whisper. "Just look at her. You'd never know she was three sheets to the wind."

Leticia was surprised that her father noticed her mother's condition, and she was appalled that he could talk about it so callously. "Daddy," she objected strenuously, "she's not drunk, you are. She's just taken a few too many of those pills Dr. Evans prescribes for her, that's all."

"Lettie my dear, I am not drunk. I am pleasantly tipsy. Let us go out to dinner before the meat gets cold." He took her arm more clumsily than she was accustomed to and led her out to the patio. Paul followed at a discreet distance, making conversation with Jeff about their golf scores. He had drunk only half of his gin and tonic and accepted no further alcoholic refreshment. Paul was attentive to both Leticia and her mother, and Leticia decided that he really was quite the gentleman with excellent manners, just the sort of man she would marry if he were a millionaire instead of a military officer.

❖

Virginia pushed open the door to the room she shared with Carolyn and strode in with unusual forcefulness. She braced herself for an argument about going to Grant's Hill for the ten days left of their vacation. Carolyn sat on their bed labeling a dozen film canisters.

"Carrie," Virginia announced, "I've got to go to Grant's Hill after all. I'm sorry."

Carolyn looked up at her. "I know. Toni's call came about a half-hour ago. How did you find out?"

Virginia cocked her head. "Come again?" she asked.

"You know, Toni, the receptionist at your father's clinic? She asked me to tell you that he fainted again and is in the hospital. She thinks you ought to get there ASAP. I know she isn't one to cry wolf, so I packed your bags." Carolyn smiled at her hesitantly. "I started in on mine as well, but I thought I ought to check with you first before deciding to come along." She paused, but Virginia said nothing. Her eyes darted around the room until they came to rest on her luggage.

Carolyn broke the silence. "I'd hesitate to interfere in your relationship with Henry, but you know I've been acting as his informal medical consultant ever since he started having symptoms. If I came along I might be useful. Do you know the attending physician? I put in a call to him, but he hasn't called back." She reached into her pocket and pulled out a piece of paper. "His name is Stanley Felton."

"Of course you're coming with me," Virginia responded with more assurance than she felt. "Henry trusts you." That sounded almost like an accusation she knew, but she didn't care. She thought of the hours Henry had spent on the phone with Carolyn. He'd revealed more about his health to Carolyn than to her, his own daughter, she thought with a trace of resentment. "Sometimes I think he trusts you more than me."

Virginia brushed past Carolyn's denial. "Did you book us on the next flight to Baltimore? Did you check us out of here? No? I'll check us out, you call the airline."

Virginia jerked open the door and raced through it before Carolyn could get another word out, so Carolyn sighed and picked up the phone.

The drive to the airport started in silence as both women recovered from the suddenness of their departure. While Carolyn had made airline reservations, Virginia had checked them out of the lodge and arranged to return the rented car in Wyoming and pick up another on the east coast. Carolyn had tried once again to reach Dr. Felton, and failing that, had left a message explaining who she was and when she was likely to arrive at the hospital.

After a silent interval, Virginia ordered Carolyn to repeat everything Toni had told her. Then without giving her a chance to respond, Virginia blurted out, "What if my father is orchestrating this whole thing? He's so determined to have me in Grant's Hill." Her mouth was dry. She hated to reveal the depth of paranoia her father could arouse in her.

Carolyn shook her head. "Toni said he got quite a bump on his head when he fell. That's why he was admitted to the hospital. He might have a concussion."

Virginia frowned, wishing Carolyn had told her that right away, but she said nothing. Carolyn squeezed her hand. "He'll be okay, don't worry. And hey, you didn't exactly give me a chance to describe the precipitating incident, you know! So don't glare at me as if this were all my fault."

"You still think he has Parkinson's, don't you?" Virginia asked, removing her hand from Carolyn's grasp.

"I'm as positive as I can be without diagnostic tests. He's such a stubborn mule though. It will take a miracle to get him to agree to the tests."

"Doctors don't make good patients," Virginia sighed. "Besides, he doesn't believe it. It will take time." She flashed back to her mother's long illness with its stages of denial and resignation.

"He doesn't want to believe it," Carolyn concurred, sounding irritated. "But the longer he waits, the harder it will be to develop effective therapy." She looked over at Virginia for a response, but Virginia was asleep.

***

At the airport Virginia returned their rental car while Carolyn stood at the counter to check luggage and get their seat assignments. By the time Virginia returned, their flights through Chicago and on to Baltimore had been canceled and Carolyn had gotten them rebooked onto a flight to Philadelphia by way of Denver. Since their departure

57

was two hours later than originally scheduled, Carolyn hunted for a pay phone as soon as Virginia appeared. She left another message with Dr. Felton's answering service, canceled one car rental in Baltimore and arranged for another in Philadelphia. By the time she returned to Virginia, she knew she was in for a difficult trip.

"Well, that should take care of everything that can be taken care of from this end," she said cheerfully, though she knew better than to expect her cheerfulness to distract her Virginia from an impending bout of despondency. When Virginia barely looked up, she continued, "I have a question for you." Still no response from Virginia, so she added, "Do you want something to eat or drink?"

Virginia glared at her. "I hate airport food."

"I know, darling," Carolyn replied gently, "but the food on the plane won't be any better."

"Thanks a bunch for reminding me," Virginia grumbled.

Carolyn rarely had to deal with Virginia in a bad mood, and she was hopelessly inept at it, she knew. But she tried one more tack before giving up. "Sweetpea, what were you about to tell me when you came back to the lodge this afternoon? You didn't know your father had fainted, did you?" She took Virginia's hand.

"No, but since I have to go to Grant's Hill anyway, what does it matter?" Virginia sounded defensive, and Carolyn resisted the urge to drop her hand and pull out a book. "Maybe it does, maybe it doesn't. Tell me what happened. Did you go to see that creepy cop?"

Virginia shrugged and pulled her hand away.

"I'll take that as a yes," Carolyn continued. Whatever he told you must have been one hell of a shocker. Was it about Leticia?"

Virginia took a deep breath and recounted as much of the conversation that she could recall. When she finished, Carolyn took her hand again. "Well, you've got some week to look forward to, don't you, sweetheart?"

Virginia nodded glumly and looked at her expectantly, but Carolyn didn't appear to have anything more to say. Virginia swallowed. "I guess I should have expected Johnson to be weird about Leticia and not exactly thrilled about you and me, but it still shook me up."

Carolyn raised her eyebrows. "I'm not the least bit surprised that the man is a grudge-bearing homophobe. But why he needs to get you involved in his vendetta escapes me." She shook herself the way a dog does when it gets out of the water and threw up her hands. "The whole thing gives me the creeps."

Virginia frowned. "I have a feeling that Johnson has been in touch with my father about Leticia as well as about you and me, but he didn't come out and say so. I can't get over that we happened to be in the same coffee shop with him. Too much of a coincidence. And the fact that he recognized me is very strange. I haven't seen him since I was fourteen, and I don't look much like my father. At least I hope I don't."

Once she'd started to articulate a load of confusing thoughts and feelings, Virginia couldn't stop. "I was worried that you'd have a fit when I told you I was going to Grant's Hill after all. And I was sure that the reason, because I need to check out this mess with Leticia, would just make things worse." She looked sideways at Carolyn, who smiled fondly at her.

"I'll save my fit for my first meeting with Leticia," she said, putting her arm around Virginia.

Virginia jerked out of her embrace. "What do you mean? You're coming to help Henry, not to confront Leticia," she protested weakly.

"Who said anything about confrontation? I think it would help if you had some support."

Virginia flinched again, disbelief written on her face. "You want to be my support in dealing with Leticia? You?" She rolled her eyes. "Carrie, you're the one who stopped me from going to Grant's Hill. You never wanted to have anything to do with the place. That's why Henry has always visited us."

Carolyn shook her head violently. "Just a darned minute there! Henry has come to visit us because we happen to live in the most beautiful city in the whole country. And you're right: I never wanted to have anything to do with that place. I still don't. But this isn't going to be easy for you, and I'd think you'd want someone to be there for you."

Virginia was still astonished. "Ideally, yes, I'd like someone to be there for me, but you?" She regretted her vehemence as soon as she saw Carolyn's face.

"I just thought I'd be the most likely person, all things considered," Carolyn mumbled, looking as if she were trying not to cry. "I apologize if that was presumptuous."

"No, Carrie, don't apologize," Virginia said softly. "I'm sorry if I sounded so...well, you know. But you get so upset about Leticia that..."

"You mean jealous, don't you?" Carolyn interrupted. "Listen, Virginia, I can't promise I won't get jealous if you and Leticia get close to each other, but I can promise not to act suspicious as long as you don't get all secretive. Deal?" She held out her hand.

"Sure, why not?" Virginia replied quickly, shaking the hand Carolyn held out. She wondered why everyone suddenly wanted to make deals with her. "You're right, I'll probably need all the help I can get."

***

Carolyn knew better than to push Virginia into further serious conversation, so she sat back and watching the people milling around near their gate, trying to differentiate the natives from the tourists with their barely broken-in cowboy boots and flannel shirts that looked as if they'd just been bought yesterday. Meanwhile Virginia chewed on her lip and worried about her father. She did not want to picture the domineering doctor who was always so comfortable giving orders to nurses and telling the parents of his patients what to do as a sick man confined to a hospital bed. She knew that Carolyn had noticed a few changes in Henry the last time he'd visited them. His voice had gotten hoarse and he seemed to be having trouble with his balance, tripping over non-existent obstacles and swaying for a few seconds each time he got out of a chair. And he'd become increasingly irascible. Carolyn had told her that some of those changes could be early indicators of Parkinson's disease, but she never insisted that Virginia do or say anything in response to her suggestion. Virginia wondered if her father really had suffered a concussion when he fell. When she thought about it, a dreadful, nauseous feeling overcame her. A concussion was the last thing Henry needed.

Virginia glanced over at Carolyn and willed herself to be distracted by the crowd of travelers the way her Carolyn was, but she failed. When she suppressed nagging thoughts of her father, her mind raced back to her last meeting with Leticia. The possibility of encountering her before she knew what to say frightened Virginia. The idea that someone she had been so close to might have committed a murder made her head spin. She didn't want to think about that any more than she wanted to think of Henry's illness, but she knew she would have to sooner rather than later. She sighed, stretched, and finally stood up to take a walk.

"Bathroom?" Carolyn murmured, but Virginia didn't answer before walking off towards the terminal's main lobby with its gift shops and

Wild West displays. Carolyn followed her with her eyes for as long as she remained in view.

When Virginia returned, she was talkative again, asking questions about Parkinson's disease. She was determined to pick Carolyn's brain, and by the time they boarded, Carolyn had told her every detail of the last dozen Parkinson's cases she had handled. She spared no details, recounting in full the drugs' side effects and the characteristic changes that marked the progress of the disease. She knew how important it was for Virginia to know what lay ahead. She wanted Virginia to be prepared, though she knew that nothing she said could adequately prepare her. On the airplane Virginia wanted Carolyn to repeat her phone conversation with Toni, but all Carolyn wanted to do was sleep.

CHAPTER 11
MR. RIGHT
1961
❖

On the morning after her first meeting with Paul Runcible, Leticia was the first person up and out of bed in the Barnes household. She made coffee for her father, who awoke at nine with a hangover. It took several sips of coffee before he was awake and coherent enough for conversation.

"Daddy," she began tentatively, "are you feeling all right?"

"I'm fine, sweetheart," he replied, smiling but bleary-eyed. "I hope you enjoyed our little celebration last night. I know your mother was slightly incapacitated, but I was impressed with how well you handled the situation. Extraordinarily well, but then you are an extraordinary girl. Our dinner was a success because of you, and I want you to know that I am very proud of you."

Leticia noticed that he didn't mention his own overindulgence, but she didn't really expect him to. She registered unwillingly how her appraisal of her father was beginning to change. The change scared her. It made her feel as if she were the only real adult in the family.

"I think that the evening's success was due to Lieutenant Colonel Runcible. He was very helpful and I like him," she said simply.

"Well, Lettie," her father replied with a patronizing smile, "I'm glad you like him. He's not at all what Old Jeff led me to expect. Not a callow young fellow in search of his first real job at all. Far from it! He's a real gem, a prize. Comes from a good family. Old stock, though not terribly well off anymore. Paul has some young men under his command who are quitting the military. They are the ones who need jobs. Very nice of him to concern himself with their prospects, I think, don't you? I told him I'd see what I could do."

"So he's not resigning his commission and settling down?" Leticia asked, already knowing the answer.

"Not a chance! Mark my words, Lettie. That young man is going places. He'll be a general by the time he's forty. He'll have a little money to fall back on when he retires, but not much. Just his military pension. Anyway, he's too old for you."

Leticia was glad that her father approved of Paul and grinned at Calvin fondly. "Well, Daddy, the reason I like Paul is that he reminds me of you. He's charming and trustworthy. Of course, even though you're older, you're more dashing. You never cut yourself shaving and show up at dinner parties with toilet paper on your face."

Calvin chuckled in pleasure. "Paul is a little old-fashioned. Insists on shaving with a straight razor. I only know because he told me. Those things are hell unless you keep the blade extremely well honed. His razor is probably just not sharp enough, that's all. No reason to be down on him for that."

Leticia knew that her father shaved with a safety razor and used Wilkinson blades. When she was small he'd regularly given her an empty razor and let her use his badger brush to lather up her face. He'd warned her not to play with his blades, but she had once picked up a blade anyway and nicked her finger. She'd panicked when she couldn't get it to stop bleeding. Instead of reprimanding her, he'd told her to hold her breath and touched his styptic pencil to the cut. It stung like anything, but the bleeding stopped. She'd yelled in surprise at the sting but didn't cry, so he had told her she was a very brave girl. Her father put a large band-aid on the nick even though it was small and had stopped bleeding. Then he found a purple marker she had been coloring with the previous evening and drew a purple heart on the band-aid. She smiled at the memory. "Well," she insisted, "I still think you're more dashing, and I'm entitled to my opinion."

Calvin swallowed. "Now, Lettie, you don't need to pay your old father compliments," he objected, but she could see that he was delighted.

Leticia was not really flattering her father. Her assessment of men was based on very little experience. She compared them to the image of her father that she had cherished for so long. The closer the match, the more she liked the man. Even though the cherished image had begun to tarnish ever so slightly, it was still overwhelmingly bright within her memory, and she could call it forth whenever she felt the need.

Leticia watched her father finish his coffee. As soon as he'd put down his cup, she asked if he knew whether her mother was up yet. Calvin shrugged. "I'm off to the links, honey," he replied with a smile. "Why don't you see to your mother? I'm sure she'd appreciate that." And then he was out the door before she could even wish him a good day.

Leticia mechanically washed his cup and saucer and laid them in the rack to dry. She didn't exactly want to walk up the stairs to her mother's room, but she didn't find the prospect quite so onerous as usual. So she wiped the table and then went to face Lucille, whom she found lying in bed.

"Mother, do you need anything? Coffee or tea or something to eat?" Leticia asked as she straightened the tangled sheet over her mother's body.

"Thank you, but no, Lettie. I'm not up to it just yet."

"Shall I run a bath for you then?" Leticia asked.

"No, not yet, dear. Thank you," Lucille replied tiredly.

Leticia found herself at a loss for words. She wanted to ask her mother if she planned to stay in bed all day feeling sorry for herself, but she felt that would be unnecessarily cruel. She resorted to cruelty only in self-defense and as a last resort, and she didn't feel the need for it that morning. Instead she smiled at her mother for a long time. It was a concerned and sympathetic smile that brought tears to Lucille's eyes.

"Lettie, you are growing up, and I must say you are turning out much better than I could have expected. You handled yourself very well last night, and unless I'm sorely mistaken, that young colonel was very taken with you."

Ordinarily Leticia would have responded with annoyance, telling her mother she was too young to think about men and marriage, but she said simply, "I liked him too, Mother. Daddy thinks he's too old for me though."

Leticia noticed the color returning to her mother's face and was relieved. "Nonsense!" Lucille asserted with more spirit than Leticia expected. Lucille sat up in bed and folded her pillow under her head. "He's only about ten years older than you, my dear, and that's not so much," she continued. "Of course, it seems like a lot to you now, but by the time you are eighteen, the young man will still be under thirty. Why, I know of many perfectly happy, married couples with a much greater age differential." She pursed her lips, and concluded, "If only his family had invested their money more wisely!"

Leticia's relief at her mother's apparent recovery was mixed with unease. Though she had played out the scenario of a marriage to the young officer in her head, it was no more than a fantasy. When her mother spoke about it, however, the scenario felt threateningly real.

"Mother, I do like Paul, but we only just met, and I'm sure he's much sought after…"

"Bah," Lucille cut her off. "Strike while the iron is hot is what I always say. I shall speak with your father." She smiled at her daughter.

"Now, my dear, would you please run my bath? Hot water, remember! I despise a tepid bath."

Leticia was glad to leave her mother's room. In the bathroom she laid out the mat and turned on the hot water tap. It was nearly a quarter to eleven, so she knew she had no time to climb her tree and order the events of the morning in her mind.

***

Virginia arrived first at the pond. "Hi, Fred," she called cheerfully as soon as Leticia came into view. "What's new?"

"New England, New York, New Jersey, Newbraska," Leticia shrieked at the top of her lungs as she skidded to a stop at the water's edge. "What's new with you?"

"New Castle, New Zealand, New Haven, Newralgia," Virginia replied, and they hugged and walked off into the shade of their favorite tree. Virginia had brought a large beach towel, and she spread it carefully. Then they lay down and rolled into each other's arms.

They held each other a long time as they always did, and Virginia's fingers traced the shadows of the leaves on Leticia's face. Leticia sighed contentedly and stretched. Then she burrowed more deeply into Virginia's arms. She tried to stay in the moment, but the morning's conversation with her mother kept forcing its way into her consciousness, making her dizzy as her thoughts raced back and forth between the pleasant fantasy she'd invented and the possibility that her mother would indeed get her way and marry her off to Paul Runcible.

Virginia felt Leticia stiffen. "What's wrong, Fred?" she asked, continuing to trace her patterns on Leticia's face. Leticia pulled away for a few seconds, then decided to forget about her mother and indulge herself in her fantasy. She leaned into Virginia and whispered softly in her ear, "I met the man I'm going to marry. He finds me absolutely irresistible."

"That's nice," Virginia whispered back with a low chuckle, hugging Leticia even more tightly. "Now can we change the subject?"

"That's nice?" Leticia echoed in an outraged voice. "Is that all you can say? Where's your sense of romance?" Suddenly she felt that she had to argue with Virginia, though she didn't know why. "You don't even want to know who he is, do you? Or what he's like, or how we met?"

"Not really," Virginia admitted. "Why would I?"

Leticia jumped to her feet and walked towards her bicycle. "You're a spoilsport and I hate you," she yelled back over her shoulder at Virginia, who'd stood up and followed her with her eyes. "You're mean and funny-looking and..." She ran out words, but instead of hopping on her bike and pedaling off, she sat down on the ground next to it and rested her arms on her knees and her head in her hands.

Virginia stood up and joined her on the ground near her bike. "Okay, Fred, why don't you tell me about Mr. Right?"

Leticia jumped to her feet and walked to the edge of the pond. Virginia followed, shaking her head. "What is up with you, Fred?"

Leticia smiled vacantly and began to recount the events of the previous evening as if she were narrating a soap opera. Virginia listened gravely, with a wrinkled forehead and tense mouth.

"But Leticia, Fred, honey," she interrupted her friend's glowing account of a life of travel and adventure she expected to lead as a high-ranking officer's wife, "you hardly know the man. He's a lot older than you, and he may not be as nice in real life, everyday life, I mean, as he seemed at the barbecue. Besides, I thought you planned to marry someone with lots of money."

"You're just jealous, Virginia Carr! Leticia snapped. You envy the life I'll have with Paul. You're going to spend your life inside a medical center or laboratory working like the slave you were born to be."

Virginia sighed, wanting nothing more than to give Leticia a swift kick. "Come on, Fred, you know I'm just worried about you. I don't want you to be disappointed or get hurt. You're making plans without knowing why you're making them. Come on, you're only fourteen. That's too early to be thinking about marriage."

"Fourteen and a half," Leticia hissed at her. "At least I don't act like an old woman of a hundred and ten the way you do!"

Virginia didn't want to fight, but she realized that trying to reason with Leticia was pointless. So she grabbed her arm and pulled her gently back to the beach towel. "I'm fourteen, just like you, Fred," she said, pushing Leticia to the ground. "If you're happy with your fantasy of marriage, that's fine with me," she added, kneeling next to her friend and burying her nose in Leticia's neck. "I hope everything works out for you. I really do."

Leticia was almost mollified, but not quite. "I'm fourteen and a half, Virginia Carr, and that means I'm older than you. You're supposed to respect your elders. You know that."

They started kissing then, and though their quarrel was history, Virginia knew she wouldn't forget it.

***

By the time Leticia left the park, she felt certain that she would marry Paul Runcible someday, but she was also very clear in her mind that it wouldn't be any time soon. She had a lot of living to do first. Nonetheless, it didn't hurt to dream. In the back of her mind she knew that everything Virginia had said was right. It was far too early to plan for marriage. She was not about to let Virginia know that though. It wasn't a good idea to let her get the upper hand, especially since she was such a know-it-all. Leticia whistled cheerfully as she pedaled home, anticipating lunch. But first she would have a good, long sit in her tree.

Lucille was waiting for her at the door, so the tree would have to wait. "Lettie," she said excitedly, "Lettie! Jeff phoned and said that Paul thought you were just delightful. I invited both of them for lunch later in the week, but unfortunately Paul has to return to his base tomorrow. He told Jeff he hoped to visit us this winter when he has Christmas leave. Isn't that exciting?"

Leticia was pleased to see her mother so lively. Had she been honest with herself, she would have had to admit that her mother was much more excited than she was. Her feelings more closely resembled relief. Paul made a good fantasy, and discovering how easy flirting was really had been very satisfying. Yet she was glad not to have to deal with the reality of the man in the immediate future.

"Did Jeff really say that, Mother? How exciting!" she feigned joyful surprise to humor her mother. In fact, she did it so well that she almost fooled herself.

"Yes, dear, he really did," Lucille replied triumphantly, adding with a conspiratorial wink, "Let's not say a word to your father about this, Lettie. You know how old-fashioned he can be."

"Yes, Mother," Leticia replied dutifully and followed Lucille into the kitchen.

CHAPTER 12
A LITTLE EFFORT
1961-62
❖

The rest of the summer passed without significant events. Virginia and Leticia saw each other on every day that the weather permitted, but their relationship never progressed beyond the point it had already reached by the time Leticia met Paul Runcible. The two young women parted in early September promising to write during the winter. Virginia returned with her father to Baltimore, where her mother had been doing cancer research all summer, and Leticia went back to her private girls' high school. Leticia's parents wintered in Palm Springs, where Calvin could play golf while handling his business affairs by long distance, and Lucille could suffer from neglect by the pool in the company of other women.

Lucille, however, had a goal in life the winter after she and Leticia had made Paul's acquaintance, and having a goal diluted her suffering considerably. She schemed and planned for what she hoped would be the exciting married future of her daughter and only child.

In December, Leticia came to Palm Springs for her winter break. On the day after Christmas the family invited a host of friends, most of whom were Mr. Barnes' business colleagues and associates, to a large formal dinner. Among the guests was Lt. Colonel Runcible in full dress uniform, looking as dashing as he had the previous summer. Leticia even consented to wear formal clothing, much to her mother's delight and her father's surprise. She lasted three hours before racing to her bedroom to change into pants and a sweater. By that time, however, Paul had left, called away on what he described as a matter of duty.

The dinner was as boring to Leticia as such dinners usually were. Having Paul there did not much alleviate the boredom, for he was far more satisfactory as a fantasy beau than as a real, flesh and blood man. However, the high point for Leticia was his description of his most recent tour of duty in Turkey. She pictured herself in the most exotic surroundings being waited on by servants and enjoying a life of elegant leisure. Mrs. Barnes was pleased by the meal but disappointed that Paul neither said nor did anything to indicate that his presence implied any intentions towards Leticia. He was cordial and friendly but behaved nothing like a potential suitor, to Mr. Barnes' great relief.

***

When Leticia returned to school for the spring semester, she found a letter from Virginia waiting for her. She added it to her collection, which consisted of fourteen scribbled multi-paged missives and a postcard exhibiting a photograph of Albert Schweitzer. Virginia wrote at length about Herbie, her school's outcast. Originally from the Caribbean with a delicate build, he was constantly persecuted with jeers and catcalls. Virginia complained about her peers' small-minded, racist attitudes for two pages. Leticia skimmed the rest of the letter for anything related to her then tore the letter to bits and flushed twice.

She had written to Virginia twice and had sent her two postcards apologizing for the dearth of letters. Leticia hated writing almost as much as she hated her schoolwork. Though quick-witted and intelligent, she was a mediocre student who saw no point in applying herself any more than was necessary to avoid unpleasant encounters with the headmistress.

Virginia's letter was not all that Leticia found upon her return to school, however. During the winter break, her mathematics instructor had decided to take a position in England, and the new mathematics teacher, Miss Stephenson, was a severe woman of about forty, who intruded upon her life in what she felt was a most unseemly fashion, insisting that she do her homework assignments on time and requiring that she repeat her mathematical exercises until she got them right. Leticia was not the only student to suffer from the new teacher's severity, and soon typically adolescent rumors began to surface in the school: that the new mathematics instructor had been a prison guard, that she was responsible for numerous suicides and nervous breakdowns at various sites where she had previously taught, and that she was a lesbian predator.

Leticia knew better than to believe the rumors. In fact, she was as uncomfortable with them as she was with the woman herself. However, she was neither brave nor mature enough to oppose the spread of the rumors. She felt that she was more than ethical in simply refusing to propagate them further.

At first she was tempted to write to Virginia about the situation, but some inner trepidation held her back. Leticia did not like disappointing others' expectations of her and she had a suspicion Virginia would expect more from her. As a result, she rather resented Virginia. She looked forward to the summer eagerly, longing for an escape from school. She yearned for peaceful visits with Virginia at the duck pond, and she struggled to do better at mathematics without compromising time with her girlfriends or her romance novels.

***

It was late on a Thursday afternoon in mid-March when Leticia, crossing the campus between her residence hall and the library, encountered Miss Stephenson. She recognized her instructor's springy gait too late to avoid her, so she pulled herself together and greeted her as they passed each other on the broad path.

"Good afternoon, Miss Stephenson," she said in the constrained little girl voice that she used in classes and with her teachers.

"Good afternoon, Leticia Barnes," Miss Stephenson responded in her usual sonorous tone. "Are you on your way to the library?"

"Yes I am, Miss Stephenson," Leticia replied, hoping for nothing so much as a quick end to their very public conversation.

"Good," Miss Stephenson boomed, "I'll walk with you then. I would like a few words with you, Leticia Barnes, if you don't mind."

"Of course I don't, Miss Stephenson," Leticia lied. They walked together in the direction of the library, and Leticia kept looking all around hoping that no one would see her walking with the dreaded Stephenson.

"Are you looking for someone, Leticia?"

Leticia looked guiltily at the ground. "No, no one in particular. I was just wondering if I might meet someone I knew."

"And have to explain what you were doing walking about with me, am I right?" Miss Stephenson demanded, but Leticia didn't reply.

If she knows what people are saying about her, Leticia thought, why doesn't she just go away or at least spare me being seen with her.

"I am quite aware," Miss Stephenson intoned, "that there are a number of ignorant rumors about me circulating among the girls at this school. I think it most ill-bred indeed, but that is not the reason I wanted to speak with you."

Leticia breathed a sigh of relief. At least Miss Stephenson didn't expect her to do something about the rumors.

"I have noticed in the past few weeks," Miss Stephenson continued, ignoring Leticia's audible sigh, "that you have been exerting yourself in mathematics class. I have also observed that you have been handing in your assignments on time. Your improvement in effort, however commendable, has nonetheless not been matched by a commensurate improvement in performance. I have given a great deal of thought to

70

the matter, for I should like very much to recognize your improvement with a passing grade at the end of the term, but I will not be able to do so unless your performance also improves."

Oh my God, Leticia thought, I'm going to fail math. She had never before failed a course no matter how little effort she put into her studies. Her face paled and her eyes widened.

"It seems to me," the mathematics teacher rambled on, unmoved by Leticia's panicked expression, "that the only thing that might conceivably account for your failure to improve is poor preparation and mathematical background, and for that there is a remedy." The woman paused briefly for breath, and Leticia tried to focus on what she was saying.

"Because, Leticia Barnes, you have made such an effort in the past few weeks to improve your mathematical skills, I should be willing to meet with you privately for an extra hour each week in order to review with you those mathematical concepts which you should already have acquired. I suggest Tuesday afternoons at four. We can meet in my office."

Leticia was appalled. Nothing appealed to her less than the idea of meeting with Miss Stephenson alone for an entire hour each week except perhaps the possibility that her fellow students might find out about the arrangement. The mathematics teacher, however, seemed to expect Leticia to comply and even to be grateful. Extra help in mathematics! Leticia dreaded the very thought, but she saw no way out, so she politely thanked Miss Stephenson for her kindness and fled into the library.

***

On the following Tuesday afternoon Leticia reported as expected to Miss Stephenson in her office at four o'clock, and they immediately began to review the basic principles of elementary algebra. The hour passed relatively quickly, and Leticia found that she hadn't minded it so much. She carefully looked up and down the hall before leaving the office. She saw no one and no one saw her. By the time dinner was served at six-thirty, she had forgotten about her hour with Miss Stephenson, but when one of her classmates made a comment about the teacher's supposed sexual proclivities, Leticia grew extremely uncomfortable and left the table shortly thereafter. She returned to her room depressed, and the depression didn't lift until the following week when she met privately with Miss Stephenson once again. She came away from her second meeting with an understanding of the difference between a constant and a variable and the suspicion that Miss Stephenson was a far better teacher than anyone gave her credit for being. Still Leticia felt powerless to stop the rumors. And she remained wary, lest anyone learn of her private tutorials. Of Miss Stephenson's supposedly aggressive sexual proclivities she saw not a trace, but that did not ease her discomfort in the least.

By the time the semester ended, Leticia was no longer failing mathematics. She had even come to halfway enjoy the subject. None of her worst fears had been realized. No one seemed to suspect that she was receiving extra help from Miss Stephenson. At least no one confronted her with the fact, and as far as she could tell, no one was talking about it behind her back. In mid-May, shortly before she was to write her examination in mathematics, she had her last meeting with Miss Stephenson, who seemed most pleased both with herself and with Leticia.

"Leticia Barnes," Miss Stephenson said to her as that final hour drew to a close, "what you have accomplished this semester ought to serve as a guidepost for the rest of your life, for it is truly a significant achievement. And I am not just speaking of your newly gained mathematical capability. No, what is truly important here is your achievement understood in purely human terms. You have demonstrated what your mind and spirit are capable of with a little effort and patience. What you wish to do, Leticia Barnes, is within your ability. You can achieve it. I hope you have learned from this that your capabilities are limited only by your desires. Choose wisely and don't sell yourself short."

Leticia passed her mathematics examination with the highest grade she had ever received in mathematics and one of the highest she had ever earned in any school subject. However, she quickly and thoroughly forgot Miss Stephenson's advice until Virginia said something similar on the day she saw her for the last time before marrying Paul Runcible.

CHAPTER 13
HENRY'S MUSINGS
1980
❖

Henry Carr woke up from a short nap and glared at the fluorescent lights accusingly. He knew he looked pale. He felt pale and wondered if what the night nurse had claimed was true. Could feeling glum really depress one's immune system and open one up to all sorts of opportunistic infections? He didn't doubt it could be true, but in his more cheerful moments he was sure it wouldn't happen to him.

He shifted in bed and concentrated on not scratching his chest. The starched hospital sheets made him itch with a persistence that was hard to ignore. He cleared his throat and thought of all the optimistic lectures, almost sermons really, that he used to deliver to his hospitalized patients on the wonders of modern medicine. He wished he could believe what he'd told them. Instead he found himself bolstering his own stoicism with reminders of how fortunate he was not to be facing amputation or back surgery.

Henry hated uncertainty. Confined to a hospital bed with no definitive diagnosis, he passed the time summoning up memories so as not to have to dwell on the uncertain future. Lately he'd found his mind fixating on the first time he'd unlocked the door to his house after Louise's death. Compared to that moment, everything else was a cookie, sweet and easy to digest. Or so he'd thought.

He grunted. Thinking of cookies brought to mind the dreaded day, probably coming soon if that fool Felton's diagnosis was correct, when even cookies wouldn't taste good anymore. He knew what meds for Parkinson's did to the taste buds and appetite, and he wasn't looking forward to it. He also knew that he couldn't rely on his legs to hold if he stood up. Still he was tempted to try, if only to prove Felton wrong.

A nurse entered, saving Henry from himself and his musings, at least for the moment. She was pushing a cart bearing pills and a water pitcher. Henry sneered when she wordlessly handed him a tiny paper cup full of capsules and refilled the water glass on his table. He looked from the nurse to the pills to the water glass and back at the nurse again. "What exactly is this, nurse?" he demanded, pointing to the cup.

She opened her mouth, but before she could get a word out, he cut her off, "Wait! I recognize some of these. Dilantin and Phenobarbitol!

What kind of idiot gives a patient with a simple concussion anti-seizure medication?"

"The doctor prescribed…" the nurse tried to reply.

"Dr. Matthews?" Henry interrupted brusquely.

The nurse looked confused. "Dr. Matthews?" she repeated. "No, your attending, Dr. Felton."

Henry snorted. "Felton is a quack. If Dr. Matthews didn't prescribe these, you can take them away." He was still in control of himself, but his voice had taken on a belligerent edge. He reached up to touch the gauze on his forehead. "Didn't you learn to read the patient's chart before handing out meds?" he demanded, fixing the nurse with an increasingly angry stare. "A simple concussion…"

This time the nurse cut him off. "Please take your medications, Henry!" she said sharply.

"Don't call me Henry! I'm Dr. Carr. And don't tell me what to do! I have more medical knowledge in my little toe than you do in your whole head." His voice got louder as he listed his accomplishments and berated her, denigrating both her intelligence and her training. Soon he sounded exactly the way he used to sound standing in his own office and dressing down incompetent assistants. The nurse made a note on the chart and backed her cart out of the room.

It took Henry a few minutes and several more sentences before he calmed down. Exhausted and out of breath, he lay back on his pillows and whispered, "Virginia, I don't know how much more of this I can take." A tear rolled out of his right eye and he angrily brushed it away before it slid down his cheek. "What have I done to deserve this?" he mumbled. Then he gritted his teeth, hating the self-pity welling up inside of him.

He took in a deep breath. As he let it out, he checked to see what he was feeling. That was a trick Carolyn had taught him. What he was feeling was anger. What he was feeling was betrayed. The anger felt energizing whereas the self-pity felt like a drain.

What was wrong with Virginia anyway? How could his daughter, his only child, fail him like this? She'd broken their bond, the gentlemen's agreement that they'd made so many years ago. He just couldn't fathom it. He remembered the first time she'd used the phrase. She stood in his office, serious, determined, and all of four foot tall, and informed him that she would take over his practice when he got too old or too sick to run it anymore. They'd shaken hands on the bargain.

And though he hadn't promised anything in return right then, his promise came later.

Henry grimaced and held back a sob. When he'd reminded her of her promise just three years ago, she stared at him uncomprehendingly for a moment, then protested, "How old was I? Ten? Eleven?" As if that mattered.

And now she wouldn't even visit him in Grant's Hill. She was always too busy. Or so she claimed. Of course, she and Carolyn had issued an open invitation to him, telling him he was welcome to visit them in San Francisco whenever he chose. And he had visited them several times. Henry acknowledged that San Francisco was a beautiful city. Virginia and Carolyn always showed him a really good time when he was there. But to his mind, San Francisco wasn't Virginia's home, it was Carolyn's, even though he knew very well that Carolyn had moved there from the Midwest, Indiana or Iowa. He always forgot exactly which state. Virginia moved there to be with Carolyn, but her home, so Henry believed in his heart of hearts, was in the East where he was.

Henry had no objections to Virginia's relationship with Carolyn. Far from it! He always told them and anyone else willing to listen that taking up with Carolyn was the best decision Virginia ever made. And he meant that. He liked and trusted Carolyn. She was a good friend and a good doctor. And most important, she was absolutely devoted to Virginia.

That meant, so Henry was convinced, that there was really no reason for Virginia to stay out West. Carolyn could easily find a place at Johns Hopkins. And Virginia could take over for him. It was simple. She belonged in Grant's Hill.

Henry glared at the cupful of pills the nurse had left. With a shaky hand he tossed the cup at the trash basket and missed. He chuckled, but the chuckle died as he resumed his musings. He just couldn't understand Virginia's aversion to Grant's Hill. Other people considered it a vacation destination. Besides, she'd spent some of her happiest summers in town. It wasn't as if he wanted to drag her off to an ugly, industrial wasteland. She'd come into her own in Grant's Hill, though the process had started earlier, when Maria Mendoza arrived on their doorstep in Baltimore.

A soft smile spread across Henry's face as he remembered. Virginia had led Maria and her little boy to the clinic on her own, but from then on, Henry and Virginia were a team. It took both of them to persuade

Louise to allow the homeless woman and child to stay with them. Henry's smile broadened to a grin. It was his idea to send Virginia home to plant the thought in her mother's head as soon as he and Virginia had done what they could for Pablo at the clinic. Since the exchange student who'd earned room and board cooking for the Carr family had moved on, Henry was fairly sure his wife could be convinced to house another young woman, especially one who could help with household tasks.

Still, Louise was dubious when Virginia sprang the idea on her. "What guest? Two-legged or four-legged this time, Virginia? Don't tell me you have an injured bird to take care of. Or is it a skunk or a possum you want to shelter just until it recovers?"

Virginia giggled despite herself. "No bird or rodent droppings, I promise! This guest is housebroken and will even help around the house."

As if she hadn't heard, Louise continued, "I'll remind you that the curtains and bedspread in the guest room are only three months old." She paused and absorbed what Virginia had just said. "Oh no! Don't tell me your father has picked up another hippie hitchhiker!" She looked dismayed, and the look didn't disappear when Virginia shook her head. "Another of his reformed fallen women then," Louise sighed. "He treats their diseases and the injuries for free, and then he wants to harbor them until they're on their feet again!"

Virginia shook her head once more. "I found her. And she's not a fallen woman." She stopped to think for a moment. "Not exactly anyway. You'll like her, and her little boy is really cute."

"A little boy! Oh dear!" Louise exclaimed. Then she sighed. "Like father, like daughter, I suppose." She laughed but didn't relent until Henry came home and added his voice to Virginia's pleas.

The young Virginia, as Henry saw her in his mind's eye, was alternately serious and bubbly, full of spunk and ideas of how to heal the world. She had loved working with him. Screaming children quieted down when she applied band-aids decorated with hand-drawn smiley faces. Henry and Virginia had special summer rituals as well. Every other night they walked to Benson's ice cream stand for hot fudge sundaes. They flew kites on the town's public beach on the weekend and handed out flyers with information on vaccinations. When Virginia came out, he was the one she told, not Louise. He had guarded her secret the way some people guard a family inheritance. That was the other half of their gentlemen's agreement.

Henry gave up and scratched his chest, cursing the itchy sheets under his breath. He didn't know where the Virginia he remembered had gone. When had she become so somber? And why? Not only had she stopped laughing at his jokes, she'd stopped laughing all together. Most of all he wondered why she had taken it into her head to avoid Grant's Hill. He just wanted his daughter to come home.

CHAPTER 14
ANOTHER SUMMER
1962
❖

During the summer after her sixteenth birthday the development of Grant's Hill led to a marked change in Leticia's home life. Lucille was the first to react to the impending effect of the town's expansion. This in itself was extraordinary, since Calvin was the one who prided himself on his foresight. Lucille gave voice to her complaint over dinner one evening late in June.

"Calvin, you know I hate to complain," she began, "but Nancy has given notice. I don't mind not having a cook or even full time cleaning staff, but I can't manage this monstrosity of a house without some kind of assistance, can I?"

Calvin was taken aback by his wife's news. He cleared his throat ominously. "What's the matter? Did you quarrel with her?"

"Don't be ridiculous," Lucille retorted immediately. "I don't quarrel with the help. No, the problem is that she can earn twice as much as a waitress at that new cocktail lounge. I forget the name of the place, but you know which one I mean. All of the college kids are leaving their housecleaning and childcare jobs to work at those new places. I just talked with Roslyn Dempster down the road, and she told me that Alicia gave notice last week."

Calvin sighed and finished his last bite of pie, but Lucille wasn't finished with her litany of woes.

"That's not all, Cal," she said, picking up speed as she realized that her husband's attention was about to wander. "Andy, the caterer, has not only raised his prices on every item, but he's feeling the impact as well. His delivery boy quit to take a job at the new hotel, and now I have to drive into town at least twice a week to pick up our supplies. He said that the influx of new people has given him so many parties to cater that he planned to curtail his ordinary meal service. So soon we won't be able to get our food from him, even if I am willing to pick it up myself."

When Lucille stopped for a breath, Calvin stood up without saying a word and walked into the living room where his newspaper lay folded on an antique end table. He picked it up and settled into his favorite armchair.

"Calvin, did you listen to a word I said?" Lucille demanded shrilly.

"Of course, my dear," Calvin replied. "I heard every word. In fact, I'm considering a remedy for our problem at this very moment."

"You are not considering anything, Cal, you're reading the newspaper for the second time today."

"Reading helps me think," he explained patiently, "and digest my dinner, which is sitting rather heavily in my chest at the moment. You know, my dear," he continued, "this may be a blessing in disguise. I haven't been particularly satisfied with Andy's cuisine lately. I think it's time I found a woman to do for us here."

Lucille looked at her husband dubiously. "But Cal, you know how expensive household help is these days. And if you are talking about someone to cook as well as look after things, well, that's exorbitant."

Leticia could tell from the way her mother's tone of voice had changed that her new complaint was not meant to be taken seriously by her father. She awaited his reply and was not disappointed.

"Nonsense, Lucille, my darling, for you, no expense is too great. Not to worry. I think I know just where to look." Without further comment, he took up his paper again.

Leticia sighed happily. Whenever her father said things like that, she remembered why she wanted to marry someone exactly like him. It made her feel so happy that she nearly went over to pat his head. She could have bounced onto the new white couch to express her pleasure, but instead she helped her mother load the dishwasher and then excused herself.

"I think I'll go out for a short walk before sunset." Neither of her parents responded, so she grabbed her windbreaker for protection against mosquitoes and slipped out the door.

***

The next morning Leticia went to the cabin on Grant's Hill. Virginia was already there when she arrived, and they embraced as if they hadn't seen each other in years, even though they had spent the greater part of the previous morning together as usual. Virginia's kisses instantly raised Leticia's temperature. They weren't playful and curious so much as sensual and loving.

Though Leticia adored her life when she was with Virginia, she refused to talk about their future as a couple. Sometimes she shivered at Virginia's touch because it seemed to ask for something she couldn't guarantee. At times she could sense that Virginia wanted to plan their future, but Leticia was on guard. She cut off any conversation that might have led to naming their relationship.

Virginia did not understand Leticia's unwillingness even to think about them as a couple, let alone acknowledge it in words. It felt like a denial of their relationship, and the depth of their commitment. Yet she had no words to voice her sense of isolation.

That morning Leticia was excited for other reasons. She recounted her parents' conversation of the previous evening and demanded that Virginia speculate about the sort of person that Calvin had in mind to take over the practical details of the household. Virginia, who had little sympathy with Leticia's tendency to fantasize, refused, saying that Calvin probably had no one sort of person in mind at all and had only said what he did to pacify Lucille and mystify both mother and daughter.

"It's just the way men are, sweetie," she said. "They like to seem in control of things, especially when they're not."

Leticia, sensitive as always when she thought her father was being criticized, snapped back at Virginia.

"How do you know what men are like? You're not even interested enough in them to want to marry one, Miss Know-It-All."

Virginia just smiled and reached out to take Leticia in her arms. She was used to her sweetie's sudden attacks of pique and found it easy to be patient with her.

"Fred, honey," she whispered, "I live with my father." Then they kissed, and as usual when Virginia stroked her, any argument was forgotten.

***

Later that week, when Calvin Barnes returned home from an afternoon at the golf course, Lucille was upstairs in her bedroom. Although she'd taken Valium twice during the day, she complained of a migraine. Calvin knew better than to try to persuade her to join Leticia and him at dinner, so he asked his daughter to take her mother a tray. Leticia spent less than a minute with her mother before she returned, the food untouched.

"She's not eating tonight, Daddy. I think those pills ruin her appetite."

"Your mother, Lettie," Calvin said, "is a very sensitive woman. I'm afraid this business with the household help is upsetting to her. I must remember to look into finding someone soon."

Leticia just stared blankly at her father. She was taken aback that he had made no moves toward hiring help. More shocking was the idea that he thought her mother's troubles stemmed from a lack of household help. She was, however, willing to give him the benefit of the doubt. Poor Daddy, she mused, he doesn't like to think the worst of anyone, especially not Mother. She was not able to see that Calvin was aware of his wife's dependence on tranquilizers. And yet this did not concern him. Although she wanted desperately to enlighten him, she did not wish to upset him. So she kept her remarks on the subject to a minimum and went into the dining room to set the table.

Calvin complimented her on the food, even though she hadn't prepared it, and she giggled happily over dinner, enjoying his company and attention. He enjoyed hers almost as much, for she was easy for him to please, and Calvin liked to please the women in his life, particularly when it took little effort to do so. He was not particularly fond of difficult women, and he had chosen his wife on that basis. If the truth were known, he felt rather hard done by since she'd grown quite difficult over time. Valium kept her out of his hair, and that is why he was more than ready to ignore signs that Lucille was abusing it. While his considerable delight in his daughter might have stemmed from her resemblance to him, it undoubtedly persisted due to his ease in entertaining her and her willingness to spare him her problems and conflicts.

"Lettie," he announced, after finishing his ice cream, "I think we need to cheer your mother up. Let's have a party early next month. By that time we should have someone on board to cook and clean for us. Let's invite all of your mother's favorite people, including that young airman she's so taken with. What was his name again? Rum-something, wasn't it?"

"Runcible," Leticia corrected him laughing. "You know very well that his name is Paul Runcible because I've seen his name in your pocket calendar. You play golf with him, don't you? And I bet he lets you win. That's why you want to invite him, isn't it?"

"Nonsense, my dear," Cal chuckled. He enjoyed his daughter's teasing. "He doesn't let me win at all. In fact I've only won two or three times, and we must have played a dozen times in the past year."

"And how many times have you won against anyone else? Except for Jeff, of course."

Calvin laughed hard. He was vain about many things, but fortunately his golf game was not one of them.

"Well, Lettie, what do you say to a party? You'll have to dress up a little, but you look so beautiful when you do."

"Flatterer," Leticia giggled at her father. "But all right, I'll do it. Just to cheer up Mother."

Calvin retired to his armchair and an after-dinner brandy while Leticia cleared the table and loaded the dishwasher. She went out into the living room to remind him that if he really intended to throw a party, he'd better check with Lucille about the date. But Calvin was asleep in his chair, so Leticia kissed the top of his head and headed outside for her evening walk.

Despite Calvin Barnes' best intentions, however, it was the beginning of August before he found household help. Leticia came home from her morning expedition to find a small, dark-skinned, gray-haired woman cooking in the kitchen. Neither her mother nor her father was anywhere in sight, so she approached the woman and extended her hand.

"Hi, I'm Leticia. Did my father hire you to run the household?"

The woman examined her with shrewd eyes for several minutes before extending her hand.

"Hello, my name is Ana Mendoza Velasquez," she said softly in an English so heavily accented that Leticia had trouble understanding her. "I am hired by Mr. Barnes to cook and to clean. I think it is your mother who runs the household."

She pronounced Barnes as Barrrnez, and Leticia laughed, discovering that she liked this small woman. She resisted the temptation to make some derogatory remark about her mother's ability to run the household.

"Mrs. Velasquez," Leticia said, "it is a pleasure to meet you, and I am certain that you will do wonders for us." She turned toward the stairs.

"I am called Mendoza Velasquez after my last two husbands, and of wonders I know little," came the woman's reply quickly, "but I will cook, and I will clean, and I hope that will be enough." She stirred the pot simmering on the stove.

"Well, whatever it is you're cooking right now smells wonderful," Leticia said before leaving the room.

At the top of the stairs she noticed that her mother's door was slightly ajar. So instead of going to her own room to wash and change her clothes, which were covered with pond slime from an attempt to rescue a duckling, she knocked softly on her mother's door and entered without waiting for a response.

As expected, she found Lucille lying in bed with an ice pack on her forehead, but she was surprised to notice that her mother was not in a Valium-induced haze. "Come in and close the door, Lettie," she ordered. "Well did you meet her? Did you meet that colored woman your father hired?"

Leticia smirked at her mother, uncertain how to express her discomfort without upsetting Lucille. "I think she's Latin American, Mother, though she didn't say what country she comes from."

"Well, I don't care, "Lucille snapped. "She's ridiculously dark, and God only knows what kind of food they eat in whatever place she comes from. I am not prepared to eat alligator stew or monkey liver for dinner."

"Mother," Leticia protested, "she seems like a nice woman, and whatever she's cooking smells delicious. Just smelling it makes me hungry."

"Well," Lucille grumbled, "I hope she doesn't poison all of us. Don't they eat horribly spicy food in the jungles of South America? You know, your father and I both have sensitive stomachs. I just wonder what Cal could have been thinking of."

Leticia could tell that her mother was genuinely upset, but she vacillated between wanting to comfort and correct her.

"Have you talked with Mrs. Mendoza Velasquez at all, Mother?" she tried to humor Lucille. "She really is pleasant and so much more mature than the college kids around here." Leticia knew that Calvin's slight attention to their former housecleaner, an attractive nineteen year old, had bothered Lucille.

"Well," Lucille admitted grudgingly, "you're right about the maturity anyway."

Leticia was glad to see her mother's mood brightening ever so slightly.

"Would you like to come down for lunch, Mother, or shall I bring you a tray?"

"I think I'd better come down just to make sure she knows what she's doing," Lucille decided, rising from her bed and dumping her ice pack unceremoniously on the nightstand.

"Good," Leticia beamed at her mother. "I'll just go and change clothes, and we can walk down together."

"Don't take too long," Lucille ordered. "I don't want to give my headache a chance to come back."

***

Ana Mendoza Velasquez knew exactly how to deal with a woman like Lucille Barnes. Never obsequious, she did manage to give the impression that she was only carrying out the wishes of her employer. She completely rearranged a household, changed the pace of life, improved the nutrition and taste of the meals, and generally took charge. The food was simple but delicious and all-American with just the slightest hint of Europe. Lucille was impressed.

"Mrs. Mendosta," she said, speaking very clearly and loudly as if that might help her listener understand English, "this is really excellent. I'm sorry that Calvin is not here to enjoy this delicious meal with us. Where did you learn to cook so well?"

Leticia was embarrassed for her mother, but when she looked over at Ana Mendoza Velasquez, she saw that the woman seemed pleased rather than offended. Leticia grinned, and Ana smiled back at her.

"Meesis Barnes," she replied, emphasizing her accent, "you do me honor to compliment my food so. I have cooked for other distinguished North American ladies, and I will try to meet your needs as I have theirs."

Leticia's grin grew even broader. Somehow she just knew that Mrs. Mendoza Velasquez had consciously substituted "distinguished North American ladies" for whatever the equivalent of "rich Yankee parasites" was in her language. She admired her skill at diplomacy almost as much she enjoyed the food.

"And you, young lady," Ana turned and wagged a finger at her, "will be very respectful of your mother who is a woman of nobility, or you will have Ana Mendoza Velasquez to answer to. Understood?"

Leticia caught the slightly dropped eyelid as the woman finished her warning. She nearly giggled as the new housekeeper inclined her head subtly in Lucille's direction. When she looked over at her mother, Lucille was puffed up like a peacock.

"Really, Mrs. Mendosta, Lettie is very good, mostly," she trilled almost flirtatiously, and Leticia realized that her mother loved having an admiring protector, whether male or female, master or servant. Now if only Lucille could get the woman's name right, Leticia thought, and the thought made her squirm with embarrassment. She could tell that Ana Mendoza Velasquez was looking at her, and somehow she could sense the housekeeper's effort to assuage her discomfort at the same time as the woman tried to keep Lucille calm. Mrs. Mendoza Velasquez caught her eye and winked broadly at her this time. Leticia smiled and finished her lunch, humming happily.

***

When the meal ended and Leticia followed her mother upstairs, Lucille didn't reach for her Valium for once. She invited Leticia to sit

85

down and pronounced herself more or less satisfied with Calvin's choice of a housekeeper, all things considered. At least they hadn't been poisoned with overly spiced and unrecognizable foods, and the woman, though terribly dark and rather savage-looking, was well-mannered and seemed to know her place.

Leticia found herself embarrassed for her mother all over again, but she hid her discomfort and listened patiently until Lucille grew tired of her company and dismissed her.

"Don't forget that your father will be home for dinner early tonight. Be sure to be home by six, Lettie," she commanded, as her daughter shut the door behind her.

Leticia was tempted to go sit in her tree and ponder the peculiarities of her mother, but she decided to go first to visit Ana Mendoza Velasquez, whom she found surveying the ingredients in their refrigerator with a less than pleased expression on her face. When she saw Leticia, she nodded but did not stop gazing into the refrigerator.

"What's so interesting in there?" Leticia inquired.

"Nothing," Ana replied. "There's nothing in there that will nourish the body or the soul. Tell me, little one, did your family not eat before I got here?"

"Oh, we ate all right. We got our food from the caterer in town. But his prices are going up, and he doesn't deliver anymore. So my father promised to hire a cook and housekeeper, and I guess that's you."

"But I cannot cook if there is nothing to cook. I used up the last beef in the house for lunch. But for dinner?" She just shrugged her shoulders expressively.

"I guess someone needs to shop for food," Leticia replied.

"And that someone will not be your mother because she does not know how?" Ana speculated. "And you, do you not know how either?"

"Oh, I know how all right," Leticia boasted, "as long as you give me a list. Only I can't bring back that much on my bike at any one time."

"Are you not old enough to drive the automobile?"

"Oh sure, I'm old enough, and I even have my license, well, a permit actually, so I'm not allowed to drive it without an adult supervising me." Leticia made a face as she revealed what she considered a shameful fact about her situation.

"Very good then, I will tell you what to buy and you will write the list, and I will sit in the automobile while you drive it," Ana announced.

Leticia thought about this for a second. "Do you have a license? I think the supervising adult is supposed to be a licensed driver."

Ana ignored her and began to dictate a shopping list, punctuating it after every third item with "are you writing this?" Leticia wrote quickly, filling up one side of an entire eight by eleven sheet of paper.

"What are we going to do for money?" Leticia remembered to ask, just as Ana pulled the door shut behind them.

"What? Your family has accounts, no?"

"There aren't any groceries in town. Just the caterer," Leticia replied sadly, fearing that her chance at an expedition was escaping. She had hoped to be seen driving in town.

"And he is too expensive," Ana said with finality. "Well then, we will go elsewhere. You will drive to the farmers."

Leticia knew little about farms. "Well, I suppose we could get vegetables and fruit direct from the farmers," she agreed hesitantly, still wishing she could drive to town. "But what will we use for money?"

"They will sell to us on credit," Ana announced as if certain. "After all you are rich people."

"But they don't know that," Leticia protested. "They don't know us at all."

"But they will," Ana promised. "They will see from the automobile that you are rich. After all, they sell on credit to the doctor."

So focused on getting some kind of expedition underway, Leticia didn't notice Ana's reference to the doctor.

"After we buy our things from the farmers, there will be more money than usual to spend at the caterer for meat, no?" Ana reasoned triumphantly.

Leticia didn't know, but she was glad to get a chance to drive. So she got in behind the wheel of her mother's car and waited until Ana Mendoza Velasquez crawled in next to her. Then she pulled slowly and carefully away from the house.

Chapter 16
Household Help
1962
❖

Leticia was distressed to find that she, rather than her companion, had been correct after all about buying from the farm stands on credit. Mrs. Mendoza Velasquez returned to the car grumbling under her breath in a language Leticia could not recognize, let alone understand. It wasn't Spanish. She did not understand Spanish, but she knew what it sounded like.

Leticia started the car and turning to the older woman, asked where she should drive. She half expected to be told to take the road directly home, but Mrs. Mendoza Velasquez told her, much to her delight, to drive into town.

"We will buy some meat from this caterer you spoke of," she declared, "and then we will go home to your mother and find out where to buy all else we need and how we can do so without carrying too much money around."

Leticia had been amazed to discover at the last farm stand they visited that Ana considered any amount above ten dollars too much money. Between them they'd had twelve, and that had sufficed to buy vegetables and fruit for the rest of the week. The housekeeper considered paying cash for food an indicator of lower class status, and she was surprised to learn that the only dealer with whom the Barnes family had an account was the caterer and that they paid that every month in full. However, when Leticia led her to the caterer's establishment, she took one look at the array of food in the display window, turned on her heel, and left the building. Perplexed, Leticia followed her, only to be ordered to drive directly home.

Leticia was not sure whether she should warn Mrs. Mendoza Velasquez of the pointlessness of asking Lucille to arrange family accounts. She knew that Lucille would, if in a good mood, hand over a large quantity of cash for shopping or, if in a bad, insist that she discuss the matter with Calvin. Mrs. Mendoza Velasquez didn't seem to want to be warned, so Leticia decided to wait and see what happened when the two women went head to head over household responsibilities. She just hoped that Mrs. Mendoza Velasquez wouldn't say anything about her having driven the car without permission. That was one of the few things about which her father and mother agreed.

Sitting at the bottom of the steps, Leticia tried to let her mind wander up to where the housekeeper was speaking to Lucille. She was relaxed yet poised to spring up and run out to her tree, should her mother call her to account for driving. Leticia could not afford, she believed, to let her attention wander for even a moment, and in that focused state of mind she began to feel very clear-headed, alive, and awake. Thoughts ran through her mind, but she dismissed them easily, listening with a kind of inner hearing for any sign from her mother's room. Virginia's image arose before her inner eye, and then the images of Paul Runcible, her father, and her mother. Of all of them, only Virginia's was clear, but as she allowed it to materialize again, it slowly turned into the likeness of Ana Mendoza Velasquez. Leticia gasped just as she heard the door to her mother's room open and close quietly and her mother's voice wishing Mrs. Mendoza Velasquez a good day.

Leticia jumped to her feet just as the old woman started down the long staircase. Her step was firm and Leticia noticed that she walked in the middle of the stairs, not touching the banister. As Mrs. Mendoza Velasquez walked by her, Leticia saw a look of positive triumph on the woman's face and could not contain her curiosity.

"What happened?" she asked, gaping as the woman showed her a handful of money. Her amazement increased, however, when she recovered enough to hear what Mrs. Mendoza Velasquez was actually saying.

"Money for seedlings, little one. Your mother is a most marvelous woman when reasoned with."

"Seedlings?" Leticia had no idea what the woman was talking about.

"We will plant, you and I. Out in the back beyond that charcoal oven where the sun reaches past the tree shadows. Vegetables and herbs. It is very late in the season, perhaps even too late for most things to bear fruit, but something is better than nothing."

"Will we really be able to grow everything we need?" Leticia asked, her curiosity piqued.

"No, not everything, but some things, yes," the old woman replied a little impatiently. "Now do not talk so much and take me in your automobile to buy what I need to prepare the ground."

"But," Leticia protested, "my father will be home soon, and I'm not allowed to drive the car."

"You and your father!" the housekeeper exclaimed. "You have permission. Your mother gave it for you to help me in any way I need. And I need you to drive the automobile. Pronto."

Leticia grabbed the car key from its hook and headed out the door. There was so much she wanted to find out about Mrs. Mendoza Velasquez' conversation with her mother, but she didn't know how to ask. They got into the car, and Leticia started it.

"Where to?" she asked, and the woman gave her detailed and surprisingly clear directions to a garden store two towns past Grant's Hill to the northwest. On the grounds outside the store they purchased three large bags of topsoil and some processed manure. Leticia was secretly delighted at hauling manure in the trunk of her mother's elegant sedan. She followed Mrs. Mendoza Velasquez into the store and helped her carry out two dozen seedlings and some small pots of herbs. Those they stowed on the back seat and floor of the car.

The old woman looked at the battered wristwatch on her arm and told Leticia they had just enough time to stop at the butcher's for meat. She still had over fifty dollars in her hand, and it was clear how she intended to spend it.

"You mean the caterer's, right?" Leticia asked, turning the car in the direction of Grant's Hill.

Ana Mendoza Velasquez shook her head vigorously.

"No, no, you are going the wrong way. If I meant the caterer, that is what I would have said. There is nothing a human being or even an intelligent animal would eat at that place. That we saw earlier. No wonder your mother is ill. She has most likely lost her B's and E's." The old woman stopped talking to shake her head in disapproval. Before Leticia could ask what it was her mother had lost and if she was missing them too, Ana continued. "There is a butcher's shop at the other end of this town. The boy working in the store told me."

So Leticia turned the car again and headed away from home. Five minutes and two left turns later, she found herself in front of a row of stores that included a butcher shop, a dairy and egg store, a bakery, and a tiny produce market.

"There," Mrs. Mendoza Velasquez pointed vigorously at the produce store, "there is where we will get our fruits and our vegetables until some of our own plants begin to bear. But first we must go to buy our meat, then our eggs and cheese. A pity there is no store to buy freshly ground flour, but then I like cornmeal better myself. I will not buy bread from a store," she continued to talk out loud but to herself, almost as if Leticia were not there at all. "It is better to make it at home. Perhaps I should try to grow some corn? No, not enough space, I think."

Leticia followed the tiny woman from store to store, helping her carry packages and count change. It took them almost an hour to complete their purchases, and Leticia was tired but excited. She couldn't wait to tell Virginia about her adventure. The only thing that disappointed her was that these shopping trips would not take her into town where Virginia would see her driving.

When Leticia pulled into the drive, she noticed that her father was not yet home. She looked at her watch and saw that it was almost seven.

"Mother will be so disappointed," she said aloud without realizing that the other woman could hear her.

Mrs. Mendoza Velasquez just shrugged her shoulders and mumbled something in that tongue that Leticia could not recognize. They got out of the car at exactly the same moment, but before Leticia could enter the house, she saw the small gray-haired woman struggling with the door to the trunk.

"Just a minute, Mrs. Mendoza Velasquez," she shouted, running back to the car. "I have to unlock it."

She helped unload the soil and fertilizer, piling them in the back shed, but the old woman insisted on carrying the seedlings herself. Then they took the food packages and went around to the back door that led into the kitchen.

Leticia smiled to herself. She felt a little like household help, but she didn't really mind. Helping Mrs. Mendoza Velasquez felt like something she'd been missing without knowing it. When she tried to unpack the bags of groceries, however, the woman shooed her out of the kitchen.

"You have done enough, little one," she said. "Tomorrow you help me in the yard."

Leticia smiled at her. It amused her to be called "little one" by this woman over whom she towered, but who she felt was in some way bigger than she. It was different from the feeling she had about her mother and father, and it interested her.

"Tomorrow I will help you, yes," she said, "but tomorrow afternoon. In the morning I will not be here."

"Fine, fine," the woman said, motioning to her to leave. "And then later on you will go with me to learn the wild herbs."

But Leticia could no longer hear her, as she had gone upstairs to try to comfort her mother, whom she found depressed as usual because Calvin had failed to arrive as promised. Lucille was just reaching for the bottle of Valium when Leticia knocked and entered.

"Do be a dear and eat dinner without me," Lucille said in a piteous voice. "I have such a headache. I just must get some sleep."

"Mother, Mrs. Mendoza Velasquez is cooking us dinner right now. It would be a shame to let her wonderful food go to waste."

"Oh," Lucille let out a little moan. "I just can't eat, Lettie. Tell her I am sorry."

"Oh very well," Leticia found herself getting angry, but she didn't know whether her anger was at her mother or her father. The idea of being angry with Calvin alarmed her, so she hurried downstairs and out the front door, avoiding Ana Mendoza Velasquez. She went around to the back of the house and climbed her tree, where she sat until her father came home at nine-thirty.

"Mother," she informed him, "has a headache."

His look asked what else was new as he leaned over to kiss her on the cheek.

"How does Mrs. Mendoza Velasquez seem to be working out?" he asked, pushing open the door and collapsing into his favorite chair.

"Very well, I think," she replied. "She had Mother absolutely cheerful over lunch. But then when you didn't get home when Mother expected you…"

"Please spare me the gruesome details, honey," he said. "I got tied up. Have you eaten dinner yet?"

"No, Leticia said, smiling at him. "I think it's still warm. Mrs. Mendoza Velasquez is still in the kitchen. Shall I ask her to serve us?"

"Please do," Calvin replied, "but in five minutes. I need to wash my hands first, and then I'll just step upstairs to see how your mother is."

He disappeared into the bathroom, and Leticia went into the kitchen to tell the housekeeper they were ready for dinner.

'Dinner for two is not for three," she said somewhat cryptically. "It is a shame when it would take so little to bring her back."

Leticia knew the woman was talking about Calvin and Lucille, but she didn't know what to make of her comments so she chose to ignore them. When Calvin returned with the news that Mrs. Barnes was sleeping soundly, they sat down at the table to eat. It was Calvin's first exposure to the old woman's cooking, and he was impressed.

"Mrs. Mendoza Velasquez," he called her into the dining room. "This is excellent."

She said nothing but just nodded gravely in appreciation of his praise.

"Take the rest of the evening off. Leticia will clear the dishes after dinner."

Again there was the grave nod, and Ana Mendoza Velasquez disappeared through the kitchen into the back of the house. Leticia joked with her father, cleared the dishes, and then left him in his favorite armchair to take her evening walk.

***

Leticia spent the remainder of the summer in a comfortable routine. She and Virginia had found an old cabin at the top of Grant's Hill that offered them privacy. So they spent mornings there, and Leticia spent her afternoons with Mrs. Mendoza Velasquez "learning the herbs," as the older woman put it. Together they planted, watered, and weeded in the garden and periodically they took walks in the park and the woods beyond to collect wild plants.

Ana Mendoza Velasquez focused on what was edible, what was not, which plants had curative powers and how those curative powers could be tapped. Leticia enjoyed collecting and drying the plants, but she especially enjoyed drawing Ana Mendoza Velasquez into conversations in which she hinted darkly at the greater potency of the wild plants in her homeland, telling stories of miraculous healing and undetectable poisoning. Whenever Leticia asked her, however, where exactly her homeland was, Mrs. Mendoza Velasquez began to mutter in her native tongue, and Leticia gave up her questioning and was content to learn what she could from the quirky old woman.

They made only a very few outings to the shops of the nearby town that they had discovered on their expedition to the garden store. Leticia never got to show off her driving or her mother's car to Virginia or anyone else in Grant's Hill, though she told Virginia about her adventures with Mrs. Mendoza Velasquez. Virginia had listened patiently and with approval, or so it seemed to Leticia.

For the first time in her life, Leticia was learning about things that interested her. While the time spent weeding was often a hot, prickly experience that Leticia barely endured, the time in the kitchen

93

combining and preserving herbs excited her. She relished the flavors that left her mouth watering and mentally noted those combinations that were astringent or bitter. When the summer ended, she experienced enormous sadness at leaving. Ana Mendoza Velasquez, who had won both her heart and her mother's, promised to return to work for them the following summer, and that comforted Leticia as much as Virginia's promise to write every week at school and phone her during the holidays. Leticia did not exactly look forward to the school year, but neither did she dread it as she had in years past. There was next summer to look forward to.

CHAPTER 17
ANA'S STORY
1962-63
❖

The winter of the year when Leticia turned seventeen was full of dances and socials co-sponsored by private boys' and girls' schools, arranged so that the male and female members of the privileged class might be encouraged to find appropriate mates.

Leticia found the high school gatherings, as she wrote to Virginia, rather tedious. She described the young men at great length to her friend, and her descriptions had a distinctly satirical slant to them. She ended each letter in the same way, informing Virginia that none of the young men she met at school could measure up to Paul Runcible, whom she only saw once during each school holiday at a party given by her parents.

She knew that her persistent praise of the young air force officer hurt and bewildered Virginia, but she could not resist including it conspicuously in each letter. It was not Virginia she wished to wound, however, but herself for lacking the courage to make her praise of Paul the penultimate line of letter and concluding with her true sentiment, which was that he could not measure up to Virginia. However, although Leticia knew that Virginia was more than willing to take their relationship a step further, she was afraid and sought to maintain it as a summer romance, nothing more.

Paul remained polite and gallant towards Leticia, but he showed no serious interest in her. He found her charming, but he doubted that she would be able to withstand the rigors of life as an air force wife. He admired her high spirits and willfulness but saw them for what they were: impediments to her adaptation to any role other than one she might choose for herself.

Mr. and Mrs. Barnes were both disappointed, she because she thought she saw in Paul the same qualities of gallantry and consideration that she thought she had seen in her husband when she married him, and he because he found Paul a singularly pleasant companion and if he must have a son-in-law, well, it might as well be one with whom he could share his pleasures and pastimes.

Leticia was aware of her parents' disappointment, but she only pretended to share it. Marriage to Paul remained a lovely fantasy for her, all the more alluring because unreal and likely to remain so. He was perfect in her imagination, though she was a bit put off when she saw him. His handsomeness was always marred by cuts on his face, which he tried to hide with flesh-colored band-aids. Someone, Leticia thought, should teach him how to shave without cutting himself.

When the school year ended and Leticia returned to Grant's Hill, she found things very much the same as when she had left at the end of the previous summer. Mrs. Mendoza Velasquez returned as promised. Virginia waited for her every morning in or near the vacant cabin on the hill. And her mother and father continued to pretend to enjoy their relationship to each other, while her father spent more and more time away from home and her mother took more and more Valium.

One afternoon late in June, while Leticia went out to gather herbs with Ana Mendoza Velasquez, they ran into Virginia wheeling a small boy in a wheelchair through the park. Leticia greeted Virginia cordially but without giving any indication of the closeness of their relationship. Mrs. Mendoza Velasquez' greeting, however, was much warmer. She walked up to Virginia, looked deeply into her eyes, said something softly to her that Leticia could not make out, and kissed her on the cheek.

Leticia was surprised, and as they walked on toward the woods, leaving Virginia and the boy behind on the park's more passable pathways, she asked Mrs. Mendoza Velasquez how she came to know Virginia.

Ana's eyes lit up, for Virginia was by far her favorite North American.

"It is a long story, little one, and if you want to hear it in detail, we must sit down and prepare to spend some time. If, however, you want a quick answer, I can tell you that I honor and love that orange-eyed healer because she saved the lives of my only grandson and his mother, my daughter."

Leticia didn't know what she had expected, but it certainly wasn't gratitude with the depth of devotion that the woman obviously felt for Virginia. She felt a little hurt, but she was not sure why. She sat down on a fallen log and motioned for her companion to do the same.

"Tell me the whole story," she said. "I really want to know."

Mrs. Mendoza Velasquez turned her gaze directly on Leticia as if she intended to discern the reason for Leticia's curiosity.

"Virginia and I are very close, very good friends," Leticia reassured her with a degree of urgency. "Our friendship is a kind of secret," she broke off, wanting to explain and yet reluctant to put words to her relationship with Virginia.

"Hmmm," Ana sighed deeply. "So that is how it is. I thought it was someone, but I did not know it was you. Very well, you shall hear the whole story. How do you say in your courts? The truth, the whole truth and nothing only the truth."

Leticia tried to hide her grin, but the old woman did not notice, for she was deep in her memory.

"It was during one of the summers before we met that my grandson was saved by your loved one," she began. "The story, however, begins much earlier, even before the year that I came here from my homeland. You always ask me where my homeland is, little one, for you think that all the peoples of Latin America speak either Portuguese or Spanish. But I and my people are Indios, and we speak our language and live as far away from the Latinos as we can. I only learned Spanish from my last husband who was not a pure Indio.

Ana Mendoza Velasquez told Leticia about the difficult times her daughter had experienced without much detail. That is, until she reached the part where Virginia took Maria to the clinic and arranged for her to stay at the Carr home. That part she told as if she had been there, though of course she hadn't.

"My daughter ran away from misery, but it found her over and over until your friend with the orange eyes saw my daughter and her son and brought them to her father, who gave the child medicine. Even he was not sure he could save the boy's life. Your friend took them in and stayed awake with them day and night.

When my grandson was finally out of danger, Virginia asked my daughter what she planned to do. She had no plans, so Virginia went to her father and begged him to find my Maria a job. The father helped, but then there was no one to look after the child. My daughter wanted me, and she asked Virginia, her guardian angel, to help her fill out the papers to bring me to her. Her father found a woman, a sick old widow in need of a paid companion, and I moved into her house with my grandson and looked after them both. I spoke no English at the time and only a little Spanish, but your friend came every day in the summer and taught me to speak English well enough to survive.

"Then the widow died, and I had no place to go with my grandson. Fortunately, my daughter met a man, a North American, who cared nothing about her past or her race. He has a good heart. He is himself partly African and partly Seminole, but he earns a good living even in this country. He married my daughter, and they are raising my grandson together to this day. I, however, your dear one said, deserved to do something for myself, so she sent me to a school to learn how to cook what the North Americans like to eat. She filled out papers for me, and the school let me attend without paying. It was a good school, and I became a cook for a rich family here in Grant's Hill. Then, when they decided to leave, your father came to me and asked me to cook for his family, and so, little one, it is due to your loved one that you know me at all."

Leticia could hardly sort out her reactions to this story. She was moved and impressed by Virginia's goodness but also angry that Virginia had never told her the story and jealous that Mrs. Mendoza Velasquez obviously admired Virginia more than her.

"That is an incredible story, Mrs. Mendoza Velasquez, but how could you have such a young daughter? And how many husbands did you have anyway?" Leticia blurted her questions.

The old woman's eyes twinkled, and Leticia realized that her questions were rude. "I'm sorry, I didn't mean to suggest that you're ancient or anything."

Mrs. Mendoza Velasquez laughed. "But I must seem so to you. I am older than your mother by many years. Maria, whom I followed here, is my youngest child. Her father, my last husband was my sixth. Some of the others died, some I sent away."

"Exactly how many children do you have?"

The old woman shrugged. "Many," she answered, "and I had more, but some died."

"I'm sorry," Leticia said solemnly.

"That is how it is with us. Our life is hard."

"Wasn't it hard for you to leave your home and come to a strange place where you couldn't speak the language?"

"My daughter needed me, so I didn't think about the difficulty, little one."

Leticia breathed deeply. "And now you work for us. Do you like working for rich people?"

The old woman laughed. "Once again, it is not a matter of liking. I do what I must."

"Well, it's not really fair, is it?" Leticia mused, half under her breath.

"Fair or not, it is life."

Leticia thought about that for a few seconds. She'd often found things unfair, but she didn't know how one lived with such massive unfairness every day of one's life. Her mind boggled.

"Mrs. Mendoza Velasquez," she began again, "I want to know about Virginia and your daughter and you. I mean, when did it all start? Virginia is only my age, seventeen. How long ago did she first meet your daughter?"

"She was eleven. I know that among you, a girl of eleven is still a child. But she showed that we and not you are right, for to us an eleven-year old female is a young woman. At eleven, she already showed the compassion and kindness of a grown woman."

"Wow," Leticia said. "I didn't know any of this at all, and Virginia and I are..." She started to say, "so close," but when she didn't finish her sentence, Mrs. Mendoza Velasquez finished it for her.

"You are lovers."

Leticia cringed slightly. Her face got very red, and she looked down.

"Do not be ashamed, for there is nothing wrong in what you feel. It is a great thing to love and you have found someone worthy of your heart." The woman reached out and patted her arm. "Among us there are some women like you and your loved one. They usually do not marry men, and if they do, they return to each other eventually, once the age for bearing children is over. They are in this life inseparable."

Leticia squirmed uncomfortably on the log and picked at its bark. She did not want to hear aloud what she feared was true. Still the old woman continued.

"Among us, women such as you and Virginia are the greatest of our healers. I know that she wishes to become a doctor like her father. She will be greater than he. And you, little one, have a gift as well, and that is why I take you out to learn the wild plants and herbs. You will heal in a different way, but you will also do much good."

"Well that's all very interesting, Mrs. Mendoza Velasquez," Leticia began to speak in a very shrill voice, not making eye contact with her companion. "But this is not your country and not your culture, and you are quite wrong about Virginia and me. We are not inseparable. She will go to college next year, and I will marry, make no mistake about that."

When Leticia finally looked into the eyes of Ana Mendoza Velasquez, they were dancing with merriment.

"Very well, the woman said. "Let us give it time, and we will see who is right, you or I. But in the meantime, we must continue with the plants. Ana Mendoza Velasquez stood up and started to walk deeper into the woods, and Leticia followed her.

"What you must remember about all the plants is that the same plants heal and harm. So it is with all life. What can cause pain and sorrow can also bring us to wholeness. The plants can teach us much: joy and sorrow, love and hate, life and death. Above all they teach us that though illness and fear are strong, knowledge that is love can overcome them."

CHAPTER 18
FOREBODING
1963

❖

When Leticia and Virginia met the next morning, both of them felt the strain. A new shyness had come between them, and Leticia did not know what to do about it. Virginia wanted to talk, but Leticia felt that too much had been said, mostly by Mrs. Mendoza Velasquez. When Virginia heard from Leticia that Mrs. Mendoza Velasquez knew they were lovers and approved, she was happy, proud, and incredibly relieved. Now that someone else knew of it, their love seemed somehow more real and more substantial to her. She told this to Leticia, who only looked sad and afraid and was unwilling to say any more.

"Let's talk about something else," she said. "I have a number of questions to ask you about Mrs. Mendoza Velasquez and her family, but most of all I want to know why you never told me about them and what you did for them, Virginia. It is terribly admirable, you know, and you might have had my admiration all this time, if I had only known."

Virginia did not like Leticia's tone, but she did not know how to counter it. "There was really not all that much to tell, Fred. I didn't do anything anyone else wouldn't have done. And as far as telling you, well, what would have been the point?"

"Admiration, my dear, admiration," Leticia said, trying to sound lighthearted and sophisticated.

"Well, I'd rather not be admired for acting like a human being. It makes me sad."

"Sad?" Leticia asked, suddenly sounding genuine. "Why sad?"

"Because I don't want to believe that simple decency is rare, I suppose. I don't know."

"But Virginia, Mrs. Mendoza Velasquez doesn't count what you did for her family as simple decency. She thinks you're a saint. You should hear her talk about you. It was really hard not to laugh."

Virginia blushed and looked down at her feet. When she looked up, Leticia stood with an expression of intense mockery on her face, and Virginia could only look away and wonder what would become of them.

It took several days for Leticia and Virginia to feel fully comfortable with each other again, and still Virginia was not at ease as she had been. She sensed that it was only a matter of time before they drifted apart, yet she was determined not to begin grieving before she had anything to grieve about. She often found herself looking intently into her lover's eyes as if seeking something to reassure herself, but all she ever found was amusement with a slight tinge of mockery and sometimes a little impatience especially when Leticia grew tired of her seriousness about their love.

"Good God, Virginia, you act as if the universe depended on our staying together."

Virginia wanted to protest, but she could not, since she was going away to college and leaving Leticia behind. Was it any wonder, she often asked herself, that Leticia talked of marrying Paul? Virginia had no way of knowing if Leticia was determined to distance herself from feeling deserted or to spread the feeling to Virginia. Virginia had invited Leticia to come with her, but Leticia had just laughed.

"I don't plan to live in a dormitory, Fred," Virginia said one morning as she sat next to Leticia who was stringing leaves together. "If I get a small apartment, well, two can live almost as cheaply as one."

Leticia didn't laugh that time. She just looked at Virginia for a long while before saying anything, but when she finally spoke, what she had to say was devastating.

"Do you expect me to take that offer seriously? What exactly would I do cooped up in a small apartment while you were spending your days and half of your nights too, if I know you, studying in the library or working in some laboratory? What kind of life would I have, Virginia? I have been raised to marry, and marry I will."

Virginia's eyes filled with tears, and for once Leticia did not mock her.

"Don't you see, honey? It can't work out for us," she said. "I can only live the life I was born and raised to. I don't know anything else."

"But you could learn," Virginia insisted. "You've learned a lot about herbs from Mrs. Mendoza Velasquez already. It's not that you can't learn."

"Oh Virginia, sweetheart," Leticia murmured, taking Virginia's face between her hands, "I'm not a good learner the way you are. Yes, I have learned a lot about herbs but what good will that do me? Can you see me serving customers at an herbalist's shop?"

"So you would just throw us away because you're too lazy or spoiled or scared to try to do anything else," Virginia finally snapped at her, defeated.

"There is no 'us', my darling, and there never was and never will be. There is only you and I, Virginia and Fred, enjoying a summer romance that has already lasted longer than I could ever have imagined. So let's not ruin it now before it's run its course."

"You make it sound so inevitable and so easy," Virginia sighed, laying her head in Leticia's lap.

Leticia stroked her hair.

"It is both and neither, Virginia. It's just life. And considering how brutal life can be, well, I'd say our summers together have been nearly idyllic, wouldn't you?"

Hearing Leticia, who considered a badly cooked meal the equivalent of a natural disaster, hold forth on the brutality of life struck Virginia as inordinately funny, and she began to laugh very hard.

"Oh, Fred," she gasped, "I do love you."

Though Leticia had no idea what was so funny, she was glad that Virginia's mood had improved, so she joined in her laughter, and soon they were racing back to their hideaway in search of some privacy. For the time being, at least, things were back to normal.

***

Leticia valued that back-to-normal feeling and wanted to preserve it for as long as she could and to have it to look back on after whatever impending threat she sensed had manifested itself, so she began to keep a diary. She wrote a little about Virginia and herself and a lot about the herbal lore and view of life she learned from Mrs. Mendoza Velasquez. She was surprised at her own eagerness to learn and even more at her retention of what she was taught. She was an indifferent student at school, but somehow she could remember Mrs. Mendoza Velasquez' words verbatim for hours. That was a good thing too, since she often had to wait for hours until she had the chance to write them all down. Ana Mendoza Velasquez gave Leticia samples of herbs and potions as well as information, and Leticia duly noted the uses and dangers of each. Rereading her notes first thing in the morning gave her pleasure.

The old woman encouraged Leticia not only to learn all she could but to trust her own intuition. When Leticia came to her, disturbed and disheartened by her sense of impending doom, Mrs. Mendoza

Velasquez neither mocked nor soothed her. She told her that she too had a bad feeling about the summer and left it at that.

Although Leticia didn't discuss her feeling of foreboding with her mother, she had the sense that Lucille felt it too. At least her mother was also behaving in an uncharacteristically restless way. For two weeks she had been busy each afternoon sorting through drawers and closets in the kitchen and livingroom. She made piles and arranged for a local charity to pick up donations of clothes and appliances. Then Lucille started in on the bedrooms. She was in and out of Leticia's room, hauling away old books and pink sweaters Leticia swore she would never wear. Mrs. Mendoza Velasquez hummed through it all, even when Lucille insisted on spending a day in her quarters. She could have easily waited a few days because the family Ana Mendoza Velasquez wintered with requested her presence in mid-August for the back-to-school errands. But Lucille was busy with her work, doing inventory of the framed pictures, furniture, linens, and anything else she found.

Ana Mendoza Velasquez had hoped that Leticia would confide in her about her relationship with Virginia, and she left opportunities for the young woman to do so, but Leticia never did. Leticia suspected Mrs. Mendoza Velasquez would be unbearably sentimental, advising her not to let Virginia go, no matter what happened. Leticia had every intention of letting Virginia go; she just wasn't ready to do so quite yet.

On the last day of August the catastrophe Leticia had anticipated occurred. Calvin Barnes was playing golf with Paul Runcible, who was on leave from his latest posting in Greece. Calvin had drunk a number of martinis with Paul at lunch, but he was nonetheless quite sober, so Paul was totally unprepared for what occurred. When the sky darkened, they agreed to play the seventh hole before quitting. At the first flash of lightning Calvin keeled over. Paul thought that he was joking at first, for the lightning hadn't struck anywhere near them. He had laughed appreciatively at his friend's antics, before he realized that Calvin was blue. By the time Paul summoned help, it was too late. Rushing Calvin to the nearest hospital did nothing but prolong the agony. The massive heart attack he'd suffered took four days to kill him.

Paul, with his impeccable manners, spent several days with the Barnes family, assisting Lucille with arrangements. In fact, his deep voice and the scent of his after-shave allowed Leticia to pretend she hadn't been left alone with her mother. Lucille made sure that Paul also spent a great deal of time alone with Leticia and that he was informed of exactly how wealthy Calvin's passing had left his daughter. Five days after Calvin's funeral, he proposed marriage and was accepted. He spoke to Lucille before broaching the subject with Leticia, so her mother had the chance to prepare her.

When Leticia first heard from her mother of Paul's impending proposal, she was shocked at its timing, but Lucille convinced her that it was what her father would have wanted. So Leticia accepted. When Paul presented her with a ring, Leticia was distracted. She was so preoccupied thinking about whether she would garden with the ring on or off that the moment for a passionate kiss passed. Paul simply kissed the top of her head, much the way Calvin would have, and Leticia felt her breath catch.

Relieved to be free of a marriage that had turned into an ordeal, Lucille began to take charge of her life and her daughter's future. Speaking by telephone with the elder members of the Runcible family, she began to plan what she'd dreamed of since Leticia was born: a magnificent formal wedding in the late spring. Leticia noticed that her mother got through days at a time without a single headache and that she had all but eliminated her dependence on tranquilizers.

A day after accepting Paul's proposal and nearly a week after her father's collapse, Leticia went to the cabin. There she left a somewhat melodramatic farewell note for Virginia, knowing that Virginia would not be satisfied with her evasiveness, yet wishing to spare herself an unpleasant scene.

They had the scene anyway, right in the living room of the Barnes residence, where Virginia showed up unannounced and uninvited early the following morning. Only Leticia and Mrs. Mendoza Velasquez were at home to hear Virginia say plainly and clearly that she thought Leticia was a coward. Then she stalked out.

The following afternoon Leticia sought her out and took her for a last visit to the cabin, where each of them packed the few things they'd kept there. It was on the way out of the cabin that Virginia gave what Leticia thought of as her little lecture about not selling herself short. It reminded her of the lecture given to her by her mathematics teacher a few years earlier. She could no longer recall the woman's name, though the rumors regarding her erotic preferences came back to her instantly.

"They're all alike, aren't they?" she told herself on the way home from her last encounter with Virginia, whom she'd decided not to invite to her wedding after all. "Yes," she said, carefully differentiating between herself and 'them', "I do believe they're all alike with their insistence on achievement."

When she got home, she went to the medicine cabinet and took one of her mother's Valium. She felt she deserved it.

CHAPTER 19
OUTSIDE LOOKING IN
1980
❖

Although the flights that eventually dumped them at Philadelphia International were uneventful, Virginia and Carolyn could barely summon up the energy to deplane when they arrived in the City of Brotherly Love. They had originally intended to drive at least as far as Dover, if not all the way to Grant's Hill, but they both agreed that they were simply too tired.

When she awoke the next morning, jolted into consciousness by the roar of an airplane flying overhead, Virginia felt as if she'd hardly slept at all. She lay at the far side of the queen-sized bed trying to slow her heart rate. Carolyn was snoring softly, and though Virginia felt vaguely resentful, she grudgingly waited until six to wake her.

"Good grief," Carolyn protested, as Virginia hustled her outside, "can't we at least have a little breakfast before hitting the road? You didn't even let me take a shower!" Virginia grimaced but didn't reply. She opened the passenger side door and climbed into the car. Carolyn rolled her eyes and got into the driver's seat.

The sky was overcast, and Carolyn made a disparaging comment about east coast weather, but Virginia didn't seem to notice. Nor did Carolyn's futile attempts to find a good blues station on the car radio distract Virginia from her thoughts. As Carolyn pushed buttons on the radio control and swore under her breath at the squawks and static her efforts elicited, Virginia started a mental list of the steps necessary to secure an extended leave from her position in San Francisco. She knew she had to cancel appointments as well as two upcoming talks she'd agreed to give. She could monitor her research projects through weekly phone calls with her assistants, so that was one thing she didn't have to worry about. She knew she'd have to break the news to Carolyn sooner or later, but she put that at the end of her list.

Demanding as Henry could be, Virginia had no intention of leaving her father alone to face what was almost certain to be a progressive, degenerative illness. Now that she was on her way to Grant's Hill, she allowed herself to think fondly of the hours she'd spent in her father's clinic. She smiled as she remembered telling him that was really her first medical practice. He'd been unable to hide his delight at her words.

Grant's Hill was not just her father, Virginia reminded herself. She knew that she was unprepared to face an encounter with Leticia. They'd had no contact for so long that any conversation was bound to be awkward. That would have been true even without her secret motivation to learn the facts connected to Paul Runcible's death. Virginia knew that she had to face Leticia and that she could not imagine doing so without feeling trapped in her past, her adolescent self, rejected, angry, and confused.

At a little past nine in the morning, Carolyn drove their rental car up to the front of the house where Virginia had spent many summers. Virginia hopped out and raced to the front door. She noticed that the screen door still squeaked and the entryway still smelled like the rubber galoshes her mother always wore when she worked in the garden after a thunderstorm. She paced restlessly around the downstairs while Carolyn made coffee. Virginia's mother had been dead for years. She had spent little time in Grant's Hill, during her life, visiting only on those weekends when she could get away from her practice in the city. Still Virginia found herself expecting to see a stack of oncology files on the dining room table or a paperback novel with Louise's reading glasses on top. She smiled wryly. How odd that traces of her mother, rather than her father, came to mind when she entered what had always been essentially his house.

Virginia had meant to show Carolyn the shelf where she'd kept her Albert Schweitzer biographies and the small cedar closet in the back of the house where she'd hidden when her parents were fighting. However she just didn't feel like it. She gripped the coffee cup Carolyn offered and darted her eyes around the place, relieved that it was clean and orderly. As soon as Carolyn had drunk the last of her coffee, Virginia rushed her to the clinic where they could see Toni and pick up a few patient records. Virginia planned to give them to her father to keep him from dwelling on his condition. Toni Donelli had other ideas though. "No, dear," she said firmly, guiding Virginia away from the file cabinets. "Your father does not need to be thinking of patients right now. He needs to be thinking of himself."

No one argued with Toni, not even Henry. She was the backbone of the clinic, a combination of medical secretary, receptionist, and unlicensed psychotherapist for staff and patients alike. She'd known Virginia since the first summer that Henry worked at the clinic and felt more like an aunt or older family friend than an employee. Toni appraised Carolyn with a single glance and clearly liked what she saw. "So this is the one doctor your father will listen to," she said, turning to face Virginia while extending her hand for Carolyn to shake. Her eyes moved from Virginia back to Carolyn and she added, "He expects you to save him from an early grave, Dr. Matthews. I expect that what you'll really have to save him from is his very own stubborn self."

Virginia grimaced. "You're right about that, Toni. He's refused to have any tests done. Carolyn thinks his symptoms are early stage Parkinson's disease."

"She and everyone else, Virginia, dear heart," Toni replied. When Virginia's surprise registered, she smiled gently. "The nurses talk, you know, and contrary to Henry's view of them, they aren't stupid or medically untrained. They all think it's Parkinson's."

Virginia sighed, but Carolyn looked pleased. "That's good. If the nurses know, then his attending physician probably does too. So it shouldn't be too hard to get Henry tested."

Virginia raised an eyebrow. "I wouldn't count on it, if I were you!" she grumbled, looking over at Toni for support.

Carolyn wasn't fazed. "If he won't agree, you can always sign for him, you know."

Virginia groaned. "If he doesn't want tests, it will take more than my signature to change his mind."

"He doesn't have to change his mind," Carolyn said calmly, as Virginia led her into Henry's private office. "He's bed-bound and probably confused after hitting his head. It would be easy to persuade anyone who needs to be persuaded that he can't make a rational decision right now." Virginia looked horrified, but Toni clucked her approval and went back to her work as the door closed behind them.

While Carolyn dug around in her pocket for Stanley Felton's number, Virginia sat on the edge of Henry's desk and played with the large amethyst ring on Carolyn's free hand. She'd given Carolyn the ring on their last anniversary, and Carolyn wore it every day. As soon as Virginia had set eyes on it, she knew it would be perfect for her Carolyn. The jewelry store clerk had informed her that it was a man's ring and too large and austere for a woman's hand. But Virginia bought it over his objections, knowing full well that Carolyn, whose hands were too big for most women's rings, would love its size and simplicity.

Carolyn dialed Felton's number and mussed Virginia's hair as she waited for the answering service to pick up. "This is Dr. Carolyn Matthews again," Virginia heard her announce, her voice half an octave deeper than usual. "Dr. Virginia Carr and I would like to talk to Dr. Felton about Henry Carr's condition and prognosis as soon as possible. We will be at St. Mary's Hospital at noon. If we don't hear from Dr. Felton to the contrary, we'll expect to see him then."

Carolyn hung up and squeezed Virginia's shoulder. "There! That should get us some attention."

Virginia smiled. She knew that whenever Carolyn referred to herself as Dr. Matthews, things started to fall into place.

***

Dr. Felton was not at the hospital. A message scribbled on a pad adorned with a pharmaceutical company logo awaited Carolyn at the fifth floor nurses' station. He would be able to see them at three in the afternoon. "He's obviously a busy man," Carolyn mumbled. "I wonder how many cases he's carrying." For once Virginia could not tell if Carolyn was being sarcastic or serious, so instead of replying, she just looked around the nurses' station to see if she recognized any of the faces. She didn't. None of the nurses was old enough to have been at work the last time Virginia had visited the hospital. She shrugged, and the two of them headed into Henry's room.

Henry sat half upright in bed haranguing a young nurse. As soon as he caught sight of Virginia and Carolyn, he began to complain to them, allowing the nurse to slip away unnoticed. "You've got to get me out of here," he whined. "That music keeps playing day and night. I can't get a bit of sleep."

Carolyn put her arm around Virginia, who looked horrified. Then she grinned at Henry. "Henry, there isn't any music playing." Virginia gasped and opened her mouth to object, but Carolyn squeezed her shoulder and continued. "You're having an auditory hallucination, my friend. That's not atypical for Parkinson's, as you know."

Henry frowned but didn't object. Virginia was a bit shocked at Carolyn's bluntness, but she said nothing. Carolyn waited for Henry's reply. His face twitched. "I see you agree with that child who just sneaked out of here," he grumbled. "They're hiring grade school children as nurses, I swear."

Carolyn's grin broadened. "Yes, the nurses are looking younger every year," she agreed. "But I think that's just because we're getting older."

Henry chuckled hoarsely. "You mean I'm getting older. You two are still in the prime of your youth." He cleared his throat, but the hoarseness remained. "It's not just the music," he went on. "Someone is coming in here in the dead of night and moving my bed down to another floor, where they're shining lights in my eyes and mumbling incomprehensibly. I can't make out what they're saying, but the whole thing is very unpleasant."

Virginia looked at Carolyn, not sure if Henry was joking or serious. He'd always had a weird sense of humor. When she saw that Carolyn wasn't laughing, she closed her eyes and whispered, "Oh, my God!"

Carolyn let go of her and walked over to Henry. She sat down on the edge of his bed. "Henry, you've always been an excellent diagnostician. That's something I've always admired about you."

Henry's face remained rigid, but his eyes lit up. He loved Carolyn's compliments. "Go on. There's something more, isn't there, Doctor?"

Carolyn nodded. "What if you had a patient who heard music that no one else heard and insisted that he was being moved around the hospital at night and having lights shined in his eyes?" Henry started to reply, but Carolyn held up her hand. "Wait a sec! He also has impaired balance, facial rigidity with occasional tremors, and marked hoarseness when he speaks. I'd guess that he has Parkinson's and that it's no longer in the earliest stages." Virginia caught her breath. She knew that Carolyn inevitably told patients the truth about their conditions, but she'd never seen her in action before.

"Well, what do you say, Henry?" Carolyn insisted. "Do you agree with my diagnosis?"

Henry managed a shrug. "You could be right, but of course, only tests could tell for sure."

Carolyn smiled and Virginia's face brightened. Henry was not going to be difficult after all. At least she hoped that's what his comment meant. "So you're willing to agree to tests?" she said, but she phrased her statement as a question.

Carolyn bit her lip. She was not sure that Henry was ready to take that step.

"Who said anything about my being tested?" he replied, glaring at Virginia. "I just fell down and smacked my head. That's all. They should have released me by now."

Carolyn shot Virginia a warning glance and then put her hand on Henry's. "Henry, if the symptoms we just enumerated belonged to a patient of yours, would you insist that he be tested?"

Henry refused to make eye contact with her. "I already said only tests could tell for sure."

Carolyn didn't release his hand. "This patient has a daughter," she continued, looking up at Virginia, "and she adores her father and would hate to have to override him if he refused testing. She could though, since it wouldn't be all that hard to make the case that he's non compos, at least temporarily." Virginia couldn't control herself. "Carolyn!" she said in a choked voice. "Don't!"

Henry looked over at her. "Well, you're obviously not talking about me," he said bitterly. "My daughter hasn't visited me in years. I can hardly believe she cares at all."

Virginia stiffened and Carolyn let go of Henry's hand. "Don't be an ass, Henry!" she said firmly. "She loves you and you know it." She took a deep breath. "And because she loves you, she'll do whatever is necessary to get you the treatment you need. Your symptoms are typical for Parkinson's, but some of them could indicate other neurological problems, including tumors or hematomas. We need to rule those out." She paused for a moment, but Henry didn't reply. "Are you following me?" she demanded.

"I'm not an idiot!" Henry shouted. "Of course, I'm following you."

Carolyn didn't respond to his raised voice. "Good!" she bit the word off. "So do we agree on how to proceed from here?"

Henry looked a little sheepish and nodded. "All right. Get them to prepare the paperwork, and I'll sign it."

Carolyn walked back to Henry's bedside and shook his hand. "Congratulations, Doctor," she said. "You've made an excellent call." When she took a step back, she saw that Virginia was pale. "Let's step outside for a minute, darling," she said gently, taking her arm.

Carolyn walked Virginia out to the nurses' station without releasing her arm. Virginia was grateful for the support of Carolyn's strong shoulder. "My God, Carrie," Virginia whispered, close to tears.

"Once he's tested we'll put him on the right meds," Carolyn whispered soothingly.

"If he agrees," Virginia replied glumly.

Carolyn smiled at her. "He did agree and I hope he'll remember that when Felton gets here." Her smile faded. "I sure wish I weren't on the outside looking in."

Virginia smiled back at Carolyn and leaned against her for a second. "I'm sure you could get hospital privileges here if you tried. After all, it's not every day a hotshot neurologist like you asks to work here. That way you could take over Henry's care."

Carolyn stepped back and frowned. "I couldn't do that."

"Not even for the summer?" Virginia wheedled. "It'd mean so much to him. And to me."

Carolyn shook her head. "I'd be an interloper. That wouldn't be fair to Dr. Felton."

Virginia snorted.

Carolyn looked at her and shook her head. "And it wouldn't be fair to my patients."

Her tone of voice was final and Virginia didn't argue even though she was disappointed. She knew Carolyn wouldn't be swayed when she thought the welfare of her patients might be put at risk. It was an annoying trait but also the one Virginia most admired. Carolyn was far more serious about her work than anyone would guess from her fondness for racing cars and outrageous clothing. Her unconventional manner was simply a front that the dedicated healer flashed at the world.

"Hey," Carolyn murmured, bringing Virginia's attention back to the moment, "are you planning to ask for extended leave?"

Virginia shrugged. "I'd thought about it," she admitted. "Henry's situation warrants it, don't you think?"

Carolyn didn't reply for a full minute. "And?" she finally said.

Virginia frowned. "And?" She sighed. "All right, there's this other thing to deal with too."

"There will be nothing you need to do for Henry once he's on the right medication, Sweetheart. And as for the other thing, well, I don't think you should get too deeply involved."

Virginia started to object, but Carolyn held up her hand. "I'm not speaking from jealousy, just concern. I don't want to see you rush into life-changing decisions unless they're absolutely necessary."

Virginia wanted to hug Carolyn, but she knew how to be discreet, so she just squeezed her hand. "I know Carrie, but I can't just walk away. I have to know."

Carolyn looked sad. "Know what? Whether she committed murder or whether you can face her without hating yourself?"

Virginia thought for a moment. "Both, I guess," she replied. "It would be easier for me if you were here too, but I do understand about your patients. Besides, if I were you, I wouldn't want to be in the middle of this Leticia thing either."

"It's not that I'd be in the middle," Carolyn protested. "And I'm not running away either. I want to be there for you, but I have a practice to run."

"I know, Carrie, I know," Virginia replied, giving her hand another squeeze. "You're the most dedicated doctor I've ever met. I hope that if I ever need a neurologist, you'll consider taking my case."

Carolyn made a face, not sure how to take Virginia's words. Virginia smiled. "So what do you say we two extremely dedicated doctors go fill up on delicious cafeteria food while we wait for Felton to show his face?"

Carolyn looked at her watch. "I don't think I can face hospital food right now. Besides, we're technically still on vacation. We can drive into town, eat, and still get back here by three with time to spare."

Virginia nodded her agreement. "Let's go tell Henry we'll be back this afternoon. I don't want him to feel abandoned."

"Are you sure you feel okay about leaving him when we just got here?"

"We're coming right back," Virginia replied. It'll be okay."

Carolyn looked morose. "Don't forget that I'll want a tour of Grant's Hill. Weren't you going to show me all the places you went with Leticia?"

Virginia glared at her. "Jeez, Carrie, you're jealous and I haven't even gone anywhere near Leticia yet. You know the only places we ever met were the park and the cabin up on the hill."

"So you've said," Carolyn grumbled.

Virginia vacillated between unease and anger. She resented feeling that she had to reassure Carolyn at every turn, particularly when she was worried about Henry. She knew Carolyn wanted her to dismiss Eric Johnson's theory, but she couldn't, not without investigating first. It wasn't as if she could forget his accusation or pretend everything was the same as it had been. She wished Carolyn could understand that. She sighed and pushed open the door to Henry's room.

114

CHAPTER 20
AGREEING ON PROCEDURE
1980
❖

"Stanley was pretty reasonable, don't you think?" Carolyn asked. "He could have been a lot more territorial."

Virginia smiled fondly at her. "It's because you're so good at dealing with people, Carrie. "Not just patients, but other doctors and hospital administrators and..." Virginia stopped and took a sip of her coffee. "Just about everyone," she added. "You could be a diplomat, even though you're not the least bit diplomatic."

Carolyn laughed. "I'd love to take the credit, but Stanley was eager to have someone else on board. Dealing with Henry can't have been easy for him."

Virginia giggled. "I wonder if Henry had ever given Stanley any indication of his true feelings about his medical colleagues before today." Her voice took on her father's pitch and intonation. "To tell you the truth, Felton, the only doctors I've ever trusted have been my late wife, and these two ladies. I find that women are better doctors than men, and lesbians are the best doctors of all." She rolled her eyes. "Poor Stanley! I thought he was going to faint."

"At moments like that I really adore your father. Stanley was trying so hard to ignore our relationship, but Henry just laid it right out there." Carolyn choked down her laughter.

Virginia agreed. "That's why I can't help but think of him as poor Stanley. He didn't know how to react. Henry certainly didn't leave him any leeway, did he?"

"Henry has a way of not leaving one any leeway." Carolyn replied.

Virginia leaned back in her chair. "I'm so glad you've decided to stay on for an extra week, Carrie. I appreciate it, and I'm sure Henry does too."

Carolyn shook her head. "I'm sure Henry expected it, especially after that performance. What else could I do?" She raised her cup and took a sip of coffee. "Yuck, if this is supposed to be good coffee, I hope I never taste bad."

"It was better when it was hot," Virginia replied.

"Sure," Carolyn retorted, "when it was hot enough to burn your mouth so you couldn't taste it. What do you say we leave the hospital and find a place for dinner?"

"A walk first," Virginia suggested firmly. "I feel like my brain has turned to sludge in this stale air. Let's go outside."

Carolyn bounded to her feet and burst through the door of St. Mary's cafeteria. The humid air was warm and made the grass smell more intense. The humidity in San Francisco always made her feel as if she were on the deck of ship surrounded by water and she would never be warm and dry again. She thrived on it.

"The air here, it's like a warm bath," Virginia observed. "I don't know how you can walk so fast."

Carolyn slowed down to allow Virginia to catch up with her, but sped up again when she saw a trail leading away from the parking lot into a stand of trees.

"Slow down!" Virginia called out. "This isn't a race."

Carolyn stopped and waited. When Virginia caught up with her again, she took Virginia's hand. "I'll try to go at the standard geriatric pace, old woman," she teased as they headed into the filtered light of the woods.

"Look at that!" Virginia hooted, pointing at a large plaque nailed to an oak tree.

"The Goldhogg Wellness and Peace Path," Carolyn read aloud, "'A Nature Walk for Staff and Patients of St. Mary's Hospital and their Loved Ones'. Good grief! The title is probably longer than the path itself." She twitched her nose. "I wonder who the Goldhoggs were. A family of gilded swine?"

"I wonder if they knew they were endowing a sanctuary for poison ivy," she added, laughing. "Watch your step! I see it on both sides."

"East coast devil weed!" Carolyn sang out, but Virginia didn't hear her. The sight of poison ivy transported her back to one of the days Ana Mendoza Velasquez led her into the woods to hunt for herbs and mushrooms. Virginia had romped on both sides of the trail, helpfully gathering fungi for Ana's inspection. Less than a week later, however, Virginia began to itch. Soon she was covered with blistery patches from ankles to elbows and unspeakably miserable. Ana had applied a tea-based tincture to every patch, and Virginia's mother had run soothing, baking powder baths. Virginia smiled wryly. It was her father, though, who quickly took over and found ways to relieve her torment until the rash disappeared.

"Sweetpea," Carolyn said quietly, "do you ever think about Henry...uh, you know, passing on?"

116

Carolyn's words jolted Virginia back into the present. She stopped walking. "Is there something about my father's condition you haven't told me?"

Carolyn shook her head vigorously. "I'm sorry. I didn't mean to alarm you. It's just that Parkinson's is a degenerative disease; it puts the body under considerable strain." She sighed. "And unfortunately so do most of the treatments."

Virginia stopped staring and looked down at the path. "I know," she said softly, "but he's not in bad shape for someone who never got any exercise in his entire life."

Carolyn smiled and squeezed Virginia's hand reassuringly. They walked on in silence for a while until Carolyn spoke again. "I'm glad we're here, Virginia. I'm glad I didn't let you come alone."

Virginia nodded. "Me too. I do feel a little guilty about your patients. But only a little."

"Don't remind me," Carolyn groaned. "Mrs. Headache will have her revenge."

"Who?"

"The woman with the blinding headaches that go away when she eats Crisco. I told you about her, don't you remember?

"Oh yeah," Virginia recalled, trying not to laugh. "Doesn't she have to have her feet massaged at the same time?"

Carolyn laughed ruefully. "If only I could figure out what her problem is. I only know she's not faking. The headaches are real."

Virginia shrugged. "I could have told you she wasn't faking. If she were, it'd be a Godiva chocolate binge, not Crisco." Virginia shuddered. Carolyn grinned as Virginia lengthened her stride and quickened her pace, as if to protest Mrs. Headache's strange appetite.

"I suggested that she see a nutritionist since nothing organically wrong shows up on any of her tests. She doesn't seem emotionally disturbed either."

"No, she's perfectly normal. She just gets blinding headaches and has to eat Crisco to cure them," Virginia repeated. "Come on, Carrie, there has to be something wrong with her. Maybe the symptom is psychosomatic."

"Sure, but it could just as easily be nutritional as emotional. Can you imagine a dozen years of therapy to resolve some issue that doesn't exist when what you really need is to change your diet or add a supplement to correct a vitamin deficiency?"

"They'll throw you out of the AMA if you talk like that, honey."

"Well," Carolyn teased, "if the nutritionist doesn't help, the issue might be glandular, so I'll just send her on up your way to endocrinology."

Virginia made a cross with her fingers, as if warding off a vampire. "Oh no, you won't, Dr. Matthews!"

Carolyn laughed, then said seriously. "As for the AMA, well, things are changing in our profession. Someday herbal medicine will be admitted to the pharmacopeia."

"Not in our lifetimes."

Carolyn shrugged. "It will happen."

"Sure, it will, you holistic weirdo. And pigs will fly."

Carolyn grinned. "No, only Goldhoggs will fly. First class!"

***

The sun had set by the time Carolyn and Virginia returned to Henry's house. While Carolyn took an inventory of what was in the fridge, Virginia walked into the living room to find a message on the answering machine from Stanley Felton. Henry had signed the necessary papers so testing would begin in the morning.

"Thank heavens," Carolyn said, as she began chopping a limp carrot.

"I guess we should plan on getting up early," Virginia called out over the sound of the rewinding tape. "You were right, honey, this is not much of a vacation."

Carolyn came into the living room. She sat down on the edge of the couch. "Sweetie, I'm not sure you ought to come in for Henry's tests. He's your father, so you can't be part of the team working on him."

Virginia's eyes flashed impatiently. "Come on, Carrie, I'm a doctor and a daughter. I'm going to be there for my father tomorrow, no matter what. Medical team!" she sniffed, masking her tears with a gesture of disgust. "You and Stanley are a medical team? Don't make me laugh!"

"It's up to you," Carolyn said gently, standing up. "I don't see the point of your standing around in the hospital while he goes through an EEG and a bunch of other procedures. But if that's what you need to do…" She shrugged and started for the kitchen without completing her sentence.

"All right," Virginia admitted grudgingly to Carolyn's departing back, "maybe you have a point. And I do need to look into that other matter."

Carolyn turned around and stared at her. "Do you really want to tackle Leticia tomorrow all by yourself?"

Virginia smirked. "I don't plant to tackle Leticia. We outgrew that sort of thing a long time ago."

"What?" Carolyn asked, taken aback.

"Nothing, Carrie. I was just responding to the image. What I plan to do is go into town and ask a few questions. If I happen to run into Leticia, I might speak with her. If not, there are other people who probably know about Paul Runcible's death and would be willing to share their thoughts."

"Gossip," Carolyn said sharply. "You're out to collect gossip about her, aren't you?"

"Don't be ridiculous!" Virginia countered. "You know how much I hate gossip. I'm just going to try to find someone to reintroduce me to Leticia, that's all."

Carolyn retreated to the kitchen. She chopped an onion and opened a can of broth before turning the flame on under the soup. "Isn't this all very roundabout?" she asked.

"I can't hear you from in there, Carrie," Virginia replied.

Carolyn popped her head through the doorway. "I was just wondering about your indirect methods, that's all. But then I don't know Leticia and you do. Or at least you did. It's your call, I guess."

Virginia smiled to herself. She could tell Carolyn was trying to be gracious about the situation. She followed Carolyn into the kitchen and leaned over to inspect the soup.

As it turned out, Carolyn was the first to encounter Leticia. They met immediately after Henry's first round of tests.

Virginia and Carolyn both got up early. Neither was in an agreeable mood. The phone had rung shortly before two a.m. Virginia hated being startled into wakefulness, and she was especially annoyed when her attempt to answer the phone met with dead silence. "Is anyone there?" she grumbled. The only reply was an exhalation and then the sound of the dial tone. "Damn it!" she snarled, crawling back into bed.

"Who was it?" Carolyn asked conversationally. She didn't have the same savage response to being roused from sleep.

Virginia grunted.

"Who was it, honey?" Carolyn persisted.

"No one!" Virginia yelled. "Go back to sleep!" She pounded her pillow.

"What do you mean? There must have been someone. The phone doesn't just ring of its own accord."

"Go to sleep, Carolyn," Virginia ordered.

"Was it Leticia?" Carolyn probed.

"Oh, for heaven's sake! Are you nuts?"

Carolyn sniffed audibly. "There's no need to be rude, Virginia Carr. I asked a simple question and…"

"Go away, Carrie! I need to sleep, and if you can't be quiet, go natter someplace else."

Carolyn was silent for a second. Then she muttered, "What's her problem?"

Virginia sat up, grabbed her pillow, and stalked out of the room.

"Aw, don't!" Carolyn protested, jumping out of bed and following her. "Come back here!"

Virginia stopped when she got to the living room sofa and dropped her pillow on it.

"Why here? Go sleep in Henry's room."

Virginia glared at her. "Henry is not dead yet!" she pronounced the words bitingly. "Now go back to bed!"

"This is stupid. I'm not leaving you out here on the sofa. You go to bed, and I'll sleep here."

"Fine!" Virginia snarled. "You can use my pillow." She returned to the guest bedroom and slammed the door behind her.

When Virginia got up before seven and marched out to the living room, she found Carolyn lying twisted like a pretzel on the sofa. Carolyn was awake and looked at her with a pathetic expression.

"You look ridiculous," Virginia snapped. "I want to visit with Henry before his tests."

Carolyn groaned and sat up. She knew that the best thing she could do was simply drive Virginia to the hospital without bringing up the events of the previous night, but she couldn't prevent herself from asking Virginia to process their interaction. She knew Virginia hated the very word "process" and always accused her of treating their relationship as if it were cheese, but that didn't stop her. Of course, Virginia reacted with disdain mixed with a bit of indignation, adding insult to Carolyn's already injured feelings from the night before.

***

"I'll meet you later in front of the town hall," Virginia said to Carolyn as they left Henry's room together. Carolyn nodded without making eye contact. They'd agreed before going to bed the previous night to meet for dinner downtown, and Virginia saw no reason to change their plans just because Carolyn was feeling sorry for herself. "Okay, bye," Virginia added and walked off briskly. She found that she was actually looking forward to beginning her investigation.

Carolyn spent the morning helping Stanley Felton interpret Henry's test results. In the afternoon, after discussing possible courses of treatment with Felton, she spent an hour cheering up the patient, who occasionally forgot himself and called her by his late wife's name. It was not the first time he'd made that slip and Carolyn didn't view the mistake as a symptom. She knew that he enjoyed discussing medicine with her just as he had with Louise, so his error was not all that surprising.

At four-fifteen Carolyn drove out of the hospital parking lot and took the main road into town. To her eyes, it was a nothing place. No vineyards, no accessible sandy beaches, and not one ethnic restaurant in sight. She drove past ice cream stands and a few stores bearing signs that read "Antique Shoppe," and parked in front of the Grant's Hill branch of the First National Bank. The only good thing about the town, she thought, was that the bank stayed open until five instead of closing at three or four the way banks did in big cities. Try to say any of that aloud around Virginia, however, and she'd get a long-winded, defensive tirade. Storefronts aside, her partner had built up more than a normal nostalgic attachment to her summer home, Carolyn felt.

Carolyn got into line behind a middle-aged man who impatiently rattled his keys while waiting for a teller. Directly in front of him stood a woman who immediately attracted Carolyn's attention. Her long unruly hair and the faded, chambray work shirt she wore made Carolyn smile, but her face seemed infinitely sad and a little tired. Carolyn wondered what events had left their imprint on her. It wasn't until her own transaction was in process that Carolyn overheard the end of the woman's conversation with the teller at the next window.

"Will that be all for today?" the teller inquired.

"Yes, thank you," the customer replied. "Good afternoon."

"Good afternoon, Mrs. Runcible. Next please!"

Carolyn grabbed her money and bolted for the door. She looked up the street, spotted the wild hair, and took off after the retreating woman.

"Mrs. Runcible, wait a moment!" she called as soon as she was within shouting distance. She noticed that Leticia had stopped next to an old car and was opening the door. As she raced towards the car Carolyn wondered what exactly she was going to say. She couldn't very well introduce herself as Virginia's lover and expect to start off on the right foot.

Carolyn slowed to a walk as she approached Leticia, who was observing her with an amused expression.

"How do you do, Mrs. Runcible?" Carolyn managed to say without gasping for breath. "My name is Carolyn Matthews. I believe we have a friend in common: Virginia Carr."

Leticia's expression did not change. She simply extended her hand. "I'm pleased to meet you," she said, and Carolyn was struck by how firm her handshake was. "I haven't seen Virginia in years." Leticia's tone was cordial. "She is well, I hope."

Carolyn nodded. "Virginia is fine, but her father is ill. That's why she, I mean, we are here. We both practice at UCSF Hospital," she added as an afterthought.

"So you're colleagues then?" Leticia asked.

"Uh, not exactly," Carolyn replied.

Leticia smiled. "I didn't think so. I hope his illness isn't too serious. I mean Dr. Carr, of course. The elder Dr. Carr," she corrected herself.

Her tone had lost its warmth and Carolyn got the idea that Leticia was not very fond of Henry. She racked her brains, trying to remember anything that Virginia had told her about bad feelings between the two of them, but she couldn't come up with anything.

"We're doing tests," Carolyn said, nodding. "I mean, Dr. Felton is having tests done and I'm consulting."

"Of course," Leticia murmured, trying unsuccessfully to hide her impatience as she glanced at her watch.

"You must be in a hurry," Carolyn smiled at her. "I don't want to keep you from your family."

Leticia opened her mouth to speak, then thought better of it.

"Good-bye," Carolyn said. "Nice to meet you."

"Good evening, Dr. Matthews," Leticia replied. Then she hesitated for a moment before getting into her car. "If you and Virginia happen to have a free moment, please do call or come by. I'm sure Virginia remembers where I live."

Carolyn barely had time to nod before the car door closed and Leticia pulled quickly out of her parking space and drove off a good ten miles over the speed limit. Carolyn shook her head and took off in the direction of the town hall. She wondered exactly what she'd tell Virginia about her encounter with Leticia. She'd expected to be jealous or at the very least suspicious of Leticia, but she wasn't. She liked her, though she didn't know exactly why. It was more than the unruly hair and the chambray work shirt, but she couldn't put her finger on the source of it.

She could see why Virginia had fallen for Leticia. She was an attractive woman. But there was more to her than conventional attractiveness. Carolyn believed that a strong sense of fun hid just below the fatigue and melancholy that she'd detected. When Carolyn remembered to look at her watch she broke into a slow trot. She was already five minutes late for her meeting with Virginia.

Carolyn's mind was filled with restless thoughts. She had no idea how to tell Virginia that she'd made first contact with Leticia. "It's not like we're in a competition," she mumbled as she picked up her pace. But she knew that if Virginia had a plan for meeting Leticia and finding out what she needed to know, she would not be at all pleased to have Carolyn disrupt it. "It's not like I planned it. She knows I'm impulsive." She knew she'd have to tell Virginia, but she wasn't sure how many of the details she wanted to share. The idea of her puffing down the street after Leticia would not, she was sure, impress Virginia. "Oh hell!" Carolyn grumbled, as she twisted her ankle slightly on a crack in the sidewalk. "It's no big deal." She chewed on her bottom lip. "At least I hope it's not."

When she turned the corner onto the street where the town hall loomed, Carolyn saw Virginia sitting on the step. She checked her watch involuntarily to see how late she actually was.

"Hi, Carrie," Virginia said, standing up to hug her. "Hard day?"

Carolyn was slightly surprised by the warmth of the hug since she and Virginia hadn't parted on the best of terms that morning. She gave a small sigh of relief and hugged Virginia back. "Today wasn't too bad. The tests came back negative, just as I expected. No hematomas, aneurysms, tumors or other lesions. No signs of epilepsy either, in case you wondered."

Virginia smiled hesitantly. "So it probably is Parkinson's."

Carolyn nodded. "Almost certainly. In fact, Felton and I spent time mapping out a likely course of treatment. Of course, we'll have an even clearer idea when the rest of the results come back from the lab tomorrow."

They started to walk towards their car. Carolyn didn't know how to broach the subject of Leticia, so she was silent. Virginia, preoccupied with her own thoughts, said nothing until they reached the car. Finally she seemed to notice Carolyn's uncharacteristic reticence. "Penny for your thoughts," she said as Carolyn unlocked the passenger door.

"In a minute, first tell me how to get to the nearest clam shack. I can't think when I'm starving like this."

They drove south and then east until they came to a restaurant overlooking the ocean.

"Very nice," Carolyn murmured appreciatively. "I hope the food is as good as the view."

Once seated, they studied the specials for a moment. Then Virginia laid her menu on the table.

"I still have that penny," she said quietly.

Carolyn closed her menu and swallowed. "Umm, I met Leticia today," she replied, looking directly into Virginia's eyes. "She invited us to phone or drop by."

Virginia whistled softly and her eyes looked past Carolyn to a net and anchor decorating the wall. "Well, how did you manage that?"

Carolyn picked up her salad fork and stared at the tines before setting it back on the table. "I was in the bank and a teller addressed her by name." She shrugged. "So, uh, I followed her to her car," she added, smiling nervously. "It was a strange coincidence. She seemed cordial enough." Carolyn's voice trailed off as she felt Virginia's gaze fixing on her ironically.

"Cordial enough?"

"Yes, not exactly friendly, but not unfriendly either," Carolyn explained.

"Good grief, Carolyn! I spent the whole day trying in vain to come up with an unobtrusive way to make contact with the woman, and you just go racing after her and introduce yourself! Did you happen to mention that you're my lover?"

"Calm down, Virginia, will you?" Carolyn responded automatically. "I didn't tell her, but she certainly seemed intelligent enough to figure it out. In fact, I think she did figure it out while we spoke."

"I never said she wasn't intelligent," Virginia said calmly. The cool expression in Virginia's eyes made Carolyn uncomfortable, but she decided there was nothing to gain by getting defensive. So she sat quietly while Virginia's face reflected a brief inner struggle, then cleared. Virginia looked at Carolyn and smiled ruefully. "You win, Matthews. I'm sorry. I was being unreasonable. Now at least I don't have to fabricate an excuse to see her."

Carolyn didn't completely trust the change in Virginia's demeanor, but she was relieved. Throughout dinner she kept looking at Virginia. She wasn't sure, but she thought she felt an unfamiliar reserve in the way Virginia looked back at her, an expression of appraisal or evaluation that she didn't like but had no idea how to interpret. Their silence on the drive back to Henry's house was fairly companionable. It was only after they'd brushed their teeth and set the alarm that Virginia dropped her bomb.

"I want to see Leticia alone, Carrie," she announced. "And I don't want her to know any more about our relationship than she's already guessed."

"Why?" Carolyn wondered if she looked as shocked as she felt.

"Because I can't trust you not to blow our, I mean my cover with one of your outbreaks of spontaneity," Virginia said sharply.

"What cover?"

"Never mind. Just look after Henry and I'll look after Leticia, okay?"

"Not really," Carolyn replied, but Virginia turned out the light, signaling an end to the discussion.

CHAPTER 22
ACCOMMODATING
1980
❖

Carolyn slept badly. She woke up early the next morning determined to have it out with Virginia as soon as possible. But Virginia slept late and was barely able to swallow some coffee before Carolyn had to leave for the hospital for a nine-thirty appointment with Stanley Felton.

"Want to meet for lunch?" Carolyn asked as she went out the door. She tried not to sound as disgruntled as she felt.

"Sure, honey. I'll come to the hospital to see Henry in a little while."

As she walked out to the car, Carolyn wondered whether Virginia really was as oblivious to the tension between them as she seemed. She'd always thought of her as acutely sensitive to other people's feelings and responses.

Carolyn looked at the morning glory flowers as she opened the car door. Magenta, indigo, and white, the colors filled her with longing for her home and office where bright, patterned tapestries and her lushly hued clothing brought a richness and warmth to her life. The morning glory vines clung to the rose bush they encircled. They were determined, Carolyn thought, to climb higher even if they suffocated their support.

Shaking her head as she slid into her seat, Carolyn mumbled, "Well, either Virginia really thinks I'd get in her way or else she's lying to me and maybe to herself." With a sigh she turned the key in the ignition.

***

Virginia had washed her breakfast dishes and swept the dust from the kitchen floor. She was having a hard time deciding what to wear for the morning meeting she planned to have with Leticia. Normally she didn't care much about her clothing, leaving the fashion statements to Carolyn. Today she wanted to be impressive though it was anyone's guess whether an impressive appearance would make Leticia more likely to reveal the details she was after. Virginia guessed not.

"Damn!" she swore softly as she noticed a large stain on the sleeve of the one silk shirt she had with her. Tossing it aside she reached for a brushed cotton top and a jumpsuit whose bright yellow she'd always liked. She held the clothing in front of her for a few seconds, then shook her head. "No way," she grumbled. "Makes me look like a kindergartener. She tossed the jumpsuit on the bed and started to rummage through the few items she'd hung in the closet. Eventually she came across a pair of slightly rumpled gabardine pants and an oversized shirt that matched the cotton top. "Got to make do," she whispered, smoothing the pants. "There, I think we're in business."

She knew Carolyn would have spent an hour looking for the iron that Henry didn't have. He had thrown away her mother's old steam iron, complaining that the cord had started to fray. He'd never replaced it because he always had his shirts professionally laundered. She herself, for all her generally conservative tastes in clothing, never ironed anything. Sometimes Carolyn rescued her particularly wrinkled pants and shirts and pressed them for her, but for the most part, except when she wore something that had been dry cleaned, Virginia always looked slightly rumpled.

She dressed quickly, looked briefly at herself in the mirror, and combed her hair, sighing as she noticed that she needed a haircut. Less than an hour after Carolyn's departures she was out the door. Since Carolyn had driven off in their rental car, she was left with Henry's ancient vehicle. Maneuvering the huge wreck onto the road, she drove towards the Barnes' house, intending to take Leticia by surprise.

As she inched up the long driveway, a wave of nostalgia washed over Virginia. She'd often come this far with Leticia, but then always turned back at the last minute. Leticia had never invited her into the house, and she'd never wanted to enter. Their relationship had been a thing apart.

Virginia parked near what had been a circular garden cut into the driveway. To her eye it now looked like a mess of weeds, though she recognized an occasional wildflower. In her memory the house was a grand affair with white pillars and a formal entryway. But the schizophrenic appearance of the place now struck her. The original building was a modest stone farmhouse onto which a larger four-bedroom home had been stuck. The larger structure aspired to plantation era grandeur, but it looked phony, like a movie set. The facade that attempted in vain to unite the disparate buildings was an ill fit. The resulting house seemed self-conscious, shrinking in on itself while the trees and shrubs muscled forward.

"What a monstrosity!" Virginia grumbled. "How odd that I never noticed before!" She looked around a bit guiltily as if afraid that her comment might have been overheard. Then she straightened her clothing and marched up to the front door where she rang the bell. She heard it clearly, but no one came to the door. Since no other car was parked in front of the house, Virginia walked around to the back. It was equally deserted. She felt a disconcerting combination of annoyance and relief. Standing in the backyard with its giant trees and rusted grill, she gazed out over the land before her, noting a few strategically placed bird feeders and swarms of insects that buzzed around the tall grasses and Queen Anne's Lace at the edge of the property.

Virginia's nose twitched. "What is that smell?" she murmured, walking swiftly away from the shorter grass that rose near the house. Only ten steps later she came upon a large weedy patch that made the mess in the front garden look almost orderly. She sniffed several times. "It's so familiar, but I can't place it," she mumbled and turned back to the house.

The bright sunlight beat down on Virginia's head and the sound of the insects seemed to grow louder. Soon she was wondering if the buzz was inside her head. "Time to go," she exhaled, hoping that the smell would be gone when she inhaled again. "She's obviously not home." She felt a slight, almost possessive smile pass over her face as she touched the rope swing on her way back to the car. "I should have called first, I guess. Could have saved myself a trip."

As she opened the car door she was shocked to find tears forming at the corners of her eyes. It was that smell! Suddenly she knew exactly what it was. The pungent smell had announced the arrival of Ana Mendoza Velasquez each time the small South American woman had come to visit. Virginia took a deep breath and pushed the memory out of her mind. Ana Mendoza Velasquez had been dead too many years to cry for her now. She wiped her eyes on her sleeve. Better by far to focus on the feeling of satisfaction she'd experienced standing on the Barnes property. She whistled tunelessly as she turned onto the main street of Grant's Hill. She drove the length of it but saw no sign of anyone resembling Leticia. So she turned left onto the highway and headed for the hospital.

***

Henry Carr lay in bed waiting for his daughter. He was in good spirits, having spent much of the morning with Carolyn. They'd entertained each other with imitations of Dr. Felton. When Virginia arrived, he greeted her with a paean of praise to Carolyn. "She's not

129

only a first-rate diagnostician," he beamed. "She is absolutely hilarious."

Virginia leaned over to kiss him, then seated herself at his bedside. "You certainly seem to be feeling fine this morning," she remarked a bit absentmindedly, wondering where Carolyn was.

"She's off talking with Stanley," Henry said, as if reading her mind. "They're reading test results." Henry propped himself up and grinned. "We think Stanley ought to be on TV as a straight man."

"Well, he certainly is a straight man," Virginia replied without thinking.

Henry laughed. "Carolyn does a wonderful imitation of him, superb. You should see it. It's wonderful."

"Ummhmm," Virginia replied with a smile, fighting the urge to stand up and pace.

"And how are you, Virginia?" Henry asked.

"I'm fine," she said automatically.

"You don't look fine," Henry determined, sitting all the way up in bed. "You look peaked, I'd say. Distinctly peaked." He hummed under his breath. "Perhaps we ought to change places."

"No, I'm really fine." Virginia responded vaguely, wishing she had phoned Leticia before entering Henry's room.

Henry was disappointed. He counted on being able to get a rise out of his daughter, as he described it to himself, by telling her she didn't look well after she'd told him she was fine. He'd done it ever since she was a small child, and it had never failed. Well, almost never, he reminded himself, except when she was a teenager moping over that Barnes girl.

Unable to contain her restlessness, Virginia interrupted her father's reverie. "Would you excuse me for a minute, Henry?" She hopped out of her chair. "I need to make a quick phone call."

"You can call from here," Henry offered, pointing towards the phone with his chin. "If it's private, I won't listen."

"Thanks, but no," Virginia smiled at him fondly. "I'll be right back. If Carolyn shows her face, tell her to sit tight."

"Ha!" Henry grunted. "She can't stay still for a minute. Always bounding around the room like a kangaroo." He chuckled at the image, and Virginia smiled appreciatively.

"Well, make sure that if she bounds around it's in here, okay?"

"I'll do my best," Henry said solemnly.

Leticia was not at home to take Virginia's call, but she had an answering machine and it was turned on. Virginia considered leaving Henry's home number and asking for a return call, but she thought better of it and just left her name and a promise to try again later. When she returned to Henry's room, he was squeezing a black rubber ball in each hand. "She was here long enough to give me these," he announced grumpily. "Then she said she needed to go. I don't know where and I don't know why. She wasn't her cheerful self. Not that I blame her. I'm not my cheerful self either."

Henry's earlier good spirits had dissolved into a bad mood, and Virginia immediately felt guilty for trying to delegate his care completely to Carolyn. She sat down on his bed and asked sincerely, "What happened to your cheerful self?"

Henry dropped one of the balls to the floor and watched it roll under the bed. "I'm ill. Haven't you noticed?" He tried to smirk, but his face didn't obey. "I doubt I'll ever practice medicine again."

"Don't say that!" Virginia called out, reaching for his hand.

"Why not? It's true and we both know it. I wouldn't mind so much if I knew you were going to take over for me." He squeezed her hand. "Think about it."

Virginia registered the quiver in her father's grasp. "I have thought about it. I'm happy where I am, doing what I do." She barely recognized her own voice. It sounded like that of a whiny eight year-old.

"But I'm not happy," Henry objected. "Doesn't that count for anything?"

Virginia released Henry's hand and stood up without another word. She left his room and turned down the corridor to the water fountain. When she bent over to drink, a hand touched the back of her neck.

"Surprised to feeeel me?" Carolyn teased, improvising a foreign accent.

Virginia was relieved that Carolyn was feeling playful. Instead of straightening up, she reached out and grabbed Carolyn's belt. She pulled Carolyn to her and tickled her.

"Really, Doctor Carr!" Carolyn's ordinarily well-modulated voice rose to a squeak. "Such behavior!"

They walked back to Henry's room holding hands, only to find that the patient had dozed off. So they tiptoed into the hall and closed the door.

"I know what you were up to," Virginia accused Carolyn. She shook her finger at her. "You were mocking Stanley Felton this morning."

Carolyn chuckled softly. "When I walked in, Henry was in a positively foul mood." She glanced sideways at Virginia. "Come to think of it, so was I." She stopped and waited for a reaction, but Virginia kept her face blank. "Anyway, I knew one of us would have to cheer up the other, and I was fairly sure Henry wasn't going to make the effort. So I gave it the old college try, and it worked. Soon he was adding his imitations, and we both cheered up."

"Good for you," Virginia said heartily. "Anything new on Henry's tests?"

Carolyn shook her head. "Nothing that contraindicates a diagnosis of Parkinson's anyway."

"So that's why Henry called you a first-rate diagnostician."

"Did he really?" Carolyn pretended to be astonished at the compliment. "What a sweetheart your father is! You should take lessons from him."

Virginia shrugged. "Actually it was just his illness speaking. He is mildly delusional, I think. By the way, what are we going to do about lunch?"

"Eat it, I suppose," Carolyn said dryly. "But not at eleven in the morning, which is the time right now. What's the matter with you, Dr. Carr? Do you live to eat or eat to live?"

"I live to eat, of course," Virginia replied. "Now that you know the worst about me, can we talk about lunch? What would you like to eat and where?"

"How about the sub shop downtown? You know, the one with the funny sign in the window," Carolyn suggested.

"You mean the place where you can order a moatball sandwitch with hot papers?"

"That's the one," Carolyn nodded.

"Okay, if we can drive the good car," Virginia agreed. "Henry's clunker is starting to get on my nerves."

"Sorry," Carolyn was quick to apologize. "I thought you'd want to drive Henry's car. I'll leave you the rental tomorrow, if you prefer. Or you can leave it for me to drive home this afternoon and take the rental after lunch."

"Great." Virginia wondered why Carolyn was being so accommodating, but she didn't want to risk ruining her luck by asking.

***

When Carolyn returned from one last check on Henry she found Virginia in the lobby, hanging up one of the two public phones.

"Any luck?" she ventured, trying to sound casual.

Virginia smiled at her uncertainly. "Yes, as a matter of fact. I'm meeting her this afternoon at her house."

Carolyn sighed deeply. "Sure you don't want me to come along?"

Virginia nodded. "I'm sure."

"I still don't understand..." Carolyn began.

"I know you don't," Virginia interrupted, "but it's something I need to do alone. I've thought about it and it will be easier that way. Now give me the car key."

Carolyn shrugged and handed her the key. "I doubt that very much," she said under her breath. Virginia didn't answer. She just carefully put the car into gear and pulled out of the parking space.

CHAPTER 23
SMALL TALK
1980
❖

Lunch went badly. The food was decent, but neither Carolyn nor Virginia felt comfortable in their silence. Carolyn picked at her pasta, and Virginia left half of her sandwich on her plate. By half past twelve they were ready to leave the restaurant.

"I won't ask you to reconsider," Carolyn said suddenly, "but call me if it gets to be too much for you, okay?"

"Don't be silly!" Virginia huffed. "I can't very well get up in the middle of a visit and phone you. It would be embarrassing. Besides, everything will be fine."

Carolyn knew better than to argue so she meekly followed Virginia out to the car and let Virginia drop her off at the hospital.

Virginia watched Carrie go through the automatic doors. She's a better daughter to Henry than I am, she thought. As her mind dredged up a long list of ways Henry and Carolyn were more compatible than her father and her, she started to feel resentful. "Damn it! Get hold of yourself, Carr!" she scolded, turning onto the highway.

Walking up to Leticia's front door she took two deep breaths and rang the bell. She heard footsteps and took another quick breath as Leticia opened the door.

Virginia stared for a second, then extended her hand. "It's good to see you again," she murmured, unsure how to greet her former lover.

Leticia's smile was almost a smirk. She shook hands with Virginia, then looked past her, her smile fading into a look of disappointment. "Where is your, er, friend, Dr. Matthews?"

"She's busy," Virginia replied quickly. It wasn't exactly a lie since Leticia hadn't asked why Carolyn was absent. "She's advising my father's doctor."

"Yes, I know. She told me." Leticia's smile returned, and it looked less like a smirk. "We met yesterday. She's a very interesting woman."

Great! Virginia thought. She's attracted to Carolyn. She felt a pang of jealousy, which she suppressed immediately. "Carolyn is interesting and my father is very fond of her. And he has total confidence in her medical judgment." She stopped and rolled her eyes. She hated it when she found herself babbling.

Leticia looked amused. "Come in," she invited, standing aside.

"Thank you." Virginia felt increasingly awkward. She followed Leticia into a large living room with a pair of simple rocking chairs, a straight-backed chair, and a modest sofa. Though the couch pillows were covered with a rich looking material decorated with interesting stitching, they were faded and a bit ragged at the edges. A tall bookshelf displayed a few reference books and a few photographs, but the surfaces of the coffee table and end tables were bare. Virginia looked around, trying to identify a keepsake or souvenir that she could use as a jumping off point for conversation about Leticia's past, but all she saw were plants and cuttings in glasses crowding the windows.

"Nice room," she remarked, sitting down on the sofa.

Leticia chose the straight-backed chair opposite her. "Thank you. Would you like coffee or tea?"

"No, thank you."

They sat in strained silence for a few moments. Finally Leticia rose. "I'm going to make a pot of tea. Are you sure you won't have anything?"

"I'm fine." Virginia stood up and started to follow Leticia into the kitchen, then thought better of it. Instead she walked to the bookcase where a snapshot caught her eye. Ana Mendoza Velasquez squinted at her, a look of calm superiority on her face. Virginia shivered; the expression was so familiar. She could tell the old woman was about to say, "We'll see who's right, little one." Two larger photos stood next to the snapshot. One showed a man with graying temples. Virginia had only seen Calvin Barnes from a distance a few times, but she recognized him immediately. The tilt of his head was like Leticia's. The other photograph interested her more. The man in uniform had to be Paul Runcible. His angular face was handsome with a kind expression, though the strong jaw line suggested pugnacity or at least stubbornness. The photographer had captured Paul's confident smile, even though his complexion was marred by what looked like a shred of toilet paper stuck to his chin. Virginia chewed her lip.

Leticia was back. She had seated herself on the sofa so she could rest her teacup on the table. "You seem very well, Virginia," she said, her voice formal. "Is your father's condition improving? I was sorry to hear that he'd fainted, but it wasn't the first time, was it?"

Virginia heeded Leticia's unspoken request and put the photograph down on the bookcase. She returned to the sofa and found herself discussing her father's health. All the while she asked herself what she was doing and why. Finally she fell silent and simply stared at Leticia, trying to find in the woman before her traces of the teenager she'd known.

"What," she began hesitantly, "brought you back to Grant's Hill? You were looking forward to life in the real world, as I remember."

Leticia's eyebrows rose. Perhaps she was taken aback by Virginia's directness. Or maybe the mention of what seemed like ancient history surprised her. "I suppose I was eager to grow up when we knew each other," she said pensively. "But then all adolescents are, aren't they?" She sipped her tea and smiled at Virginia. Virginia found the smile condescending and bristled slightly, but Leticia didn't appear to notice. "After all," she continued, "as children we all have illusions about being grown up."

"We weren't children," Virginia said stiffly.

Leticia smiled again, and Virginia wanted to slap her. "Be that as it may. We certainly weren't the adults we took ourselves for, were we?"

Virginia frowned. An exchange of truisms about adolescence was not what she had come for, and her mind raced with the effort to change the subject. However, she found herself tongue-tied and wished heartily that Carolyn were there to take up the slack.

"I only recently learned of your husband's death," she finally blurted out.

Leticia made eye contact with her for just a moment, waiting for her to continue, but Virginia did not know how to elicit the information she wanted without giving offense. She looked down at her hands, hoping that her silence would entice Leticia to say something revealing about her husband. Leticia just sipped her tea.

Finally, Virginia broke silence. "We never really could talk to each other, could we, Fred?" she asked, bitterness and resignation vying with each other in her voice.

Leticia rose and wandered to the window. "No one has called me Fred in ever so long," she said so softly that Virginia could barely hear. She was tempted to join Leticia at the window and started to rise, but then sat down again.

"I told Paul my nickname, but he just made a face. He seemed to be uncomfortable using a boy's name to refer to his wife."

Virginia finally dragged herself to her feet and joined Leticia at the window. "Were you happy?" she asked, dreading the answer.

136

Leticia looked at her vaguely and smiled. "Happy?" The word seemed to perplex her for a second, but she caught herself quickly. "You mean with Paul?"

Virginia nodded.

"Yes," Leticia murmured after thinking about the question for a while, "yes, I'd have to say I was happy. That is," she reconsidered, "I was happy enough once I got over my romantic fantasies about marriage. And about Paul himself." She smiled at Virginia again. "You know, living as a man's wife is quite different from living with one's father or brother. Not that I ever had a brother," she added unnecessarily.

"I can only imagine," Virginia said in her driest, most ironic tone of voice.

"Oh yes, that's right. I almost forgot," Leticia whispered with a small giggle.

I'll just bet you did, Virginia thought. She returned to her seat and looked at her watch, hoping to end the pointless visit, but not certain how to do so. She knew she needed to say something.

"How is your mother?" The question rang false, but it was the best she could do.

Leticia's expression brightened. "Actually she's doing well." She seemed amazed by her own answer, but she continued, "She came to life right after Daddy died. I thought she was starting to become depressed again, but after Paul's death she livened up again." She let out another small giggle. "You'd be astonished at what a trooper she was. She helped me arrange his funeral. And then, though she didn't really understand why I wanted to move back here, she organized my move. I barely had to do a thing. After she sold the house in California and moved to Florida, it was as if..." Leticia paused and started over. "I don't know. Maybe it was the Valium. Maybe she didn't really like Palm Springs. Or maybe it was just life with my father." She shook her head and went on, almost as if Virginia weren't there. "All through my childhood she was missing in action, as Paul put it. Then suddenly it was as if someone had taken the cover off a parrot's cage, and there was Mother, colorful and louder than I could ever have imagined." Leticia swallowed quickly and then took a sip of tea.

"That's nice," Virginia said, wishing she'd never asked about Lucille Barnes. Leticia, however, wasn't finished. "Since her move to Florida she's been a bundle of energy. She's even found herself a young man."

She grinned at Virginia in a slightly embarrassed way. "Seriously! He's a race car driver, no less, and he's at least thirty years her junior. She usually comes up here for a week or two during the summer. Without the race car driver. In fact, I'm expecting her next week."

Virginia wrinkled her nose in distaste. When Leticia noticed, she was annoyed, but her annoyance simply caused her to revert to her role as hostess once again. "Are you sure you wouldn't like tea or coffee?" she inquired. "I have lemonade and ginger ale too."

"No, thanks." Virginia stood up and started to move towards the door. "I've taken enough of your time. And Carolyn is expecting me to meet her at the hospital." Virginia hoped she wasn't blushing at the lie.

Leticia brightened at the mention of Carolyn. "The next time you visit, I hope Dr. Matthews will accompany you," she said. "She is really fascinating. So spontaneous."

So you said, Virginia thought with a grimace. "Good-bye, Fred," she said softly and opened the door. As she walked towards the car, she sighed in relief. It felt good to be leaving the Barnes' house and Leticia.

Although Virginia and Carolyn had made no arrangements to meet, Virginia drove to the hospital. Henry was alone in his room, and he tried to engage her in shoptalk—how could he give Toni time off this summer, what should he do about long-term patients—but Virginia refused to commit herself to helping him with his plans. She hoped he might talk himself into a solution, but instead he dozed off. Virginia wandered down the hall, expecting to run into Carolyn. She sighed. "I give up. Carolyn isn't here," she said out loud. No one seemed to notice her. As she walked through the hospital doors, she found herself hoping against hope that her next encounter with Carolyn would be more satisfying than those with Leticia or her father. Somehow she doubted it though. She doubted it very much.

CHAPTER 24
RESTLESS AND GETTING NOWHERE
1980
❖

When Virginia got back to Henry's house late that afternoon, Carolyn was still out, so she puttered around and then settled down to read. An hour later, when Carolyn had not yet returned, Virginia grew restless and started dinner. After putting rice on to cook, she inspected the few sorry vegetable remnants in the refrigerator. Pathetic, she thought and wondered how Henry managed to survive. She cleared away the rotten bits and rescued the handful that still looked edible. After a quick glance at the clock, she chopped the edible bits and heated some oil in a cast iron pan. "Can't wait for her forever," she mumbled.

She was examining chicken breasts on the bottom shelf of the refrigerator when she heard the door slam. "I'm in the kitchen, Carrie," she yelled, "trying to pull something together for dinner."

"How was your afternoon?" she asked when she felt Carolyn's presence right behind her.

"Okay, I guess," Carolyn responded quickly. Then she corrected herself. "Honestly? It was stressful. Henry was in a foul mood because I really couldn't engage with him. I kept wondering what was happening to us, Virginia."

"I had firsthand experience of Henry's mood," Virginia said, cutting into the chicken package. "I went to see him after my visit, but I couldn't engage with him either. He was manipulative as usual though." She tossed the chicken into the hot oil. "I wasn't really there to see him; it was you I was looking for, but you weren't around."

"I needed some time alone," Carolyn explained. "You know how it is."

Virginia threw the vegetables in the pan with the chicken. Then she turned to Carolyn. "I know you were upset about my visiting Leticia alone, and you were right. Our conversation was totally stupid and pointless. And I felt horribly uncomfortable the whole time. All we talked about were her mother and my father. I didn't get a smidgen of information." She wrinkled her nose in disgust. "The only good thing was that I found out she likes you. She invited me to visit again, next time with you."

Carolyn made a face. "Wouldn't you know it? I came to the conclusion that you were right and that my best bet is to keep out of the way. I mean, I'm glad to be here for you to talk with and to help you figure out what you feel. But I'm here to help with Henry's treatment, not to play detective."

Virginia exhaled. "I'm not playing detective."

Carolyn said nothing for a moment, then said calmly, "I don't want to visit Leticia with you. It doesn't feel right and you don't need me to do it."

"Of course I need you to do it!" Virginia exploded. "Didn't you hear a word I just said? She likes you and will be more likely to spill the beans to you than to me."

"Listen to yourself," Carolyn replied quietly. "You sound as if you plan to manipulate Leticia to get at the truth. But she's much less likely to be forthcoming if she feels like you're a prosecutor rather than a friend."

Virginia bristled. "We're not friends. We were once, but that was a long time ago."

Carolyn put an arm around her. "Why don't you just ask her about her marriage and her husband's death?"

"I did ask about her marriage," Virginia insisted, squirming away from Carolyn to reach for bowls and plates in the cabinet. "She didn't reveal anything."

Carolyn took the dishes from Virginia, walked into the dining room, and started to set the table. "Sweetheart, you have to level with her instead of beating around the bush. And before you can do that, you have to level with yourself."

Virginia stiffened. "What's that supposed to mean?" she asked coldly. She stood across the table from Carolyn, adjusting the silverware, taking elaborate care with the precise location of each piece. Carolyn recognized the controlled fury in her actions and said nothing.

"Are you suggesting that I'm lying to myself?"

Carolyn cleared her throat. "No, I don't think you're lying to yourself. But you have to admit that you're not clear about what you feel and that makes your actions suspect."

"Suspect? To whom?"

"Probably to Leticia," Carolyn replied. "You want conflicting things. You'd love for Leticia to admit that her marriage to what's-his-name was a mistake and that she'd have been better off staying with you. However, you also want her not to have killed the guy." Carolyn centered a bowl at its place on the table and added, "A disastrous marriage is excellent grounds for murder, so you're asking her to incriminate herself, if you see what I mean."

"I don't really," Virginia snapped, spooning food into a serving dish. "Lots of people have bad marriages and don't kill their spouses. If she was unhappy with Paul, she could have left him."

Carolyn sighed. "Listen, you have to stop thinking about reality for a minute and look at appearances."

Virginia smirked. "That was what Leticia did, and look where it got her."

"No, no, no! Use your head for a minute, Virginia. Put yourself in Leticia's place."

"But that's just what I can't do, Carrie," Virginia protested. "I never dumped my lover for a man I didn't even know."

Carolyn sighed again. "I can see this is getting us nowhere. Let's talk about something else."

"Fine," Virginia agreed. "How about the weather? That's a neutral topic."

They sat down facing each other across the table, but neither had any appetite. Virginia drank some water and picked at her food, while Carolyn just sat looking at her. "What's the matter?" Carolyn teased halfheartedly, "Can't stand your own cooking?"

Virginia's fork fell onto her plate. She drank more water and stood up. "Your turn to clean up since I cooked." She strode into the kitchen, calling back over her shoulder, "I'm going to get some fruit and go for a drive."

Carolyn began to clear the dishes from the table. "I take it you don't want company on your drive," she said.

"What?" Virginia shouted. "I can't hear you over the clatter."

Carolyn carried the dirty dishes into the kitchen. "I said that I expect you don't want company on your drive."

"I'd love company," Virginia said heartily, much to Carolyn's surprise. "We can drive out to the miniature golf course and get some ice cream the way Henry and I used to do. Then I want to head over to Leticia's and try to talk with her again."

Carolyn's mouth twisted. "Have a nice drive then." She walked towards Henry's study.

"Wait a minute! I thought you were offering to come along!"

"Not to Leticia's. I told you I had no intention of getting involved."

"Talk about having a supportive partner. What a laugh!" Virginia grumbled, making sure that the words were loud and clear enough for Carolyn to hear, if only barely.

Carolyn stood still for a second and looked at her. Then she started towards the study again. "When you really need and want the support I can give you, I'll be there. Right now there's nothing I can say or do that will help, so I'm butting out."

"Okay, okay. At least you could do the dishes." But Carolyn was no longer within earshot.

***

During the hour after dinner Virginia phoned Leticia three times. There was no answer. Since she was too restless to settle down and read, she did the dishes and felt morally superior to Carolyn for a full half-hour. Then the feeling faded, so she tried Leticia's number again. But again she got no answer. She considered simply driving out into the country, but she knew her insatiable curiosity would lead her to Leticia's house and she would feel frustrated if Leticia weren't home. She laughed ruefully, knowing that frustration would be her lot even if Leticia were home.

Her thoughts shifted to the tension between her and Carolyn. You'd think, she'd be just the least bit worried about my wanting to go off to Fred in the evening, Virginia brooded, but no, she thinks she's so irresistible that I'd never be tempted by another woman. Of course, I'm not thinking about Fred that way. Not anymore. But Carolyn could at least be a little jealous.

Virginia ran her fingers through her hair and sighed, wondering how she had managed to get caught up in such a twisted thought pattern. "Good grief!" she said under her breath. Grabbing a pad of yellow legal paper and a pencil from beside the phone, she seated herself at the kitchen table. "Okay, Matthews, you win. I'll spend fifteen minutes figuring out all the ins and outs of my feelings, fears, and expectations. But only fifteen minutes," she announced, as if complaining directly to Carolyn.

Over an hour later Carolyn entered the kitchen and found the dishes done and Virginia filling sheet after sheet of paper with illegible scrawl. She came to the table, but Virginia was so engrossed in her writing that she only noticed Carolyn when she felt the gentle pressure of a hand on her back.

"What are you doing?" Carolyn's voice was as gentle as her touch.

142

Virginia looked up and smiled warmly at her. "Making notes." She laid the pencil aside and took Carolyn's hand. When Carolyn sat down next to her, Virginia's first reaction was to hide the pages she'd filled. She relaxed when Carolyn didn't ask to see what she'd written. Carolyn studiously avoided mentioning Leticia, and soon they were discussing Henry and the impact of his illness on their future.

"You just need to tell him you don't want to take over for him if you don't," Carolyn said firmly.

"I know, I know."

"I know you know, but I want to keep saying it so you don't forget. It's hard for you to make anything stick when you deal with Henry. You seem to feel you have no choice. Why is that exactly? Do you feel like you owe him?"

Virginia shook her head. "No, not exactly. I hate to disappoint him though." She paused to recall how the idea that she would take over her father's medical practice came into being. "You know," Virginia said slowly, "I think it wasn't his dream at first. He came up with the notion that we would practice together to encourage me when I was still cleaning up the office and handing out band-aids for him. He said it so often that he came to believe it was what he really wanted. Now that he's slowly accepting the idea that he'll have to curtail his practice, if not give it up all together, I can hardly talk to him without hearing that if I really cared for him I'd move here and work with him. He simply can't understand when I say I have to live my own life, not his."

Carolyn nodded sympathetically. "And I have to live my life, not yours, which is why I won't go visit Leticia with you. At least not until you're ready to be honest with her. But if issues come up that I can help with, you can count on me. I hope you know that."

"Sure I do," Virginia said brightly. "It's enough that you're here for me."

The words sounded sincere, but Carolyn wasn't sure she trusted the bright tone of voice. The look of intense openness on Virginia's face made her suspicious as well. It seemed contrived somehow. However, since she'd made up her mind about what she was going to do, Carolyn had nothing more to say. The two of them read in companionable silence until they climbed into bed at eleven and fell asleep easily.

CHAPTER 25
HALLUCINATIONS AND THEIR AFTERMATH
1980
❖

The ringing started at a quarter to three.

"Turn off the damned alarm, it's the middle of the night," Carolyn mumbled. The noise persisted, however, and after almost a minute of fumbling with the clock, she tossed it to the floor just as Virginia managed to pick up the telephone receiver.

"Hello," she growled. "Do you realize what time it is?"

That was all Carolyn heard until Virginia shoved the telephone receiver in her face. "Help me! You have to help me!" a voice quavered. "You have to get me out of here. They've put me in jail."

"Oh shit!" Carolyn groaned, sitting up. She glanced at Virginia whose face looked shell-shocked. "His dosage is off," Carolyn whispered, putting a hand over the phone's mouthpiece. "He's hallucinating."

"Hurry! Please hurry! They're going to torture me for information, but I don't have any information." The sound of Henry's sobbing was so loud that Virginia could hear it. Her pupils expanded and then shrank to pinpoints.

"We'll be right there, Henry," Carolyn spoke calmly into the phone. "Just hang up and wait for us." She got up and started to pull on her clothes. Virginia didn't move.

"Are you coming?" Carolyn asked, running a comb through her hair.

Virginia moved slowly, as if swimming through molasses. "Yes," she said weakly, "yes, I'm coming."

"Okay," Carolyn called out as she left the bedroom. "I'll start the car."

Virginia stumbled around, stubbing her toe on the dresser. "Ow!" The pain jammed the sleepiness out of her brain. She pulled on jeans and joined Carolyn in the car.

"Are you okay? Carolyn asked, pulling onto the street.

Virginia nodded out of habit. Because she knew Carolyn was watching the road and couldn't see her, she added, "Yeah, I'm okay. At least I think I am."

Carolyn grunted and turned onto the highway.

"How bad is this?" Virginia asked in a shaky voice.

"Can't say for sure. Probably the dosage just needs adjusting."

Virginia shivered even though the night was warm. Carolyn put her arm around Virginia and pulled her close.

Virginia took a long breath. "I'm scared. I've dealt with irrational patients, but this is my father."

"This probably won't make you feel better, but he's delusional, not irrational."

Virginia snorted. "You're right. It doesn't make me feel better."

"He's not crazy. His brain chemicals are just out of balance."

Virginia shrugged. "It's hard to feel so useless," she admitted. "I'm a doctor after all."

"I know. When my mother got sick I couldn't do a thing for her. What does a neurologist know about bone cancer?"

Virginia had no answer.

***

When they got to Henry's floor, the head nurse told them to leave. "We have ample visiting hours," she asserted, "but they don't occur in the middle of the night."

Carolyn's explanation, that she was a neurologist and had received an emergency call from a patient fell on deaf ears. "You may or may not be a neurologist, but in either case you're not affiliated with this hospital." When Carolyn instructed her to call Dr. Felton, the nurse called hospital security instead and had them escorted out of the building.

The irony of the situation was not lost on Carolyn. At home in one of the nation's leading teaching hospitals she and Virginia were treated like the rising stars they were. Hospital staff showed respect and deference in every interaction. Here at a fifth rate hospital in a nothing town Carolyn found herself tossed out on the sidewalk. She had no time to savor the contradiction however. Virginia was starting to get that shell-shocked look again.

Fortunately, a public telephone stood less than fifty feet from the emergency room entrance, so Carolyn called Stanley Felton herself. After a little prodding, he agreed to meet them at the hospital. Carolyn apologized for dragging him out of bed in the middle of the night.

Stanley Felton resented being called at four in the morning, but Carolyn's personality and credentials intimidated him, so when he arrived, he put the best professional face on the matter. He led Carolyn and Virginia past the protesting nurse into Henry's room.

"That patient has been uncooperative all night," the nurse insisted, following them. "Be careful. He was violent earlier and I had to have him restrained."

"Good God, Nurse!" Felton exploded, finding a convenient target for his annoyance. "His bed is wet. He's tangled in the sheets. And he's ice cold. Do you want him to contract pneumonia? The man is a doctor, for heaven's sake!"

The night nurse refused to be cowed. "I don't care if he's Jesus Christ! He was incoherent and out of control."

Felton stepped out into the hall and hauled her along.

"Do you want this hospital to get sued?" he hissed. The nurse stared at him. "He's on anti-seizure medication," Felton explained slowly, as if speaking to someone with a mental handicap. "Didn't you bother to read his chart?"

"Of course I read his chart. He wasn't having a seizure, Doctor, he was violent."

Carolyn entered the conversation. She could see that Stanley was at the end of his tether. "It's all right, Nurse," she said calmly. "Sometimes patients respond to the medication prescribed for Dr. Carr by becoming temporarily delusional."

Carolyn's intention was to soothe her, but the nurse shrieked: "That's not Dr. Carr. I'd know Dr. Carr anywhere. He delivered my oldest child." Her chin jutted out and when neither of the doctors responded, she stalked over to the clipboard.

"Well, he's got Parkinson's syndrome, and he's not quite himself," a now calmer Stanley Felton took over again. "So could you untie him, please, and get his linen changed?"

"I'll see to it right away, Doctor," the nurse snarled.

Virginia approached Henry's bed, worried because she hadn't heard any sounds from him. He lay quietly with his eyes wide open yet unseeing. Every now and again his body twitched briefly. Virginia gasped each time.

"He'll be all right, sweetie," Carolyn soothed.

Virginia looked at her questioningly.

"He's just temporarily out. We'll wait until he comes to and adjust the dosage. He should be his own ornery self in a few hours."

Virginia continued to stare at her father's unconscious form on the bed.

"Kind of horrible, isn't it?" Carolyn said softly. "I see it a lot and am sort of used to it."

Virginia pulled herself together. "I see lots of unconscious people too, but they're usually hooked up to life support and rarely having seizures every couple of seconds."

"He's not having seizures," Carolyn informed her. "The tremors are typical."

Virginia looked up at her. "That's not really much help, you know," she said in a conversational tone.

Carolyn squeezed her shoulder. "I know, but I just want you to know that he'll be okay in a little while. Why don't we step out into the hallway for a few minutes?"

"Carolyn, for Christ's sake," Virginia exclaimed, "I'm a doctor!"

"And you're also Henry's daughter," Carolyn replied, pulling her gently by the arm, "so just trust me on this, okay?"

Virginia yielded and allowed herself to be led out into the hall. Carolyn did not stop at the door of Henry's room, as Virginia had expected, but she continued to maneuver her over to the elevator.

"Hot chocolate for two as soon as this damned elevator gets us to the cafeteria," she announced, and when the elevator arrived, she half led and half shoved Virginia into it.

When they reached the cafeteria, Virginia collapsed into a chair while Carolyn went for cocoa. Virginia rested her head in her hands, trying not to think about how Henry looked lying unconscious in bed. When Carolyn set a styrofoam cup in front of her, she sipped at it without noticing how hot it was.

"Jeez, Virginia, let it cool," Carolyn ordered, pulling the cup closer to her side of the table. "I don't want to have to your treat third degree burns in addition to Henry's problems."

Virginia smiled apologetically, but the smile looked like a grimace. "Speaking of Henry's problems," she said, "what do you think?"

"About what?" Carolyn replied immediately.

"About Henry's problems," Virginia snapped at her. "What the hell was I just asking about?"

"I think Henry has Parkinson's Disease, but this is not news to either of us."

Virginia sighed deeply and pulled the cup back to her side of the table. "Right. And are you going to tell me that everyone with Parkinson's has Henry's reaction to the medication?"

"Come on," Carolyn chided her lightly, "does everyone react to any medication the same way?"

Virginia grimaced again. "Christ."

"Look," Carolyn said suddenly, pointing to the window. "The sun." The sun was, in fact, just clearing the treetops, shining on the dew-covered grass. Carolyn hoped the sight of it would cheer Virginia. "The worst hours for patients are between three-thirty and sunrise," she said softly, "so the worst is over."

"Yeah, for today anyway."

"We should be singing and shouting Hallelujah," Carolyn boomed, grabbing Virginia by the hand. "Let's go check on Henry. I bet he's better."

Virginia extricated her hand from Carolyn's grip. "Calm down, Carrie, we've only been here a few minutes. I'm sure Henry is just the same as when we left him."

"Bet he isn't," Carolyn challenged, sticking out her little finger in the timeless gesture of children.

Virginia gave half a laugh. "You're never going to grow up, are you, Carrie?"

"Nope. Now have we got a bet or not?"

"No, I don't want to bet. I hope you're right," Virginia answered. Then she stood up and offered Carolyn her hand.

***

When they returned to Henry's room, they found him sleeping peacefully. Carolyn left Virginia and went off in search of Stanley Felton to discuss further treatment. Virginia sat in the chair by Henry's bed and just watched him breathing calmly and deeply with only an occasional facial twitch and no sign whatsoever of agitation.

After a while, Henry woke up. He seemed surprised to see her.

"A little early for visitors, isn't it?" he asked, glancing at his travel clock.

Virginia wasn't sure how much of the previous night Henry could recall, nor was she certain whether or not it was a good idea to remind him, so she just nodded.

"Well, what happened?" Henry persisted. "Did you suddenly wake up this morning and find you missed your old dad?"

Virginia smiled fondly at him. "That's exactly right, Henry. You got it on the first try."

"That's what I thought," Henry said smugly. "I felt mighty strange last night, let me tell you. At around two in the morning I got dizzier than I've ever been in my life, and that, my dear, is the last thing I

148

remember until I woke up this morning and found your bright eyes looking into mine."

"Well, Carolyn is working on making sure you don't have a repeat of last night any time soon," Virginia reassured him.

"Okay," Henry agreed. After sipping some water, however, he quizzed her. "So what happened last night?"

"Not much," Virginia lied. "I think you had a small run-in with the night nursing staff, demanding and disagreeable patient that you are."

Henry nodded. "Yes, that night nurse seemed a bit slow on the uptake. I remember that much." He looked at her suspiciously, and Virginia was momentarily alarmed, fearing that her mention of the night nursing staff might trigger his paranoia.

But Henry wagged his finger at her reprovingly. "Virginia, there is something you're not telling me. I can always tell, you know. Even when your mother couldn't tell, I could. I did something awful last night, didn't I?" Henry asked, anticipating a story in which he would be the focus of all attention. "You have that look you get when you don't want to hurt my feelings."

"No, I'm not worried about your feelings, Henry."

"Tell me what I did," he demanded.

Virginia gave up. "Well, you phoned us sometime around three and said you'd been moved from the hospital to jail and were about to be tortured. So we came to see what was going on. I think you had a bad reaction to the drug you've been taking."

"And you've been here since when? Four in the morning?"

"Just about," Virginia replied, shrugging her shoulders. "I suppose I should start boning up on drug treatment for Parkinsonism."

"Planning to change your specialty, are you?" he teased.

"Just curious about what they're feeding my old man, that's all."

Carolyn entered, interrupting their banter. She announced her intention to take Virginia home for some rest before returning to the hospital and neither Carr voiced an objection.

As Virginia was kissing his forehead, Henry said, "Virginia, your mother left so many linens, books, and momentos in the house. If there is anything you want, ..." he stopped short of giving her the go ahead to take the objects away with her.

Sensing this was bait to engage Virginia in a discussion of the right place for her as well as the Carr heirlooms, Carolyn broke in: "I want to be here when you get your new dosage, so tell Stanley to wait, all right?"

"Since when does he listen to me?" Henry complained. "You're the only one who listens to me, Carolyn. You know that."

Carolyn grinned at him. "You know, Henry, as long as I can hear you complaining about being treated like a patient, I know all is well with the world. Never mind. I'll tell Stanley to wait for me. You give him a hard time about something else."

CHAPTER 26
A LITTLE HONESTY
1980
❖

Virginia needed to sleep. She wanted to sleep. But as soon as she closed her eyes, images of Henry in distress filled her mind. So she got up and read about Parkinsonism for an hour, seeking reassurance that aggressive treatment would provide him with a good measure of relief and a reasonable quality of life. When she found no guarantee, she put down the medical journals and paced through the house. She was irritable and jumpy. She yawned, feeling sorry for herself.

The morning was unusually cool. She hoped physical work would tire her enough to make sleep inevitable. So she retrieved a bucket, some rags, old newspapers, and an ancient bottle of ammonia from the basement and went to work washing windows. The ammonia smell made her gag, but she turned her head away and carried the bucket, rags, and paper outside. She set to work on the windows at the front of the house, but after ten minutes she gave up in frustration. She just didn't remember how to get the windows clean. She remembered watching her father dry them with newspaper, but he hadn't left gigantic streaks. "This isn't helping," she grumbled. "I don't need any more confusion in my life."

Back inside the house, she wondered why she had thought the word confusion. She wasn't confused, was she? Her life made perfect sense. She had her work, Carolyn, their house in San Francisco... Well, it was actually Carolyn's house, but she'd never felt excluded from ownership. She took a deep breath. Where were these thoughts coming from?

She remembered that Henry had invited her to raid the attic. She hesitated. Her bedroom had been in the attic. It wasn't a bedroom exactly. She remembered how Henry had put up a partition with a door cut into it. "This," he'd announced, pointing to the large, makeshift room with the window looking out onto the back yard, "shall henceforth be known as Virginia's Realm." He then produced a wooden sign with those very words carved into it. He'd let her nail it to the door. She'd enjoyed that, undaunted even by her mother's look of disdain. Louise had wanted her to sleep in the room that was now the guest room, the room she and Carolyn were sharing.

She'd never told Carolyn about Virginia's Realm, and she could tell from her initial response to the guest room that she'd believed it to be Virginia's old bedroom. "Not bad at all," she'd said, but her voice lacked conviction. Virginia had never asked herself before why she'd kept the existence of Virginia's Realm secret from Carolyn. She'd just assumed the opportunity to reveal it had never come up. But now she wondered if there wasn't more to it than that.

She walked into the guest room and looked around. How could anyone who knew her at all possibly think this had ever been her room? She sat down on the bed, knowing she was being unfair to Carolyn. But she felt like being unfair. Carolyn hadn't exactly been making her life easy since their arrival in Grant's Hill.

Virginia knew that few, if any, of her possessions were still in the attic room. She'd gotten rid of nearly everything when she left for college. The big pre-college clean-up was what she called it. That was what she told herself anyway, herself and her parents. Her mother had been impressed with her thoroughness, which she interpreted as a hopeful sign of maturity and a willingness to put away childish things. Virginia knew better, of course, though she accepted her mother's praise without blinking an eye. "Virginia is dead," she used to whisper in bed before falling asleep.

She shivered and walked back into the living room. "Oh, I suppose I might as well go up and see if there's anything I want from the attic," she mumbled at the sofa. "Maybe there's something Carolyn would let me bring into the house." She chuckled. The woman slept on silk. What would she think of the scratchy, old bedspread that Virginia loved?

Virginia walked slowly to the pantry behind the kitchen. There was a trapdoor next to it that had to be pushed open with a broom. She looked around and saw the broom standing right where it had always stood. It even looked like the same broom. "The only thirty year-old broom in captivity!" she announced, reaching for it. She remembered when Henry had bought it: right after that feral cat had broken in and torn the old one to shreds.

One short push popped the trapdoor open. "Now let's see if I can still do this." She reached up and caught the edge of the ladder with the broom handle. "Got it on the first try!" she crowed, pulling the ladder down. She walked over to the back wall and pressed the switch that controlled the two light fixtures in the attic. Nothing happened. "Oh well," she murmured, "I see that Henry's flashlight is still here on the shelf." She grabbed it and climbed slowly up the ladder.

When she got halfway to the top, she stopped. "Odd," she murmured, switching on the flashlight. "On such a sunny day I'd expect more light streaming in through the window." She assumed the door separating her bedroom from the storage area comprising the rest of the attic was closed. At the top of the ladder she took a few steps towards the doorway, but when she shone the flashlight, there was no door, just a pile of old furniture. "Oh my God," she whispered, casting the light back and forth across that end of the attic, "my room is totally gone!" Not only the door but the partition that had divided the attic was absent. The entire attic had become one large storage area.

Virginia turned and moved swiftly back to the ladder. She came down quickly and ran through the kitchen to the living room without returning the ladder to its proper position or closing the trapdoor. She noticed that she was shaking because she couldn't hold the flashlight still. She fell onto the sofa and turned the flashlight off. After putting it carefully on the table, she sat with her head in her hands. "I guess whoever said you can't go home again wasn't kidding," she said under her breath. Her hands still shook, slightly, making her teeth chatter, so she shifted her position on the sofa. "Jesus," she whispered, "I have to get out of here."

All the while she was dimly aware of a voice in her head saying, "What did you expect? You haven't been back here since you finished high school. You no longer have a place here, but that was your own doing."

Virginia shuddered, suddenly feeling very alone. "I really have to get out of here," she said aloud. "Who's stopping you?" the voice in her head replied. "Go ahead! Run away again!"

With effort Virginia stopped herself from racing out the door. Instead she picked up the telephone and dialed Henry's hospital room. Talking to Carolyn would make her feel better. She might even tell Carrie about Virginia's Realm. Certainly she'd sympathize. Virginia sighed. No one was picking up the phone in Henry's room, so she dialed the nurses' station. "I'm trying to locate Dr. Matthews who's assisting Dr. Felton. This is Dr. Carr," she said firmly.

"Dr. Carr is in physical therapy, Dr. Matthews. Dr. Felton may be back in his office. I can connect you."

"No, this isn't Dr. Matthews. I'm Dr. Carr, Virginia Carr," Virginia snapped in annoyance, but she caught herself. "Never mind," she said calmly. "I'll try later." Then she hung up.

The restlessness, which had started to ease in anticipation of talking with Carolyn, intensified again. Thinking being outdoors might help, she went down into the basement and pulled out an assortment of gardening tools. She hauled them upstairs and went out to the front of the house. "Should I prune the hedge or weed the morning glories?" She made a few swipes at the hedge with a pair of antiquated clippers, but they were too dull to have much effect. "Ow!" She had gotten too close to the rosebush. She put her thumb in her mouth. "Damned thorns!" she swore softly. Then she sighed and gathered up the tools. "This isn't working," she mumbled and dragged them back into the house and down the cellar stairs.

Having returned to the kitchen, Virginia washed her hands and inspected the tear in her thumb. "Just what I need! The way things have been going I could end up in the hospital in septic shock! Wouldn't that be fun?" Finding nothing alarming in the wound didn't relieve Virginia's stress. She paced around the kitchen, eyeing the kettle that stood empty on the stove as if it were a potential attacker. She decided she wanted a cup of tea, filled it, and turned on the gas. Then she thought better of it and turned off the burner. The clock on the kitchen wall read half past twelve, but she felt as if it should already be late afternoon. "Guess that's what happens when your day starts in the middle of the night," she mumbled, and sat down to try to draw up some sort of plan for the investigation of the death of Perceval Paul Runcible.

Forty-five minutes later she had a page full of doodles and had written nothing except: "Send Carolyn to see Fred? No, too risky." The more she thought about Carolyn and Leticia, the more jittery she felt, so she stood up and rummaged in the cupboard until she found crackers and peanut butter. Then she returned to her planning pad. By two o'clock she decided that if she were going to waste the day, there had to be more enjoyable ways to do it.

***

Virginia parked near the bank and meandered up the main street, hoping she could walk off her restlessness. She stopped to look in an occasional shop window but couldn't distract herself enough to quiet her racing mind. "Damn, I probably need more strenuous exercise," she mumbled irritably, as she turned away from the stationery store window.

"I quite agree," she heard a voice say and looked up to find Leticia gazing at her in amusement. "I came out of the pharmacy five minutes ago and saw you staring fixedly at those file folders. Or was it the three-by-five cards?" Leticia grinned. "But never mind."

Virginia was stunned by her own reaction to Leticia's presence. Her feelings alternated between passionate delight and equally intense rage. Part of her wanted to run off with Leticia to their old cabin, but another part wanted to kick her in the shins. She took a deep breath. "The file folders, I think," she said, hoping her voice wouldn't shake, "though I'm not really sure. I was looking without seeing. You know."

Leticia nodded. "Walk me back to my car. There's a coffee shop nearby, where the old Linton's restaurant used to be. The coffee is almost good enough to drink."

Virginia felt strangely elated, almost lightheaded. "Are you buying or am I?"

"My treat," Leticia replied with a laugh. "After all, I invited you."

As she walked up the street next to Leticia, Virginia realized that her restless irritability was gone. She smiled.

In the coffee shop they chose a booth. After they'd ordered their coffee, Leticia examined Virginia's face carefully. "I hope you'll forgive my saying so, but you look like hell." She flushed. "Sorry! I mean, you don't look at all like yourself." Her flush deepened. "Not that I know what you normally look like these days, but yesterday you seemed more like the Virginia I remember." Leticia stopped and laughed nervously. "Boy, am I ever putting my foot in my mouth! Sorry about how that came out. I'm not trying to be insulting. I'm just concerned."

The annoyance that Virginia had begun to feel disappeared. Feeling oddly pleased, she waved away Leticia's apology. "No offense taken. I'm just a little tired. We didn't get much sleep last night."

"You and Dr. Matthews, you mean," Leticia spoke softly. It wasn't a question, but Virginia nodded and looked intently at Leticia's face for a reaction to that confirmation of Virginia's and Carolyn's relationship. Leticia's face revealed nothing, however. Her expression of gentle concern remained unchanged.

"I know it's none of my business, but if you'd like to talk about what kept you awake, I'd be glad to listen."

Virginia sighed and folded her hands on the table. Looking down, she tapped her index fingers together and then spoke as softly as Leticia. "My father phoned from the hospital in the middle of the night. He was…irrational…delusional. So we had to race over there."

"Is he all right now?"

"No," Virginia's mouth twisted. "Not all right, but better, I think. Carolyn and his doctor will adjust his medication. She thinks the dosage set him off." Leticia nodded encouragingly, and Virginia went on, "Carolyn is a really great neurologist and I have complete confidence in her. But last night was scary." She breathed deeply. "Henry was having spasms. His whole body contorted every few seconds. His face too." Virginia looked up and managed a weak smile at Leticia, who reached across the table for her hand. "I've been a doctor for several years, Fred, and I've worked on lots of cases and seen even more. But when it's your own father…" She shook her head and stopped talking so her voice wouldn't crack. She didn't want to show weakness. Still Fred's hand on hers was comforting.

Leticia didn't seem to be aware that she was holding Virginia's hand. Her eyes were clouded. When she spoke, her voice seemed to come from far away. "My father died when you and I were…when you and I knew each other, but he wasn't sick. One minute he was fine and then he was gone. And it was the same with Paul. So I've never experienced what you are, but I know a lot about feeling afraid and disoriented. If there's anything I can do for you, please tell me."

Virginia smiled and squeezed her hand. "That's really kind, Fred. I'm sorry if I was rude during our visit. Things haven't been easy."

This time Leticia waved away Virginia's apology. "I understand," she said, then hesitated, biting her lip. "I kept trying to put myself in your place after you left," she continued. "I didn't sleep much either. The whole situation is so awkward."

"It doesn't have to be," Virginia said firmly. Determined to get everything out into the open, she plowed ahead. "Look, I think that if we're honest with each other, we can manage to get along despite our history."

Leticia smiled mockingly. "Ah, now I recognize my good, old Virginia. Who else is so convinced that a little honesty can make everything all right?"

Virginia felt her pulse speed up, and she extricated her hand from Leticia's grasp. "No," she said quietly, suppressing her anger. "I don't believe that a little honesty can make my father all right or bring back my mother. Or your father or husband either, for that matter. But it might be a good place to start, Fred. I never felt you were honest with me in the past, and I don't now."

Leticia started to protest but then thought better of it, so she just shrugged.

"And the fact is," Virginia continued, "that I haven't been completely honest with you either. I haven't lied, but I haven't told you the whole truth."

Leticia smirked. "So what else is new?"

"My father's illness isn't the only reason I'm here. Carolyn and I encountered someone from our, that is your and my past while we were on vacation. He told me of your husband's death. He thinks the death was not from natural causes and is convinced..."

Leticia looked at Virginia was an expression of overwhelming irony. "Here we go again," she interrupted. "Why not let me guess? Eric Johnson, right? He told you that I cold-bloodedly murdered my husband. And you believed him."

"Not exactly," Virginia protested. "He did tell me and he wanted me to investigate on his behalf. I told him to go to hell." She stared intently into Leticia's eyes. "I didn't believe him, Fred, but he did disturb my peace of mind. I need to know what happened."

"Why?" Leticia shouted at her, suddenly furious. "What the hell business is it of yours how my husband died? You didn't know him. You never wanted him to take me away from you." She took a deep breath and glared into Virginia's eyes. "Maybe you killed him. Makes about as much sense as Johnson's theory. And since when does being a doctor qualify you as a detective and prosecutor, Virginia Carr?"

Her vehemence took Virginia by surprise. "I...," she began, but she had no idea what to say, so she just closed her mouth and looked down at her cup of cold coffee.

CHAPTER 27
LETICIA'S PLACE
1980
❖

Leticia wished she were somewhere else. Anywhere else would do in a pinch, but if she had a choice, she'd always choose to be in her garden. As she sat struggling not to look at Virginia, she tried to let her mind take her there. That was a trick she'd learned shortly after getting married and moving with Paul to Turkey. Though she found the country fascinating, she missed her favorite tree. So she visualized herself sitting on a thick branch halfway up. When she worked at it, she could smell its greenness and feel its bark rough against her hands and the backs of her legs. The tree was gone now. Her mother had written to her a year after she'd left to tell her that a severe windstorm had brought it down. Leticia had found that hard to believe; it was such a solid tree and very healthy. And one never knew whether Lucille was reporting facts or inventing them. But since she had no evidence to the contrary, she chose to accept her mother's word. With a heavy heart, she'd let go of her tree and transferred her loyalty to the garden, especially the front garden.

She and Ana Mendoza Velasquez had dug that together during Ana's second summer with the Barnes family. They had planted the usual herbs for cooking, rosemary, oregano, thyme, and marjoram, but that area was also their experimental plot where they transplanted thistles and Queen Anne's Lace from the surrounding meadows. Ana had also planted some seeds that she'd brought from her homeland, but the plants had not survived the first winter. Leticia's own garden of medicinal herbs was in back of the house. The plants were local and hardy and barely needed tending.

Immediately after returning to Grant's Hill, Leticia felt uncomfortable going into town. So she spent most of her waking hours outside in her garden. Thinking back on that time, she realized that her reticence had a lot to do with Virginia. Living in Grant's Hill where Henry Carr lived and practiced medicine full-time made it likely, she feared, that she would run into Virginia. But that didn't happen, and after the first few years she gave up worrying about it.

Now sitting across from Virginia she tried hard to visualize herself clipping back the heads of the daisies that lined the path to her back door. However, the presence of Virginia made it hard for her to see the

158

daisies and feel the pressure of the clippers against her hand. She frowned, remembering her adolescent callousness. Looking at Virginia she felt a twinge of guilt. Not only had she dumped Virginia, she'd never made any attempt to reconnect with her once they were adults, who'd outgrown, so she told herself, the tempestuousness of those adolescent feelings. She wasn't even sure she liked this adult Virginia. Though she could recognize the continuities in Virginia's personality and appearance, the woman before her seemed like a different, less interesting person than the girl she'd known. Why did Carolyn Matthews seem more alive and attractive than Virginia? Was Virginia simply worn down by the stress of caring for her sick father? Henry Carr was a difficult man, and Leticia had no reason to feel fond of him or sorry for him. Still she felt a pang of sadness when she thought about him, lying sick in the hospital. He was no friend of hers, but she did not wish him ill.

Leticia wondered what it was like to watch your father degenerate and die. Her own father's death had been so quick and unexpected that she could not to this day say a casual good-bye to anyone she cared for deeply. Not that there were many people in that category. Her mother, but of course that went without saying. Who doesn't love her own mother? Leticia smiled a bit grimly. Then there was Cyrus, though she'd never thought she'd get so attached to him. And Susan, who had started out as Paul's friend.

Leticia could never think of Susan without smiling. In her mind's eye she saw the intense, serious young woman she'd met right after Paul's tour of duty in Turkey had ended. They were in Wyoming then and Paul told her he'd invited someone for dinner. "You don't need to cook anything too fancy," he'd said with a grin. "This one thinks mess hall chow is tasty."

Susan didn't really enjoy air force rations, but her taste in food was fairly primitive. She put catsup on nearly everything and her favorite beverage was chocolate milk. Leticia had prepared some ground beef kabobs and spiced them the way she'd learned to in Turkey. "Wow, what cute little burgers!" Susan exclaimed, drenching them in catsup. Leticia looked over at Paul who mouthed, "I told you." He frowned to hide his smile.

It was hard to believe that Susan had a brilliant legal mind, but she did. First in her class at Boalt Law School, she had gone on to make a name for herself as a prosecutor. Then suddenly she enlisted in the air force. She was immediately assigned to the Judge Advocate General's Department.

"She's an outstanding investigator," Paul had told Leticia the first time he mentioned Susan, "but she's awfully stubborn. Susan needs to learn you have to go along to get along. She's incorruptible but naïve; it's a recipe for disaster."

Leticia had no idea how Paul had gained such insight. She wondered at first if the two were having an affair, but that struck her as unlikely once she met Susan. It wasn't that Susan was unattractive. Quite the contrary. But having an affair with a married officer went against the code of military justice, so it was out of the question for Susan to consider it. That's what Paul had meant by incorruptible but naïve, she decided. Susan threw herself wholeheartedly into whatever she did, and she followed the rules to the letter.

They never invited her again for dinner, but they did see her at Christmas and New Year's parties on the base. She was always very pleasant to Leticia, but no more than that. Then Paul died, and Susan came to Leticia and told her that she had reason to believe his death was suspicious. Other people, especially Paul's relatives, felt that way, but most of them suspected Leticia. Susan had a different take. She was convinced that Paul knew too much, and she brought Leticia a pile of documents, which, she claimed, demonstrated that he had information about smuggling and money laundering that implicated a handful of higher-ups. Leticia didn't believe her, but it was on Susan's advice that she insisted the medical examiner include toxicology screening in the autopsy. When Susan continued to insist that Paul had been poisoned despite the negative test results, Leticia decided that the woman had lost her grip on reality. Although she was sure there had been no affair, Leticia surmised that Susan had been in love with Paul and was therefore unable to accept that he had simply died. She felt no jealousy, just a sense of kinship. Since she too had loved Paul, their grief became a bond. Eventually they put their loss behind them and their relationship began to blossom in its own right. Susan's honesty made it easy for Leticia to confide in her. Her trust in Susan grew, and what had initially been gratitude that someone did not go out of her way to think ill of her turned into a rich friendship. Leticia found she could talk to Susan the way she had never talked to anyone else. She often thought that she would not have survived the first weeks after Paul's death without her.

However, Susan's persistence in trying to uncover corruption on the part of higher level officers hadn't won her any friends, and she transferred out of her unit and was reassigned to a post in California within a few months of Paul's death. That, as much as anything else, persuaded Leticia that she had to leave Wyoming. She considered moving out to California, but when she found herself expecting Susan to call her Fred during their infrequent phone calls, she decided to head in the opposite direction. Despite the distance, the two women wrote regularly, and Leticia was glad to know that she had one person she could call a friend.

Leticia's connection to Cyrus Marshall was something else all together. The only resemblance that he bore to Susan was that he too was brilliant, albeit in an entirely different way. Whenever Leticia met with Cyrus she had to think about Ana Mendoza Velasquez, who had taught her so much about medicinal herbs. Ana had always insisted that everyone had a gift to bring to the world and that Leticia's would have to do with healing. Though Leticia had always regarded this prediction as suspect, she did share the natural remedies she knew with the population of Grant's Hill, especially with those who either couldn't afford or didn't trust standard medical treatment as meted out by Dr. Henry Carr. Dr. Carr had frequently scolded her and even threatened to have her arrested for practicing medicine without a license. She had never understood why he was so upset since the people she treated were not his patients. However, one afternoon, in the middle of a scolding, the reason for his anger became clear. "You," he'd shouted, "are promoting quackery instead of science. You could kill someone with your concoctions. Just because you got away with eliminating your husband, don't think you can poison people and not be held accountable!"

Leticia had been astonished and dismayed. She stopped distributing herbs and seriously considered leaving Grant's Hill. Then one evening her telephone rang and a woman's voice informed her that Professor Cyrus Marshall wished to invite her to lunch at the Johns Hopkins Faculty Club. She thought it was a joke at first, but when Cyrus followed up with a call of his own, she agreed to meet him. As soon as he began to describe the ethnobotany program he'd founded, she realized that the best use of Ana's knowledge would be to share it with Cyrus. Perhaps that way her gift to the world could be healing after all. In Cyrus she had a partner with academic credentials and access to the networks that could legitimate what Ana had given her. Once Cyrus got his work into print, she thought, Dr. Carr would never again accuse her of promoting quackery instead of science. And maybe someday down the line Ana's knowledge would actually enter into medical practice and help more people than Leticia could ever have helped on her own.

It was a noble idea, Leticia told herself, but sometimes she resented being dependent on Cyrus. He worked so slowly that she despaired of his finishing the work they had started together. Though he seemed healthy enough, he wasn't young. Ana's lore was so vast that Leticia just hoped he'd live long enough to get it into print.

Cyrus never seemed to be in a hurry. He delighted in the process of learning. In fact, there was hardly any activity she could think of that Cyrus didn't delight in. She was sure he rhapsodized over his daily shower and his shaving cream as much as he did over the herbs that she described. She admired his capacity for enjoyment, though sometimes she found it tedious because he felt called upon to verbalize everything he experienced in great detail. When he ate the baklava she occasionally baked for him he offered extensive commentary on the taste and the texture. Indeed he swirled each morsel around in his mouth as if it were expensive French wine.

She knew that the public lectures he gave were increasing respect for the field of ethnobotany and awareness of the importance of the rainforest. And his meticulous explanations of the properties of the herbs Ana Mendoza Velasquez had brought with her were gaining some attention from pharmaceutical companies. Still she wished he would get on with the written record. He was on the brink of retirement after all.

She sighed and released the image of Cyrus Marshall. As it floated free of her mind, she suddenly was able to visualize herself in her garden, to smell the mint and rosemary. She felt the dirt under her fingernails and the thistles and burrs in her hair. When she glanced down at her muddy clothes, she cackled. She looked like nothing so much as her childhood idea of a witch. The thought made her laugh aloud. "I'll get you, my pretty!"

CHAPTER 28
RESCUE MISSIONS
1980
❖

"What was that?"

Leticia exhaled loudly, jolted out of her reverie by Virginia's voice. She felt a flash of irritation. "I beg your pardon?"

Virginia smiled uncertainly at the sharp edge in Leticia's voice. "You laughed and then said something, but I missed it."

Leticia took a deep breath to master her annoyance. "I didn't," she replied curtly.

"Didn't what?" Virginia looked confused.

"I didn't say anything."

"Yes, you did," Virginia insisted. "I heard you."

"You're imagining it," Leticia insisted, and Virginia remembered how frequently Leticia used to insist on the accuracy of assertions that were patently false. She sighed.

Leticia shrugged and peered into her coffee cup. "Eric Johnson," she said emphatically, "is obsessed. He has hated me ever since he lost that job way back when. He's held me responsible for it all these years. Paul's death just gave him the opening he was looking for."

"Well, weren't you?" Virginia asked sharply.

"Wasn't I what?"

"Responsible for his losing his job."

"Don't be ridiculous!" Leticia snapped.

"Just wait a minute, Fred," Virginia continued. "Didn't your father have him fired?"

"What my father did or didn't do was not my responsibility. It isn't now, and it certainly wasn't then. Good God, Virginia, I was all of fourteen years old. Impetuous, wild, immature..."

"Oh no you don't, Fred," Virginia interjected angrily. "You can't get off that easily. You complained to your father because Johnson hurt your pride, and that cost him his job. It's no surprise that he remembers."

"I didn't say it was a surprise," Leticia responded. Her voice sounded tired and annoyed. "I simply pointed out that he has hated me since then. Surely there must come a day when it's time to move on. Instead he's harassing me by trying to turn my husband's death into a murder."

Virginia fiddled with her spoon. When she finally spoke, her voice was very soft. "Whether or not he's harassing you is beside the point, Fred."

Leticia lips tightened. "What exactly is the point then?"

"Did you do it?" Virginia whispered. "Did you kill him?"

Leticia shook her head very slowly. When her eyes finally met Virginia's they were icy. "You don't know me, Virginia. And I don't know you. So what exactly is it that you want from me?"

Virginia just sat and stared. She had no idea how to answer Leticia. Her first instinct was to avoid the question. "The truth," she replied at last, her voice hoarse. Her voice echoed in her mind, but the sound was hollow.

Leticia stared blankly back at her. Virginia couldn't read her gaze. Was she afraid? Antagonistic? For a second Virginia was tempted to take back her words, but she resisted the impulse. It had to be said, she thought. I have to know. She lifted her cup and sipped at the cold dregs. "I thought you said this coffee was almost good enough to drink," she teased, allowing disgust to dominate her facial expression.

"Don't change the subject!" Leticia commanded. "Have you come to torture me or to help me?"

"You know," Virginia said conversationally, replacing her cup on the table, "when I said I wanted the truth, I was lying. I suppose I want to know that you didn't kill your husband. Though of course I don't want you not to have killed him because you were madly in love with him." She looked down at her cup. "That would be a blow to my pride."

Leticia blinked. "What difference does it make if I was madly in love with him or not? He's dead. And you haven't exactly been pining away after me all these years. You and Dr. Matthews are a couple. A happy couple, I assume."

"Yes," Virginia replied, "we are. But that's not the point."

"Damn it, Virginia! Everything I say is not the point. You never were this repetitive when we were young. If I'd known you'd turn out to be such a know-it-all, I'd have had nothing to do with you."

Virginia smiled faintly. "Your memory must be failing. I've always been a know-it-all. We used to fight about that all the time."

"I don't remember fighting with you," she said softly, then shrugged. Virginia noticed the skin around Leticia's collarbone was pinker than her face. "So tell me again, what is the point? And I'd like the truth this time."

"The point," Virginia replied, busily tracing the pattern of the cup on her damp napkin, "is that Eric Johnson is trying to find evidence to indict you for a crime he thinks you committed. And I have somehow ended up in the unenviable position of looking into the matter. I'm not at all sure there was a crime. And even if there was, I don't know that you committed it. But," she added, "neither am I sure that you're incapable of killing someone. By that I mean that the young woman I knew might have been able to kill. I don't know you well enough now to be able to judge if that's still true."

Leticia's expression was deadpan. "If the woman I am now were capable of killing, let me assure you that you'd be my first victim."

Virginia looked up, alarmed.

Leticia merely looked bemused. "Let me understand you. You would like to find out whether I killed my husband, assuming he did not die of natural causes as determined by the autopsy. And you would also like to be reassured that the young woman I was could not have done so. Isn't there a contradiction at work here, Virginia?" She smirked. "I suppose we could hold a séance to answer the first question." Her smirk expanded into a mocking grin. "Then maybe we could go to the bank and get a notarized statement to answer the second. Would that be sufficient?"

Virginia shook her head impatiently. "Stop it, Fred! This isn't a sitcom. I need to know if you killed him."

Leticia raised her eyebrows. "And?"

"And I want to know if you are the same person you were when we were together."

Leticia snorted. "Oh come on, Virginia! Are you the same person you were at fourteen or fifteen? No one is the same from minute to minute, let alone over a span of years."

"When you snort, you certainly seem the same," Virginia observed. "The impulsive young woman who got her father to fire Johnson could very well have killed her husband if he didn't live up to her expectations. As I recall, your expectations of What's-his-Name were pretty unrealistic."

Leticia narrowed her eyes. "Paul," she said softly, "his name was Paul. Perceval Paul Runcible. And my initial expectations of him were unrealistic, but I certainly did not kill him. After all, I had unrealistic expectations of you as well, and I didn't try to kill you, did I?"

Virginia smiled, but the smile didn't reach her eyes. "No, you found an easier way to get rid of me. But then marriage is a more difficult arrangement to get out of than a lesbian affair."

Leticia sat back in her chair as if willing a larger space to open between Virginia and herself. "I don't like that word. Please don't use it in reference to me."

"Which word?" Virginia challenged. "Marriage? Affair?"

"You know perfectly well which word, Virginia Carr. Lesbian," Leticia replied, her voice icy. "It offends me."

"Well, what word would you prefer, Fred?" Virginia's voice dripped sarcasm. "Should I call our relationship a Sapphic interlude? Or maybe you'd favor female homoeroticism as a descriptive term."

"Stop it, Virginia! I didn't come here to be bullied." Leticia stood up. "I see no point in continuing this conversation," she announced. "I'll pay for the coffee at the counter."

"Great! Have a nice life!" Virginia called out after her. She winced at the sound of the door slamming behind Leticia. "Well," she said out loud, "no one ever said I was cut out to be a diplomat." She stood up slowly and made her way out the door. Leticia was nowhere in sight.

***

Carolyn agreed that Virginia was not cut out to be a diplomat. When Virginia told her of the meeting with Leticia, Carolyn listened carefully and refrained from comment at first. She knew that she'd get a clearer picture of what happened if she didn't say anything.

Virginia lay on Henry's scratchy sofa with her head in Carolyn's lap, and while Carolyn gently massaged her forehead, she gave utterance to her frustration with Leticia. "You can't have a conversation with her," she began. "She either withdraws or flies off the handle. Sometimes she does both!" Virginia took a deep breath. "Umm, that's nice!" she murmured. "My head feels like someone wrapped it in cement."

Carolyn smiled. "You were saying?"

"Yeah, well, Leticia can seem restrained and mature, but underneath she's still that spoiled rich kid who's used to getting everything she wants. She certainly could have killed her husband in a fit of temper."

Virginia shifted the position of her head so she could more easily see Carolyn's face. Carolyn kept her expression neutral. "Nothing about Colonel Runcible's death suggests a crime of passion. Leticia may indeed have a temper, but she doesn't sound particularly calculating or cold-blooded."

166

Virginia tried to shrug, which wasn't all that easy with her shoulders wedged in against Carolyn's body. "Don't you think her past dealings with Eric Johnson indicate cold-bloodedness?" she demanded.

"Not really," Carolyn said after a moment's thought. Her hands moved down and began to massage Virginia's shoulders. "You're angry with her, and that makes you see her in the worst possible light."

"Maybe so," Virginia conceded, but she didn't sound convinced. After a few seconds she added, "I don't think I'm really angry at her. I'm disappointed that we don't seem to be able to connect."

"Hmm," Carolyn mumbled. Taking that as permission to continue, Virginia snuggled down into Carolyn's lap. "I can't shake the feeling that I could have done better by her."

Carolyn stopped rubbing her shoulders. "Do you mean today or in the past?" she asked gently.

"Both, I guess. I hate feeling like I've failed."

"That's your subjective conclusion!" Carolyn said briskly. "And don't try to take responsibility for Leticia's life. She's a grown up; her life is her own."

Virginia smiled.

"The first question that we need to answer," Carolyn went on, "is whether her husband was killed at all. The man might simply have died."

Virginia frowned. "Do you think Johnson will get the body exhumed?"

"I doubt it. He'd have to get a court order, and I don't think he has grounds. He'll just keep bugging potential witnesses until he finds something he can use to build a case."

Virginia sighed. "Why does he care so much? Why do I? Whatever happened is over. Fifteen years have passed."

Before Carolyn could reply, the phone rang, and Virginia jumped up. "Henry!" she said through gritted teeth, afraid that her father's condition had worsened.

Carolyn sat back while Virginia greeted the caller. She knew why Virginia cared. Virginia was like a St. Bernard; the urge to rescue people seemed bred into her. It made her a devoted doctor, Carolyn thought, but it took its toll. She began thumping one of the cushions on the sofa, raising a cloud of dust. She chuckled under her breath. In her place, Virginia would have picked at the cushion, pulling off every shred of lint. That was how Virginia was, picking at everything that wasn't quite right. Carolyn, however, didn't believe in picking at scabs or worrying a cold sore. Once she'd taken whatever major action a crisis demanded, she was content to let nature take its course.

As she sat staring past Virginia, Carolyn, who'd always acknowledged the differences in their approaches to life, suddenly saw a pattern she hadn't detected before. At fourteen, Virginia had been unable to rescue Johnson's job, and she wanted to make up for that now. At eighteen, she hadn't managed to rescue Leticia from the life she imagined she wanted, and, as she herself had just acknowledged, she still felt she'd failed her even today after fifteen years. Carolyn's intuition went into overdrive. "She holds herself responsible for whatever has happened since then, even though she doesn't know what happened." But before she could analyze that insight, Virginia's voice cut through her thoughts.

"Another damned hang-up," Virginia groused. "Who are these people anyway? At first I thought Henry's patients might be calling to see if he'd come home, but they wouldn't just hang up. Could someone be checking up on us?" She bit her lower lip. "Let me tell you, it's starting to give me the creeps." She sat down on the couch and rolled her shoulders. "That sure ruined the good effects of your massage," she continued. "I haven't had a stiff neck like this in ages." She looked as if she wanted to cry, but then her mood suddenly improved. She smiled at Carolyn. "Enough of my melodrama. Tell me, how was your afternoon?"

Carolyn observed her closely for a moment to satisfy herself that Virginia was really finished with the topic of Leticia, at least for the moment. "It's a little tense at the hospital," she began, then sighed. "Actually it's very tense. Felton and I can't agree on the best way to proceed. It took me hours to convince him it was too early to give up on L-dopa. He finally agreed to give it another couple of days."

Virginia sucked in her breath. "Well, that's something, I guess. How is Henry reacting to the disagreement?"

"He doesn't know?"

Virginia laughed. "Wanna bet? Henry knows everything that's going on around him all the time."

Carolyn smiled sadly. "That used to be the case, but I think it's all he can do right now to keep his head above water." She glanced at Virginia to see her reaction. If she expected her to be disheartened she was surprised. Virginia shook, her head vehemently. "Don't underestimate him," she said softly.

Carolyn shrugged. "Okay, maybe he knows, but neither of us has spoken with him about our disagreement. Satisfied?"

Virginia nodded. "Shall I drive us to dinner?" She reached into Carolyn's pocket without waiting for an answer. Carolyn didn't object.

***

In Baltimore Virginia drove to a Mexican restaurant overlooking the bay. Carolyn watched her eye the water dreamily. She was reluctant to break the peaceful silence, but she felt she had to say something.

"Leticia wasn't wrong," she began. Virginia snapped out of her reverie and gave Carolyn a puzzled look. Carolyn went on, "You need to figure out what you want from her. You're tied up in knots."

Virginia's expression didn't change. "Isn't it amazing that gulls can stare at the water all day with no eye protection? You or I would end up with a headache. I wonder what they have. A built-in UV filter? Or is it the shape of the eye or its position on the head?"

"Virginia, what do you want from Leticia?" Carolyn tried again.

"Nothing!" Virginia exclaimed. She didn't try for lightness of tone, though her face took on an ironic look. "I wish I'd never started this ridiculous investigation. Do you think it's too late to break it off?"

"Not if that's what you want to do. You don't owe Johnson anything. And I'm sure Leticia wouldn't mind."

"Don't bet on it," Virginia replied quickly. "She wanted to know if I was going to help her or harass her. No, wait a minute. It was torture her. Johnson was the one who was harassing her. She offered me two choices that didn't include packing it in."

"You don't owe her anything either, honey," Carolyn said. "Her expectations don't have to govern your behavior."

Virginia's face went blank, as if she couldn't make sense of Carolyn's words.

"You're in charge of what you do," Carolyn barreled on, convinced she could make her point, "not Leticia, not Henry, not me, not anyone else. You need to do what's best for yourself."

Virginia wiggled her nose for a second. Carolyn's tone had sounded preachy to her. She struggled to hear the words through the urgent whine. Finally she looked up and smiled. "You're right, but if I hadn't responded to your expectations, Carrie, where would we be today? Probably not together."

169

For a fraction of a second Carolyn wasn't sure how to respond. She looked at Virginia sharply. "I hope you didn't get involved with me just because I expected you to," she said, shaping her expression into a mask of horror. "After all these years, now is a fine time to learn that!"

"Of course, not!" Virginia giggled but she wasn't willing to let the matter drop. "Your expectations did influence me though. Positively, we both agree, but nonetheless…"

"There is no nonetheless this time," Carolyn interjected quickly. "You have to decide what to do about this Leticia business on the basis of what you need and want. The same is true for your dealings with Henry, by the way."

Virginia rolled her eyes, yet she was determined to avoid being dragged into a discussion of father-daughter dynamics, "How much soul-searching do you expect me to do before appetizers?" she demanded, signaling the waiter.

Virginia watched Carolyn devour a heaping plate of chicken with molé sauce, the greater part of a fried banana dessert she'd claimed to want to share, and two beers. In spite of eating huge quantities of food, Carolyn was tall and thin and would probably always be tall and thin, like her mother. Virginia had liked Carolyn's mother. The woman was competent, kind, and capable of minding her own business. Virginia's own mother had shared only the first two of those traits.

It took her a second to realize that Carolyn was speaking. "You know, even though I know that Ana Mendoza Velasquez was not from Mexico, I can't help but think of her when I eat this kind of food."

Virginia nodded, but she said nothing.

"Were you jealous that Leticia got to spend so much time with her?" Carolyn asked bluntly.

Virginia thought for a moment. "I saw her every week on her day off during the summers. And I spent time with her on my college vacations." She sighed. "Of course, I missed her when she moved away. And she did have a good effect on Leticia. Anyone could see that."

Carolyn didn't say anything. She could see that Virginia was still thinking. "It would have been nice to have her around more of the time during my adolescence," Virginia admitted. "But she needed to work and we didn't have the money to pay a housekeeper." Virginia smiled wryly. "I was with her the week before she died. Leticia and her husband were in Turkey then. It happened fast and unexpectedly.

Undiagnosed thyroid cancer." She sighed. "That's why I became an endocrinologist. But you knew that, didn't you?"

Carolyn nodded, and Virginia continued. "Ana talked about Leticia a lot. She told me that she was giving Leticia a way to live in the world that would let her be herself the way her parents couldn't. She was convinced that Leticia needed her, and maybe she did. But I needed her too. She didn't seem to take that into account.

"Leticia's mother was a mess, completely hooked on Valium, but my mother wasn't exactly available when I needed her. And when she was around she didn't really know how to help me find my way. She interfered when I needed privacy and backed off when I needed help. I always thought her work interested her more than I did. In some ways, Ana Mendoza Velasquez compensated for the mothering Leticia and I both needed but didn't get from our mothers. The woman was remarkable on so many levels. The only thing she got wrong was her absurd insistence that Leticia and I would be forever inseparable."

CHAPTER 29
THINGS THAT DON'T MIX
1980

❖

Henry was still not responding to treatment, and Virginia was worried. Though there had been no more panicked phone calls from him, he was not improving. When she visited him, he seemed like his old, irascible self during most of the visit. Then suddenly he would stop and ask, "Did you hear that?" Virginia hadn't heard anything, but he insisted a bell had rung or a buzzer had sounded and became quite incensed when she disagreed. Two days after her dinner by the bay, she was sitting with Henry when he suddenly demanded loudly, "What do you think you're doing here?" She looked around but saw no one else in the room.

"Were you talking to me?" she asked.

He scowled. "Don't be ridiculous. I know what you're doing here. You're visiting your neglected, old father. But what was he doing here?"

She had no idea whom Henry meant, but when she asked, he just answered, "Never mind. You've never been very observant, Virginia. It makes me wonder how you can possibly be a good diagnostician."

Virginia ignored the criticism, much to Henry's disappointment. "Come on, tell me, my neglected father," she asked, trying for a light tone, "to whom were you just talking if you weren't talking to me?" Henry sniffed disdainfully. "That intern who stuck his head in and asked me if I was sleeping. Stupid young twerp! How could I be sleeping if I was talking with you?"

Virginia didn't remind him that there were no young interns since it wasn't a teaching hospital. She was beginning to wonder though if Stanley might be right. Maybe it was time to give up on L-dopa and try some other combination of drugs. She said nothing to Carolyn, but she was actually relieved when Stanley phoned her the next day and invited her for a conference. She wanted to know what was going on, and Carolyn had not been very forthcoming once she'd announced that they were continuing with L-dopa for the time being.

"How about tomorrow at three?" Stanley asked graciously. "It would be a pleasure to get your opinion, Dr. Carr. I know what Dr. Matthews thinks, but she is not Henry's daughter."

Virginia agreed to a three o'clock meeting and to his request, albeit with considerable misgivings, that she not tell Carolyn about the conference until after it was over. She didn't want to get in the middle of a turf battle between the two of them, but she had been getting only Carolyn's take on Henry's treatment and realized she was eager to hear Stanley Felton's opinion.

Nonetheless she felt guilty and a little angry during the drive to the hospital. Why had Stanley thought he could ask her to go behind Carolyn's back? And why had she acquiesced? Why hadn't Carolyn arranged a meeting for all three of them? A tall brunette crossing the parking lot distracted her and she nearly nicked a car as she pulled into a parking space. She forced herself to breathe, folded her sunglasses, and idly wondered if Carolyn were at the hospital. If not, was she off having a tête-à-tête with Leticia? Virginia walked into the tiny neurology waiting room and asked for Dr. Felton.

Felton was late, so Virginia spent an hour skimming through outdated magazines. As patients filed in and waited, Virginia had an urge to call her own office. For the first time in days, she missed her practice and her patients. What the UCSF Medical Center's offices lacked in comfortable furnishings, she tried to make up for by having interesting paintings on the walls. Unlike Henry, she was respectful toward residents, interns, and nurses, and she demanded that they show the same respect toward her patients.

Anxious and bored, she distracted herself by inventing symptoms and diagnoses for the patients sitting in the waiting room. Some of her ideas were so absurd that she started to giggle. The laughter made the receptionist look up. Virginia made eye contact with her and smiled, and when the receptionist blushed and smiled back, Virginia realized that she was flirting and enjoying the experience. When Felton finally arrived and escorted her into his office, she was almost disappointed.

Stanley Felton did not sit down. Projecting, as if he were speaking to a far larger audience, he told Virginia that Parkinson's Disease was not causing Henry's symptoms. She stared for a moment at his receding chin. Finally she cleared her throat. "That's good news, if it's true," she said cautiously. "But what makes you think so?

He smiled at her condescendingly. "It's quite simple actually," he intoned. "The medications routinely prescribed for symptoms of Parkinson's Disease are not impacting his symptoms. Therefore it behooves us to consider the possibility that the diagnosis is not correct."

"But you've only tried L-dopa," Virginia interjected.

"Until today. Today I began treatment with Bromocriptine."

"Well then, you've hardly had time to determine the effectiveness of that medication," Virginia objected.

Felton looked annoyed. "Unfortunately your father had an adverse reaction to the drug," he said, sounding as if Henry had let him down. He shrugged. "It was severe enough to contraindicate continuing the medication."

Virginia felt panic rising into her throat and swore under her breath. Why hadn't she told Carolyn about this conference? She took a deep breath, then asked, "Does Dr. Matthews know?"

Felton made a sour face. "Yes. She's with the patient now."

Virginia noticed the shift in terminology from 'your father' to 'the patient' but didn't comment. She stood up.

"Where are you going?" Felton demanded. "We're not finished with this conference yet."

"I'm going to my father," Virginia said, emphasizing the words. "I need to see him and to find out what Carolyn, er, Dr. Matthews thinks. You can come along if you wish. Or not."

"An exercise in futility," he spat the words out. "Your friend is stubbornly insisting on continuing with L-dopa. The young woman is quite irrational. Further tests are obviously necessary."

Virginia, halfway to the door, shook her head. "No further tests until I talk with Dr. Matthews." She opened the door.

"I am his doctor," Felton announced. "And I will order tests if I see fit."

"And I'm his daughter," Virginia called out, as she left the room, "and I'm withholding permission!"

Felton followed in her wake. "Goddamned women doctors," he hissed under his breath, as the elevator door opened and he joined Virginia inside.

***

Henry was in the midst of an uncontrolled spasm when Virginia entered his room. His body twitched as if electric current were running through it. Carolyn stood by his bed, looking on helplessly. When she heard footsteps she turned. As soon as she became aware of Virginia, she stepped towards the door in order to block Henry's body from view.

"Too late," Virginia said softly and brushed past her. "What's going on, Carrie?"

"I'm glad you're here," Carolyn said. She looked as if she were in shock. "I was finally getting the L-dopa dosage right this morning. Henry was cheerful and proud of himself for having walked to the bathroom without assistance. But when I came in after lunch, he was like this." She nodded in the direction of the contorted figure. "I don't know what happened. I've never seen anything like it."

Virginia took her by the arm and pulled her out into the hallway, where Felton stood waiting. He glared first at Carolyn, then at Virginia.

"It's not your fault," Virginia began. "Stanley changed the medication." Carolyn's jaw dropped and her face went white and then very red. "I can tell from your reaction that you didn't know."

Felton stood up straighter and cleared his throat. "The L-dopa was clearly ineffective." He held up his hand as if expecting Carolyn to object. "I am his physician and I changed the course of treatment."

Carolyn glared at him. "I checked Henry's chart when I came back after lunch..."

"It's not in the chart yet. He had his first dose of Bromocriptine an hour ago. Since it's no more effective than the L-dopa, I have suggested to Miss Carr that further tests are necessary. She would not agree until..."

"Shut up, you incompetent asshole!" Carolyn yelled. "Are you trying to kill the man?"

He looked at her coldly. "Control yourself, woman!" he ordered. "I am Dr. Carr's physician, and you are here by my leave. I can and will have you removed from this hospital if you continue to be abusive and insubordinate." He turned on his heel and walked away.

"You're a fucking jerk!" Carolyn yelled after him. She pounded her hand hard against the wall and yelped in pain. "What a prick! What a competitive prick! He could kill Henry."

Virginia grabbed Carolyn's arm and steered her firmly into the elevator and then out of the hospital into the parking lot. Sometimes she really wanted to throttle Carolyn. Why did she have to throw a public tantrum? Did she want to make Henry's situation even worse?

When they reached their car, Virginia took a deep breath. "Felton called me in for a conference," she said tonelessly. "He thinks Henry needs more tests."

"Felton and think are two words that don't belong in the same sentence," Carolyn shouted. "Why didn't you tell me you were going to talk to him?"

Virginia shrugged. "It didn't seem necessary. Of course, I didn't know he was going to pull a stunt like this."

Carolyn looked at her skeptically. Her voice returned to its normal volume. "All you have to do is say the word and I'll bow out, you know. I can go back to California any time. If I'm making things worse for Henry I really shouldn't be involved in his treatment."

Virginia shook her head. "I don't think Henry would like that."

"Henry's not in any shape to make his wishes known." She didn't make eye contact with Virginia. "It's up to you. If you don't have confidence in me…"

"Of course I do!" Virginia forced herself to sound certain. "But you can't go on working with Felton."

Carolyn made a sound halfway between a growl and a groan. "Get a listing of all the neurologists on staff," she ordered. "Let's see who else is available besides Dr. Dimwit. Then I can make a few calls."

***

Carolyn and Virginia spent the rest of the day back in Henry's room. Virginia sat staring into space while Carolyn was busy on the phone. Fortunately Stanley Felton didn't appear and try to assert his authority as Henry's attending physician, and by seven in the evening Carolyn had found a local neurologist to take over Henry's care.

She got off the phone and beamed at Virginia. "You remember Sandra Keller, don't you?"

Virginia nodded. "Your favorite professor. Why?"

"She just recommended someone named Leonora Epstein. Sandra said Leonora is one of the best neuro people on the east coast. She's on the staff at Hopkins, but she also happens to have privileges here. Sandra said Leonora and her husband have a summer home right outside Grant's Hill."

Virginia nodded again. She felt exhausted. "I hope she's easier for you to work with than Stanley was," she said, closing her eyes and running her hands down her face.

"Come on," Carolyn said. "Let's go home."

Virginia looked at her father's sleeping form. "Are you sure it's okay?"

Carolyn nodded. "He'll be fine. Leonora will come in tomorrow morning and we'll work out his meds. He's so wiped out from Felton's mistake that he'll sleep until then."

Virginia sighed.

"What is it?" Carolyn demanded. "You look like you lost your favorite puppy dog."

"I feel guilty." Virginia confessed so softly that Carolyn could barely make out the words. "If I'd told you about the meeting with Stanley, maybe you could have stepped in and prevented Henry's ordeal with the Bromocriptine."

"I doubt it. He'd already dosed Henry before you came to the hospital. That asshole..." Carolyn stopped herself. "Never mind. It's over now."

"But he could have killed Henry!" Virginia protested.

"Yes, but only if he'd gone on medicating him without telling me. If we both kept on giving Henry drugs at the same time, well, you can imagine. But one overdose was just that, one overdose. The combination itself isn't dangerous."

Virginia stood up. "Well, I didn't expect Stanley to be such a jerk. He seemed like such a mild-mannered guy when we first met him."

Carolyn shrugged. "Some men can't work with women, that's all. He probably felt threatened. That doesn't excuse him, but it explains a lot, I think." Her tone was brusque, and Virginia was glad to let the subject drop.

Still she felt uncomfortable with her role in the conflict. She'd always thought she trusted Carolyn both as a doctor and a human being. The idea that she'd gone behind Carolyn's back made her wonder if that was true. Worse, it frightened her because it made her distrust herself.

By the time they got back to Henry's house, Virginia was wondering what Leonora Epstein was like.

"How come you don't know Leonora Epstein?" she asked as they got into bed.

"What?" Carolyn replied, setting the alarm for six-thirty.

"If Leonora is so good, how come you don't know her?"

"I don't know every neurologist in the country, honey."

"But don't the names of the really good ones get around?" Virginia persisted.

"She's younger than we are and ..."

"Still," Virginia interrupted, "you ought to know her name if she's so good."

Carolyn yawned. "I trust Sandra Keller and Sandra trusts her. And I love you."

Virginia grunted and turned over. As she fell asleep she summoned the image of Felton's receptionist.

CHAPTER 30
BETS AND ODDS
1980
❖

Leonora Epstein said she had no professional problem taking over Henry's care. Carolyn insisted that Virginia notify the hospital and Felton himself of the change to make it official. Virginia did both by phone from Henry's room while Leonora read Henry's chart and tried to make small talk with him. Felton just growled, "Good riddance" and hung up after Virginia had said her piece.

When she got off the phone with the hospital administrator, Virginia turned to take the measure of Leonora Epstein. Her first reaction was surprise at how young the woman seemed. Her second was dismay. Although she liked what she saw, a competent, pleasant, young doctor with obviously good diagnostic skills, she could tell that Henry did not like Leonora one bit. Though still somewhat hazy from his overdose, he was uncooperative and even more irascible than usual. When Leonora tried to get him to demonstrate the range of his movements, he glared at her and told her to go to hell.

"Come on, Henry!" Carolyn ordered. "Stop acting out! This is an assessment to see what you can do and what you can't."

"What do you need her for?" Henry demanded, managing a shaky nod in Leonora's direction. "You're my doctor."

Carolyn shook her head in exasperation. "You know that I don't have hospital privileges here, Henry."

"But you could get them easily enough," he insisted. "Get yourself established here on the east coast. There's no reason to live out in California. You never have time to go to the beach."

"I'll consider your recommendation, now could you please cooperate with Dr. Epstein?"

Henry complied with bad grace. When Leonora had finished and left his room, he complained about her for a solid hour, first to Carolyn and then, after Carolyn left to talk with Leonora, to Virginia. "Where the hell did you find her? At a military prison? Are they turning out eighteen year-old doctors nowadays?" His litany went on and on, and Virginia had trouble keeping herself from yelling at him.

When Carolyn returned to tell father and daughter that she and Leonora had come to an agreement about the course of Henry's treatment and the right dosage of L-dopa, he fired his final salvo.

"Christ! The woman isn't even a lesbian! With a husband to look after, how much attention will she even pay to my care? She'll probably be on maternity leave when I need her most and we'll have to start over again with a new doctor."

***

Sometimes Henry's professed preference for lesbians tickled Carolyn, but as his rudeness to Leonora intensified, she became increasingly irritated. Reasoning with him didn't work and threats to leave and go back to California left him unmoved. He seemed like a man on a mission, and the mission was to chase off Dr. Epstein.

After a particularly harrowing day, during which Henry actually struck Leonora with his telephone receiver, Carolyn turned to Virginia in desperation.

"Will you please do something about your father? He's driving me nuts," she complained. Virginia, busy washing dinner dishes, coughed knowingly. "Welcome to the club."

"Seriously," she grumbled, cracking her knuckles, "we need Leonora. Henry must realize that. He's a doctor after all. But he acts like such a...such a..."

"Spoiled brat?" Virginia suggested, handing her a dishtowel. "You're supposed to be drying the dishes, remember?"

Carolyn took the towel. "I just don't get it," she continued, reaching for a plate.

"He wants us to move back here. He thinks that tormenting Leonora until she quits is the way to make us do it."

Carolyn scowled. "Well, it isn't!"

Virginia shrugged. "I agree! He's being manipulative and foolish." She stopped washing dishes for a moment and took a deep breath. "Do you think his illness might be responsible for that?"

"Maybe, at least in part. But even if it is, that doesn't solve the problem, does it? You need to talk to him, Virginia."

Virginia sighed. "If he won't listen to you, what makes you think he'll listen to me?"

"I don't really, " Carolyn sighed, "but I can hope, can't I?"

"Yeah, you can hope," Virginia agreed, "and you can stop cracking your knuckles and dry some more of these damned dishes."

***

Virginia tried to talk with Henry the next morning, but Dr. Epstein walked in shortly after Virginia got started. "Don't look now," Henry

180

announced, "but General Westmoreland's twin sister has just entered the room."

Virginia shot him an angry look but he grinned proudly. Leonora ignored his comment. "Good morning," she said. "I've come to talk with you about something quite specific." She turned to Virginia. "I'm glad you're here. It saves me a phone call."

Leonora's brusque manner reassured Virginia, who associated it with competence. She knew that the brusqueness infuriated Henry though. He preferred cozy interactions with women or bantering exchanges of the sort he enjoyed with Carolyn and with the nurses at his clinic.

Virginia roused herself from her contemplation of Henry's likes and dislikes when Carolyn entered the room. Swinging her stethoscope like a lariat, she winked at Henry and drawled, "Howdy, pardners." Henry brightened and sat up shakily in bed.

"Good morning, Doctor," Leonora said formally.

Carolyn smiled and walked up to Virginia. She put an arm across Virginia's shoulder. "Good morning, Dr. Carr," she said with mock formality. "And good morning for the second time today, Dr. Epstein."

Leonora smiled uncertainly and cleared her throat, but it was Henry who spoke up. "Hey, how about me?" he demanded. "Don't I get a good morning greeting? I certainly deserve one after being glared at by my daughter."

"I'll tell you what, Henry," Carolyn replied jovially, "I'll wish you a good morning if you say good morning to Dr. Epstein."

"Shit!" Henry barked sullenly, lying down in bed. "I'll say shit to her, the humorless pile of cow dung."

Leonora Epstein's expression remained neutral, but Virginia's face went very red. She felt so mortified that she wanted to run from the room.

"Henry, stop acting like a jackass!" Carolyn scolded him firmly.

Leonora's expression turned to disapproval. Virginia tried to imagine her calling one of her patients a jackass, but she couldn't. Pulling herself together she said, "I second the motion." For the first time Leonora Epstein cracked a smile, and Virginia felt inexplicably pleased by that.

Henry sat up again. "Ladies," he started up again, "my tremors will intensify if you…"

Carolyn interrupted him. "Can it, Henry!" she snapped. Undaunted he let saliva run out of the corner of his mouth. "That's it! Virginia and I are out of here. And I mean now!"

Henry stopped drooling and whined, "You wouldn't leave a helpless, old..."

Carolyn started towards the door before he could finish. "Let's go!" she said sternly to Virginia, then added with a glance at Leonora, "Can we discuss this case in private, Dr. Epstein?"

Startled, Leonora cleared her throat. "Yes, of course." She led Virginia and Carolyn into a small conference room, where Carolyn promptly seated herself and began drumming her fingers on the round table.

"What are we going to do about Henry?" she demanded, looking from Virginia to Leonora then back to Virginia again.

Leonora raised her eyebrows. "We are going to treat his illness, of course. What else?"

Virginia, who had been looking down at the table raised her head. Surely, she thought, Henry's dreadful behavior must bother her. But she's acting as if nothing is amiss. She felt a faint smile form on her lips as she listened to the young doctor,

"I would like to check his cholesterol levels and do some tests on his arteries. I was surprised that his previous physician omitted a few procedures." She explained to Virginia exactly which tests Henry would undergo and the sequence and timing of the procedures.

Virginia and Carolyn nodded their approval after exchanging a brief glance. "Fine. We're done then," Carolyn said, "for now anyway."

Virginia was the first to stand up, but she didn't leave right away. "I, uh, I want to apologize for my father's abominable behavior," she said, making eye contact for a second with Leonora before blushing and looking away. "He's not usually this bad. I mean, he's not bad at all generally. Just a little manipulative at times, but he has good manners. Except for now, of course. I mean he can be abrupt, but he's rarely rude. Except..." Virginia took a deep breath. She realized she was babbling. When she looked up, she was astonished to see Leonora and Carolyn grinning broadly at each other.

"You win!" Leonora announced. She reached across the table and handed something to Carolyn.

Virginia was confused. "What's going on? What did you just hand to Carolyn?"

Leonora looked slightly abashed, but Carolyn smiled triumphantly at Virginia. "Ten bucks!" She waved the bill in the air. "I told her you'd apologize for Henry, but she didn't believe me. So we made a bet."

Virginia clenched her hands, suppressing the urge to slap Carolyn. She stared intently into Leonora's eyes. "Didn't you think I'd have the decency to apologize?" she demanded.

Leonora smiled. Unlike Carolyn's smile, hers was gentle. "Decency has nothing to do with it," she said softly. "You haven't been the least bit uncouth. Your father has. So you don't owe me an apology."

Virginia contained her anger. "My father's behavior reflects on me," she said earnestly. Please don't think he's always been this way." She blushed. "And I hope you won't believe that rudeness runs in the family."

"Of course not!" Leonora replied quickly. "I don't hold you responsible for your father's behavior. Dr. Matthews said you believe you are responsible for others' actions. That was why she bet that you would apologize. I probably shouldn't have taken her up on the bet. I'm afraid I'm the one who's been rude."

Virginia forced herself to smile. "No, not at all," she lied. "I understand."

Leonora capped and uncapped her pen. "But we've hurt your feelings. I really did not intend to do that. I'm not usually so thoughtless."

Virginia felt genuine affection for Leonora. "It's all right, really. I'm not offended."

"You're very kind. But that's no surprise. Sandra Keller said that the two of you are the nicest women she's ever met."

"Nice!" Carolyn objected. "Couldn't she come up with anything better than nice?"

While Carolyn pretended outrage, Virginia attempted to collect herself. She was still a little irritated, but she noticed that her irritation was mainly at Carolyn. It didn't extend to Leonora. She's the one who's nice, Virginia thought, though you wouldn't necessarily think so if you only saw her dealing with Henry. She didn't understand what I was getting at with my apology. "The apple doesn't fall far from the tree." Virginia knew it was a cliché, that had some truth to it. She just wanted Leonora to realize that Henry wasn't as bad as he seemed. She still wanted her to realize that. After all…

Virginia followed her train of thought with some reluctance. "After all, I want her to think well of me" was what she wanted to say to herself, but she didn't like the questions that raised. Why did it feel so important that Leonora think well of her? Aside from the obvious advantage they'd have in dealing with Henry's illness if they respected each other, there was no need for her to want to make a particularly positive impression on Leonora. She chewed on her lip. She knew that Carolyn wanted admiration from everyone, but she had always considered herself above the kind of grandstanding that Carolyn indulged in for attention. Anyway, Leonora wasn't everyone; she was a colleague and Henry's doctor.

If Leonora had misunderstood her, Carolyn had contributed to the misunderstanding. Virginia found Carolyn's insistence that she took responsibility for other people intensely irritating. Why, she argued with herself, is it wrong to want to help people? Isn't that what makes us human? Why else did I become a doctor? Why else did Carrie become a doctor? Of course there were limits to what one person could do for another. She knew that. But she also knew that her decisions had an impact on other people. Hadn't leaving Grant's Hill to pursue her medical studies left Leticia alone with her dead-end dreams? The thought oppressed her. She preferred to think of Leonora's surprisingly sympathetic response to her than of her failures with Leticia.

"Anyway," Carolyn's voice interrupted Virginia's musings, "Sandy Keller was always a detail freak, so I doubt she'd recognize creative chaos if it bit her on the butt."

What she was going on about Virginia could hardly guess, but she had to laugh when Leonora responded, "She talked about your creative chaos, Dr. Matthews, but she called it 'raging lunacy coupled with an intuitive gift for diagnosis'. In other words, you're gifted but crazy."

Carolyn laughed out loud. "Ah yes, that sounds like the Dr. Sandra Keller we all know and love."

"We know and you love," Virginia interjected. "She scares me half to death."

"Me too!" Leonora said quickly. "She's a brilliant teacher but a real martinet." She and Virginia exchanged warm smiles. Then all three of them walked out into the hallway.

Virginia returned to Henry's room to sit with him for a while, but she realized quickly that she was out of patience with her father. The third time he turned the conversation to the details of his practice and what she'd have to do when she took it over, she excused herself and went to the nurses' station, where she left a note for Carolyn. "I don't want to be here," she said to herself as she waited for the elevator. "I'm taking the afternoon off."

When Carolyn came around a few hours later, Henry was grouchy. "Is my daughter coming back to see me today?" Carolyn shook her head.

Henry snorted, but the snort turned into a cough. "She's busy with that Barnes woman, I bet. I never liked her, you know."

Carolyn sat down. "I didn't even know you knew her. You never mentioned her."

Henry smiled crookedly. "I'm discreet. It would have been bad manners to mention Virginia's former lover to you, don't you think?"

Carolyn hooted. "Since when are you worried about manners, Henry?"

He looked offended. "I'm never rude. Well, hardly ever. Just ask my nurses."

"How about if I ask Dr. Epstein?"

Henry rolled his eyes. "She's a bitch, but I think Virginia is taken with her. You need to keep your eye on my daughter, sweetheart. You're the best thing that ever happened to her, but she's daft enough to lose you."

Carolyn frowned, convinced that Henry was just trying to make trouble. "Come on Henry, Dr. Epstein is a married woman. And Virginia is just preoccupied, that's all." He peered up at her from his bed. "Since when did being married stop anyone from having an affair?" He shook his head, and it kept shaking until he lay back down on his pile of pillows. "I'm only concerned about the future of your relationship. If you were to split up, I'd be heartbroken."

She wanted to laugh, but she knew he meant what he was saying. If he wanted Virginia back in Grant's Hill, the odds favored him more if she and Carolyn were no longer a couple. He knew that Carolyn would never leave San Francisco, and she knew he knew. Henry really did want them to succeed as a couple. So she sighed and changed the subject. "Tell me about Leticia Runcible, Henry. Why don't you like her?"

"She's a murderess and she practices medicine without a license."

"A murderess?" Carolyn probed.

"Don't get cute with me, Carolyn Matthews! I know that the real reason Virginia dragged you here has to do with investigating the death of that woman's husband, poor fellow. I have no doubt he's better off dead than married to her, but that didn't give her any license to kill him."

"What makes you think she killed him?"

Henry shrugged. "Everyone knows it, but no one can prove it."

"Everyone? The police determined that he died of natural causes, didn't they?"

"The police? They never really investigated," Henry replied, his eyes gleaming. "Don't get me wrong. I have enormous respect for the police, but they never pursue a rich suspect unless someone pressures them."

Carolyn could see that Henry would not be diverted from discussing the privileges of the rich, but that would not help her get a handle on the death of Paul Runcible. So she told Henry she had phone calls to make and took her leave.

"It's all over but the shouting," Carolyn said cheerfully. She stood looking out the window at Henry's front yard as she made coffee.

Virginia, sitting at the kitchen table, said nothing. She was doodling on a prescription pad and humming tunelessly under her breath.

"Are you listening to me?" Carolyn called out, "Once Leonora and I get back the last of Henry's test results, we'll be able to fine tune the treatment plan. He's improved a lot in a couple of days, so it's time for us to head home. I'd just as soon not spend a day longer than necessary in this town."

At the mention of Leonora, Virginia looked up attentively, but she soon started doodling again. Carolyn, caught up in what she was saying, didn't notice.

"I'm sorry you didn't get things straightened out with Leticia, but there was probably nothing to the accusation. She seemed okay to me. Not a killer. That cop was just indulging an old grudge."

Virginia's thoughts were elsewhere. She was still looking for an opportunity to confront Leticia one more time. But Leticia wasn't the only person on her mind. Virginia was sure Leonora Epstein was going to turn Henry's treatment over to someone else as soon as Carolyn and she had gone home. She desperately didn't want that to happen.

"Virginia, are you listening to me?" Carolyn demanded. The use of her name instead of an endearment caused Virginia to look up. She smiled hesitantly.

"I just said that we need to make plane reservations for Friday."

"Um-hmm," Virginia murmured. "Fine, as long as Henry's treatment is settled by then."

"Of course," Carolyn grumbled, "I just said we'd have that settled by the end of today."

"Will Dr. Epstein keep working with him?" Virginia asked softly.

Carolyn looked surprised. "I don't see why not."

"Can you arrange a meeting with her before we go, Carrie, I'd like to be sure."

Carolyn raised her eyebrows. "Okay." She took a deep breath, remembering Henry's absurd warning that Virginia was attracted to Leonora. "You know," she said, trying to sound casual, "there are lots of top-flight neurologists at Hopkins. If Leonora's caseload is too heavy, I'm sure she'd recommend someone." She watched Virginia's face for a reaction, but Virginia's expression didn't change.

"It'd be hard for Henry to get to Hopkins. She can treat him locally."

"True," Carolyn conceded, "but it would probably be good for Henry to have someone at Hopkins, at least for the future. The facilities are better there. He's not going to go back to the way he used to be. Parkinson's is progressive, you know."

Virginia sniffed. "Of course I know! Leonora's on staff at Hopkins, isn't she?"

Carolyn nodded. "So's her husband. He's a nice guy. A cardiologist." She kept her tone light.

"Good for him," Virginia mumbled.

"So you're okay with leaving on Friday?"

"Fine," Virginia agreed. "Do you want to call for the plane reservations or shall I?"

Carolyn shook her head. "Paging Virginia, come in please! I just asked if you'd mind only five minutes ago."

"I don't mind at all," Virginia replied, not reacting to Carolyn's taunt. "What day was that again?"

Carolyn sighed in frustration. "Friday. That'll give us three days to make sure Henry's drugs are working."

"Fine," Virginia said again with a bright smile this time.

Carolyn was uneasy. "Is there something you want to talk about?"

"No, I was just zoning out a little. I'm okay."

Carolyn shrugged. "If you say so." Even that failed to get a rise out of Virginia the way it usually did. "I'm off to the hospital," Carolyn announced heading for the door. "See you around five."

"Shall I meet you? When is your appointment with Dr. Epstein?"

"Whenever the results come in," Carolyn replied. "Don't bother coming to meet me unless you want to pay a late afternoon visit to Henry.

Virginia shook her head. "No, not today. I spent three hours with him yesterday and all he did was nag me about moving back here. He seems to think that if I do, you'll follow."

Carolyn rolled her eyes. "I'll be back around five. Then we can eat and go to a movie if there's anything decent."

Virginia nodded as Carolyn picked up the car key. Carolyn blew her a kiss across the room. Before Virginia had a chance to respond in kind, the door slammed and the car engine started. Finally, certain that Carolyn was really gone, Virginia settled on the sofa to plan her next move.

***

Virginia's absentmindedness was only slightly disturbing to Carolyn. She knew her partner was under considerable strain. What bothered her more was Henry's insinuation coupled with Virginia's increased interest whenever Leonora's name came up. "I seem to be surrounded by women my sweetheart is or was attracted to," she said to herself. She wished Henry hadn't put the notion of Virginia's fickleness into her head. "She wouldn't," she whispered, "not with all we have together." She wondered what was going on in Virginia's mind, but she knew better than to guess.

Henry was sitting up in bed when she entered his room. He looked morose.

"You've been neglecting me," he greeted her.

"Sorry about that, Henry, old pal," she teased him, "but I've been busy playing poker with a really tough opponent."

Henry eyed her skeptically. "Virginia doesn't play poker." He thought for a moment. "Epstein? If you've been playing with that bag of bones, I hope the stakes were high and you cleaned her out."

Carolyn grinned at him. "Nope! I lost."

"To Epstein?" Henry's voice went shrill. "I'm disappointed in you, Carolyn. How could you lose to that?

Her grin broadened. "I never said I was playing with Dr. Epstein."

"Who then?" Henry demanded.

"For me to know and you to find out." She noticed that his color was good and the game she was playing with him had brought brightness to his eyes.

"Come on, Dr. Matthews! Just between the two of us."

Carolyn let her face fall. "Me," she said. "I lost four games to myself and I can't get a rematch."

Henry laughed and slapped his thigh. "You really got me. You're such a card." The unintentional pun made him laugh even harder. Carolyn noticed that his hand and head still shook, but the tremors abated quickly.

"Well, Henry, you do seem to be feeling better."

"I'm ready to go home," he growled. "Any fool can see that I should be discharged today--or tomorrow at the latest."

189

"What does Dr. Epstein say?" Carolyn asked. Before Henry could reply she added, "Without insult or invective, please!"

Henry smiled. "I haven't seen her yet today." He reached for Carolyn's hand, and she noticed that his grip felt strong. "I still can't stand the woman, but I admit she's a better doctor than Felton. Can you believe that fool did his medical degree at Harvard? Just goes to show the place is overrated. I always thought so."

Carolyn nodded. The inferiority of Harvard to his alma mater Johns Hopkins was one of Henry's hobbyhorses.

"Leonora Epstein is a cold fish," Henry announced, looking slyly down at his bed sheet, "but say hello for me anyway if you see her before I do."

Carolyn nodded. "I will." She knew she shouldn't ask, but she couldn't help herself. "Why the change of heart?"

Henry grinned at her, his eyes gleaming with mischief. "I remembered that she's not really my doctor; you are."

Carolyn sighed. Henry was hard to resist when he was complimentary.

"Is my daughter coming to see me today?" he asked before Carolyn had a chance to leave.

"I don't think so, Henry, but if you want to see her and promise not to pressure her to live here, I'll pass on your wish to her. Of course you could just call her yourself."

Henry shook his head. "It'd be more effective coming from you."

***

Virginia stood looking out the window at the morning glories. The flowers had closed for the day, but the pattern the vines made creeping in and out of the hedge held her eyes while her mind wandered. Just a few more days and she'd be out of time. She was more confused now than when she'd arrived in Grant's Hill. She shook her head. It wasn't just Leticia. She found herself spending too much time and energy, fantasizing about Leonora Epstein. "Some sleuth!" she grumbled, just as the phone rang.

It was probably just another crank call, but it might be Leticia. Or maybe Leonora Epstein calling to schedule that meeting Carolyn had agreed to arrange. Virginia picked up the receiver and had to regroup when it was Carolyn's voice she heard. She wasn't exactly disappointed, but she wasn't thrilled either.

"Hi, honey, how are you doing? Any word on Henry's tests?" she asked automatically.

"I'm fine. The last of the tests still haven't come in, but Henry is showing signs of major improvement."

Virginia waited. She knew Carolyn wasn't calling just to check in.

"Speaking of Henry, he wants you to visit. Maybe you and I could meet here."

"We'll have both cars at the hospital," Virginia protested.

Carolyn laughed. "It'll be okay, sweetie. You're so practical sometimes."

"Wait, just a second …" Virginia began, but Carolyn had already hung up.

"That's just so typical," Virginia snarled, banging the receiver on the cradle. "It'd be nice to have a choice! If it's not Henry it's Carolyn trying to run my life." She found herself thinking about Leonora Epstein, wondering if Carolyn had set up a meeting with her. "Probably not!" Virginia growled, pacing angrily through the kitchen to put on water for more coffee. "Just because I asked her to is no reason she'd do it. Not like Henry asking her to summon me to the hospital." She slammed the freezer door after failing to find the coffee. "Where's the coffee? Carrie always hides it."

Virginia resisted revisiting her plan for the day. She phoned Leticia's number again to no avail. "Damn, where is the coffee?" she complained aloud, surprised to find herself near tears. After checking the freezer again, she grabbed a pencil and prescription pad and banged out the door to the screen porch. Doodling on the pad she considered her options. She could leave a note for Leticia on her way to the hospital. She stopped doodling and glared accusingly at he prescription pad. "I know there's decent notepaper somewhere," she mumbled, standing up and going back into the house.

She found notepaper and an envelope in Henry's desk. Since she'd given up on coffee, she decided to make a pot of tea to drink while she penned her note to Leticia. In the tea cabinet she found the coffee. This struck her as funny, and she was still giggling when she seated herself at Henry's desk.

***

The note was short and simple. It explained that she and Carolyn were leaving on Friday and would like to visit before then. Sealing the

191

envelope, she reminded herself that she still had to convince or coerce Carolyn into coming along.

No one answered when Virginia ran the doorbell at the Barnes house, so she left the note and drove to the hospital. Henry was asleep when she entered his room. "He looks so frail," she thought. "I don't know what's going to happen." She ran her hands through her hair, but of course that did little to dispel the anxiety that had started to build. "No use indulging in morbid thoughts," she scolded herself. "Make yourself useful!" She smiled briefly, remembering how often Henry had uttered those words to her. She started to clean up and organize his bedside table.

Working carefully so as not to wake her father, Virginia threw away a number of old menus, scraps of paper, and an empty tissue pack. Having cleared off the top of the table, she then attacked the single drawer so stuffed that it didn't close all the way. It held a dozen packets of sugarless gum, a paperback history of the War of 1812, two prescription pads, pencils, a pair of sunglasses, and Henry's favorite keychain with a plastic four-leaf clover attached to it. The reason the door wouldn't close, however, was four pairs of argyle socks jammed in on top of the other contents.

"One pair of socks can stay," Virginia mumbled. "The rest go into his suitcase." She found the suitcase in the closet under a pile of pillows. Then she opened it, it was as messy as the drawer: clothing crammed into it in no discernible order along with two half-full bottles of milk of magnesia. She shook her head, glad that the bottles hadn't leaked, and laid them on the closet floor. How like Henry to be prepared for indigestion!

Virginia unpacked and repacked the suitcase, folding everything carefully. After organizing the main compartment, she reached into a side pocket where she'd stashed the socks she'd extricated from the bedside table. "Ow!" she looked up to make sure she hadn't disturbed Henry's sleep. She stared at her hand. "Just a paper cut," she muttered, sucking on her finger. She was relieved she hadn't sliced herself on a razor blade.

She gingerly reached back into the pocket and pulled out a sheaf of letters still in their envelopes. The envelopes had been slit open neatly. As Virginia read the return addresses, she inhaled audibly. The letters were all from the same address in Jackson Hole, Wyoming. The sender was Eric Johnson, Jr.

Virginia weighed the packet of letters in her hand. Then she looked at the postmarks once more. The top letter was the most recent. She could hardly resist the temptation to read it.

With a sigh she put the letters back in the suitcase and replaced the suitcase in the closet. Her father had always respected her privacy when she lived with him. That was one of the things she'd loved most about him during her adolescence. She felt she couldn't read his letters, but she intended to ask him about them as soon as he woke up. In the meantime she'd walk the hospital grounds. Henry's room was making her feel claustrophobic.

CHAPTER 32
DISCOVERIES ABROAD
1980
❖

Leticia sat at the desk in her study, the room that used to be her father's bedroom. It was a large, airy room that got more sunlight than any of the other bedrooms. Her mother, whose bedroom had become the guest room, had insisted that Leticia choose one of the parental bedrooms as her own once it become clear that no one could dissuade her from moving back to the old place. But Leticia preferred to sleep in the room she'd always slept in, though she didn't really know why.

On her desk directly in front of her rested three pieces of paper and her planner. The first sheet was Virginia's note. It looked as if it had been crumpled, then smoothed. Leticia picked it up, glanced at it, and shook her head. She sighed as she picked up the second piece of paper. The handwriting was her own. On it was a flight schedule. Lucille was due to arrive within twenty-four hours, and Leticia didn't feel ready for her visit.

She put the sheet of paper down and picked up the last one. It was a letter from Susan Russell. Leticia smiled as she reread it. Susan was due to testify before a congressional panel in Washington and wanted to include a brief visit to Grant's Hill at the end of her trip. Leticia tapped her fingers on the surface of the desk. Susan's visit would overlap with Lucille's stay. That would inevitably mean fireworks.

Leticia reached for the phone. It would be a treat to talk with Susan. She picked up the receiver and held it for a moment, then set it down again. What would she say? What could she say? She wanted to tell Susan to re-schedule her visit, but she knew that was absurd. Susan had to come east for the hearing, so that was when she would visit, if she visited at all. It wouldn't work any other way. Leticia sighed again. She'd have to tell Susan not to come, and she resented that.

The only time Susan and Lucille had met was after Paul's death. They had taken an immediate dislike to each other. Lucille referred to Susan in conversation with Leticia as Paul's whore. To Susan's face she was condescending and barely polite. Susan was angered by the haste with which Lucille disposed of Paul's possessions. "It's like he couldn't die soon enough to suit her," she told Leticia. "Or maybe she's trying to get rid of evidence."

Leticia had attempted to calm her down. "She wasn't even here when he died," she said. "It's just that she knows I get upset when I look at his stuff and remember he's gone."

Susan had hugged her then and said, "I'm sorry. It's just that I miss him too, and seeing his belongings is comforting. Of course, it's different for you. I feel bad, but you must feel ever so much worse."

Leticia hadn't felt bad though. She had just felt blank, as if her life had ended with Paul's. Unlike him, however, she was about to begin a new life. She had felt very much the same way when her father died so suddenly. One day she was Leticia Barnes, or even more authentically Fred the tomboy, and then she was Mrs. Paul Runcible. It was as if she'd been the object of a magical transformation. When Paul died, she went from contented air force wife to widow under suspicion of foul play, and the feeling of dislocation was similar. Sometimes she'd wondered if there was a real person behind the roles she played.

Of course, she couldn't share any of those thoughts with Susan, so she'd just accepted Susan's sympathy and vowed that she'd never allow Susan and her mother to be in the same room at the same time, insofar as she could prevent it. Afterwards, she'd had a recurring nightmare in which the two women met in California and tore each other to shreds. In the dream she'd looked on, unable to stop the carnage. It was her fault somehow, or so she felt upon awakening.

If it were her choice, Leticia would much prefer a visit from Susan, who never failed to entertain her. She found her mother anything but entertaining. Still it never occurred to her to tell Lucille to cancel or postpone her visit. There would have been no point.

Leticia decided not to think about Lucille. Instead she imagined the letter she'd write to Susan. Even though she'd have to turn down Susan's offer of a visit, she could tell her about the progress of her herbal research and send her a few recipes. Susan was slowly learning how to cook something besides scrambled eggs and hot dogs, and it was about time.

Leticia's mind wandered back to her days in Turkey, where she had started to learn to cook. At first, like all the other wives of high-ranking officers, she had taken her meals with Paul at the officers' club. When Paul had entertained his fellow officers at home, the meal, if there was one, was always catered. Leticia was amazed at how self-sufficient the military was. The meals were roast beef, roasted chicken, or pork chops. Not one catered meal betrayed the fact that the base was in a foreign country with a unique cuisine. Most of the officers and their wives drank more than they ate anyway, and Leticia, who had no use for drunkenness, quickly found them tedious company.

Thinking about the past, Leticia had to admit that it was odd she'd never learned to cook from Ana Mendoza Velasquez. The old woman had offered to teach her, but Leticia despised cooking, considering it one of those feminine tasks. She knew better than to express her contempt to Mrs. Mendoza Velasquez, however. "I'd never cook as well as you," she'd complimented the old woman. "And since you're here to cook for me…"

Mrs. Mendoza Velasquez ground her molars together at that and said she was an old woman and would not live forever. When that had no effect, she asked, "And when you are married and go away, little one, and I am not with you, what will you eat then?"

Leticia just smiled. "I'd never marry someone who couldn't provide me with household help, including a cook," she replied. "That's the very least a husband can do."

Leticia laughed faintly at her memory of that conversation. She wondered if Mrs. Mendoza Velasquez had had to restrain herself in order to keep from slapping her. Sometimes Leticia could hardly understand the young woman she had been.

She hadn't intended to learn to cook in Turkey. It had happened by accident. A fortunate accident, Leticia reminded herself, one that had made her stay in Turkey a high point of her life so far.

The officers on the base rarely went into town. When they did, it was usually at the urging of their wives, eager to shop for antiques or oriental carpets. Since Leticia had no interest in that kind of shopping, she was the only wife who hadn't managed to coerce her husband into making the short trip from the base into town. She took a certain pride in her difference from the other wives, and Paul was grateful for not being dragged to the bazaar.

His commanding officer's wife, whom he referred to behind her back as Mrs. Bargain, was not content to let Leticia off the hook. "She's been here three months and hasn't bought a thing," she told her husband, Major General Walsh. He then asked Paul if there was something the matter with Leticia. Was she depressed or simply shy? Or didn't she like the other wives? Was she a communist or had she taken some kind of vow of poverty? Paul, knowing better than to refuse, accepted an invitation to take his wife shopping with General Walsh and Mrs.

Bargain on the following Saturday. When he told Leticia it was important not to be viewed as eccentric or unfriendly, she reluctantly agreed to the excursion.

"It's just a day trip," he'd assured her, noting her reluctance. "I couldn't stand more than a day of Mrs. Bargain myself."

Leticia smiled automatically. "I suppose I can feign interest in antiques for a few hours, but I really don't think we should waste our money."

Paul agreed, and they let the matter rest.

***

Saturday was warm and sunny, and when Leticia stepped into the major general's staff car, she wished that they were going to the beach rather than into town. Rose Walsh and the general himself were already seated in the back of the vehicle, so Leticia made for the front door. "No, no, Mrs. Runcible," Major General Walsh called out, "let your husband sit next to my driver. It's more comfortable back here."

So Leticia squeezed into the back seat, while Paul settled comfortably in front. He turned and flashed a grin at her as he closed the door.

"Well," Rose Walsh began enthusiastically, "you won't believe the wonderful prices! I found such a bargain last week. An antique hand-knotted rug for less than I'd spend on a good meal back home."

Home was a small town in Indiana. Leticia smiled politely.

"I also discovered the most amazing collection of brass implements," Rose went on. "Candlesticks, platters, even incense burners. All in a tiny shop less than a quarter of a mile from the old bazaar. The shop's owner was an old man who swore that I was robbing him blind. Of course, he had no idea how valuable the brasses were. To him they were just merchandise."

Leticia doubted very much that the shopkeeper had been fooled by Mrs. Walsh, but she kept silent. Maybe the woman was right. Or maybe the man had been obliged to sell off family heirlooms to feed his offspring. The thought depressed her, and she heartily wished she were not about to spend the day bargain hunting with the Walshes.

"Rose will show you all the best places to get great deals, Mrs. Runcible," the general piped up, gazing fondly at his wife. "She has a real nose for a bargain."

The image that arose in Leticia's mind made her reach for Paul's shoulder and squeeze it hard. She saw the amply endowed Rose Walsh as a giant bloodhound, nose to the ground, sniffing through

197

overturned refuse bins. She could barely contain her laughter. Paul resisted the impulse to turn to look at her, knowing that if he did, she'd lose control.

"Well, here we are," Rose said happily. "James, tell the driver to let us off. There's the entrance to the old bazaar."

Leticia smiled faintly. Why couldn't the woman tell the driver herself? And why did her husband look so pleased to be ordered around? He was a major general, after all. She'd never ordered Paul around, and he was a mere colonel. Yes, Leticia had been impatient back then, she admitted to herself. It took several months and the acquaintance of what she still thought of as her Turkish adoptive family for her to learn that patience really could be a virtue. Or as her friend Damla was fond of reminding her, humans who live by clock time instead of in God's time don't generally live very long or very well.

When Leticia stepped out of the car she was struck by the antiquity of the buildings surrounding her and by the incredible liveliness of the street. She could express it to herself in no other way: the very street seemed alive, full of people and smells and sounds and motion. She was dazzled by it.

"Come along, Mrs. Runcible," the general said. "Don't gawk! The natives don't like it." He chuckled. "Stick close to us."

Rose took Leticia's arm, and she felt like a small child with an imperious nanny. Leticia gazed imploringly at Paul, who just shrugged. "There's a very good carpet store a few buildings behind the old bazaar," Rose chirped. "Mr. Kizirian is actually Armenian."

Her husband cleared his throat. "Bet you thought the Turks had killed them all off, didn't you?"

Leticia managed to nod, as Rose pulled her into a small shop. "Mr. Kizirian, hello!" she called out. Leticia reached back and took Paul's hand, hoping that Rose would release her grip, but she didn't right away. "I want you to meet our friends, Colonel Runcible and his wife," she said to the thin man who'd stepped forward to greet her.

Mr. Kizirian offered them Turkish coffee and suggested that Paul and Leticia look around his shop, while he showed Rose and the general a few carpets he'd selected especially for them. Only then did Rose finally let go of Leticia.

***

"Let's get out of here!" Leticia whispered in Paul's ear.

He grinned at her. "Give it a little more time so we don't come across as rude, okay? Just a half-hour or so." He caressed her arm and then stopped abruptly.

Leticia sighed and stared unseeing at a row of carpets hung on the wall. "I'm sure these are very nice, but I don't know a thing about them."

Paul laughed softly. "Neither do I. But I'm certain Mrs. Bargain would be glad to help you pick one."

Leticia groaned softly. "Can we go yet? Please!!"

Paul pulled her back to the center of the shop where Rose stood haggling with Mr. Kizirian. "Major General Walsh," Paul began, "since this is my wife's first trip to town, I'd like to show her a few of the sights. With your permission, of course."

The general nodded. "Of course, Colonel. Just remember not to let her go wandering off on her own. The streets aren't safe for a woman like her."

Leticia wondered exactly what he meant by "a woman like her," but she didn't ask. Instead she pulled Paul to the door of the shop and stepped out into the brilliant sunlight.

"Where to?" Paul asked.

Leticia shrugged. "How should I know? I've never been here before, remember?" She looked around. "Mrs. Bargain said the old bazaar was not in use anymore. Does that mean there's a new bazaar?"

Paul smiled. "There's the open market near the river." He raised his eyebrows. "I thought you weren't interested in shopping."

"I'm not. I'm looking for an herbalist."

Paul's smile faded. "An herbalist? What for? If you're sick, you should see Major Phipps. He's a very good doctor."

Leticia rolled her eyes. "I'm not sick. I'm interested in herbal remedies. You know that."

Paul looked startled. "I had no idea you were interested in Turkish herbs. That woman from the Andes whom you knew when you were a teenager…"

"Mrs. Mendoza Velasquez," she interrupted him.

Paul shrugged. "She never told you to go out and accumulate herbal cures across the world, did she?"

Leticia smiled and took his hand. "No, not exactly. Can we go to the market now?"

Paul didn't look very happy, but he led Leticia through the winding streets to the riverside, where the market stretched out for at least a mile. "I don't think you're going to find an herb doctor in the middle of the market," he told her. "I think the government has been cracking down on everything pre-modern."

"There's nothing pre-modern about herbs," Leticia snapped.

"Right," Paul conceded immediately, knowing better than to argue. "But I'm sure herbal medicine is seen as part of the superstitious past by the reformers in power."

Leticia poked him to reinforce her point. "I'm not looking for a herbal practitioner here, just for someone who sells herbs. Any kind of herbs. Cooking herbs will do fine."

"What?" Paul's expression mirrored amazement. "But you don't cook!"

"Trust me," Leticia replied.

Leticia smiled broadly as she remembered walking into the small shop that emitted heavenly aromas. Paul followed her hesitantly. When the shop's owner, a man of about sixty, greeted him in heavily accented but understandable English, he sighed in relief and explained, pointing to Leticia, that his wife was looking for herbs.

"Ah, so your wife is a good cook," the man announced. It was not a question. "My daughter can introduce her to the most important herbs in Turkish cuisine." He called out a few words in Turkish and a young woman entered the room. "This is my daughter Damla."

Damla, who was little more than a teenager, glowered at Leticia and Paul. Whatever she had been doing certainly interested her more than dealing with the American couple. Her father, noticing her irritation, said something else in Turkish. His tone was scolding, and the young woman gave Leticia a weak smile.

"Can I help you?" she asked, sounding very much as if she'd learned her English in America.

Leticia smiled back at her and said, "I'm interested in herbs."

"Come, sir," Damla's father said to Paul. "In the back room we will share coffee."

Paul glanced at Leticia and smiled. Then he followed his host into a space separated from the small store by a heavy curtain.

"Herbs," Damla repeated the word. "You want to cook with them, drink them in tea or make medicine?" Her smile turned slightly mischievous. "Of course tea and medicine can be the same, but Americans don't even cook with herbs."

Leticia's smile widened. "Well, this American doesn't cook at all. I never learned."

The young woman's eyebrows rose. "You never cook? How come your husband doesn't divorce you?"

Leticia started to laugh. She couldn't help herself. "I am interested in herbs that can be used as medicine," she said.

"But you must learn to cook!" Damla insisted. "I learned from my mother. Why didn't you?"

Leticia sighed. "My mother didn't have to cook. She married a wealthy man. We had a cook, a woman who also taught me about herbs."

Damla looked perplexed. "She taught you herbs but not to cook?"

"Damla!" came her father's voice through the curtain. "I asked you to help the lady, not to interrogate her."

"Yes, father." Damla blushed. "My grandmother is an herb doctor," she whispered. "You will come with me to her. Not now. But soon."

Leticia nodded. "Will I find you here?"

"Always."

***

That was the beginning. Though Leticia could not persuade Paul to accompany her to the small shop, he didn't object to her visiting as long as an aide, a young man who was as happy to get away from the base as Leticia herself, went along with her. The aide left her at the shop and went off for a couple of hours of sightseeing while she went about her business. Not content with merely introducing Leticia to her grandmother, a pipe-smoking old woman who was more than willing to share her knowledge for a very small fee, Damla insisted that Leticia learn to cook. "My mother will gladly teach you," she offered. "That way, when you are old and wrinkled, your husband will still love you." Leticia agreed to the cooking lessons and was surprised to discover that she had considerable talent for the skill she'd previously considered beneath her. Damla's mother, often invited neighbors to sample the results of Leticia's lessons, and soon Leticia found herself part of a community of women who seemed able to ignore her foreignness and welcome her wholeheartedly into their world. After a month she realized that she felt more comfortable in town among her new friends than she did on the base.

The first time she cooked for Paul, he was wary until he tasted the food. "This is wonderful!" he exclaimed, helping himself to more. "I think that next time we entertain, we'll have a dinner party instead of the usual cocktails and hors d'oeuvres. If that's all right with you, I mean. You can cook more than these two dishes, can't you?"

Leticia could and did. Mrs. Bargain had taken credit for Leticia's newly developed talent. "If I hadn't insisted she come to town, this never would have happened," the general's wife announced at the first dinner party. At the second party, however, she not so jokingly warned Paul that his wife was in danger of going native. "Look at those bangles on her arms! And that long embroidered skirt! It's as big as a tablecloth. Back home women are starting to wear short skirts."

Paul smiled. "I think the embroidered skirt is quite pretty," he defended his wife. After the party, however, he reminded Leticia how important her conformity was to his military career. "We have a good thing going," he said, putting his arm around her shoulders. "Your cooking has made us a couple worth noticing. Don't ruin it for us with this oriental whimsy. You're spending too much time with the women here, especially that girl with the bad attitude."

Oriental whimsy? Girl with a bad attitude? Leticia just nodded. "Maybe you're right, Paul. Next time I'll wear something different."

She had no intention of deserting her friends or changing her style of dress. But it did no harm to seem to agree. Paul didn't keep track of her visits to town, and she could always put on her Turkish clothes in the curtained off room behind the herb store. Damla would consider fooling Paul a great adventure. "We women," she said, "have to be cunning like a fox outsmarting dogs." Leticia had never thought of Paul or Major General Walsh as dogs before. But though she'd never say so to anyone else, when she sat alone in her room on the base and thought about it, she had to admit that the description fit.

CHAPTER 33
LUCILLE'S ARRIVAL
1980
❖

Virginia desperately wanted to talk with Carolyn about Henry's letters from Eric Johnson. She stepped out of the hospital elevator and looked around. Her gaze halted momentarily at the pay phone near the door to the parking lot. She knew she couldn't reach Carolyn by phone since she had no idea where Carolyn was at the moment. With a sigh she walked past the admissions desk to the cafeteria. She peered in, half expecting to see Carolyn at a table with Leonora Epstein. She knew it was wishful thinking, but she couldn't help but feel disappointed.

Dispirited, Virginia trudged through the front door and started to walk around the hospital grounds. She reminded herself to breathe deeply. That was what Carolyn always told her when she felt anxious. Her anxiety was mixed with bewilderment. She knew that her father liked Johnson and kept in touch with him, but she had a bad feeling about the letters. Why had Henry taken them with him to the hospital? Was he hiding them? If so, from whom? She didn't like feeling paranoid.

Carolyn, she was sure, would be able to put everything in perspective. That was one of Carolyn's strengths: the ability to perceive patterns and analyze them correctly. Of course, she hated it when Carolyn turned that talent on her and humiliated her the way she had in front of Leonora Epstein. It was as if Carolyn had no control over how and when she expressed her considerable insight. That was one of her biggest flaws, Virginia thought. Funny how the same quality could be both a strength and a weakness. She had to admit that she'd been more tuned into Carolyn's weaknesses than her strengths lately, but that was only because she didn't feel that Carolyn was really on her side. She sighed again and stepped off the path to pick up an iridescent feather lying near the base of a tree. When she looked up, she could see a wild turkey watching her. She pocketed the feather and continued walking away from the path. Occasionally she tripped over a root or a pebble. "Got to watch where I'm going," she mumbled each time she lost her footing, but she was too wrapped up in her thoughts to pay attention.

She reached into her pocket and fingered the feather. It reminded her of Leticia, specifically of the times she'd tickled Leticia and made her guess what it was that was moving lightly along her spine. She shook her head. Thinking about Leticia made her anxious all over again.

The pieces didn't fit together. Reviewing what Eric Johnson had told her, Virginia struggled to make sense of Paul Runcible's death. Cardiac arrest made the most sense. Carolyn had observed that pre-meditated murder required planning, deep resentment, or a grudge. Perhaps Leticia resented Paul, perhaps she even bore him a grudge, but Virginia just couldn't see her as someone who could plan and execute a homicide. Leticia had resented Eric Johnson, but her outrage had been right on the surface, the way her indignation always was. Had that changed so much?

Virginia smiled involuntarily, remembering how she'd distracted Leticia from her pique with kisses and caresses. Yet she had seen the cold side of Leticia. Remembering Leticia's good-bye note and her own tantrum in response was mortifying. That old, familiar feeling of not trusting her own reactions was still part of her, though it had rarely troubled her in recent years. Living with Carolyn had gone a long way towards erasing that particular insecurity. Loud, spontaneous, and flamboyant as she was, Carolyn was also reliable and trustworthy. Virginia knew this to be the case, though lately she had had doubts. Carolyn was also totally disarming. While she analyzed, she charmed, and the person being charmed had no idea how busily Carolyn's mind was working. Virginia just knew that Carolyn could clarify what was happening with Henry and Leticia. All Virginia had to do was find her.

On her way back to the hospital, Virginia picked a few dandelions for Henry. Although there was nothing elegant about a dandelion bouquet, she hoped that when he saw them he would have his usual reaction and tell her the story of how once, when she was still very young, she'd picked dandelions for the vase in his waiting room. Unable to estimate the proper amount, she'd gathered enough to fill ten vases and was in tears at the idea that she had to discard so many. That was when he'd taken her to a local rabbit farmer who'd allowed her to hand feed the dandelions to his rabbits. Memories like that made her glad Henry was her father. She hoped that he would remember that day, and that narrating the story of a disaster averted would make it easier to broach the topic of Johnson's letters. She expected him to be defensive about her having found them at all. "I was just cleaning up a little," she said under her breath, as she walked out of the elevator and turned up the corridor to Henry's room. "It's not as if I were snooping. If anyone needs to explain, it's Henry, not I."

"Talking to yourself?" she heard a voice say and looked over her shoulder to see Leonora Epstein smiling at her. "Some people say it's a mark of genius, you know."

Virginia blushed, but Leonora gave no indication that she'd noticed. "The test results came in early, and you'll be happy to know they were pretty much what we expected. Treating his blocked arteries won't reverse the Parkinson's, but it should slow down the progression."

Virginia smiled and expressed her gratitude. "Have you seen Carolyn?" she asked the young doctor, hoping that the flush she'd felt from her crown down to her toes was no longer visible. Leonora didn't have much information about Carolyn's whereabouts. "The results came in early, as I said," she reiterated, "so of course, there was no good reason for her to wait around. I'm off." Leonora waved.

Virginia watched Leonora walk down the hallway towards a different wing. The young woman waved again as she went around the corner, but Virginia ignored that. No good reason indeed! Carolyn was supposed to meet her at the hospital. Surely that should have been reason enough to wait.

Virginia walked into Henry's room and found her father sound asleep and no sign of Carolyn. She could barely resist the impulse to have another look at the letters, so she walked out again and marched to the nurses' station to see if someone could locate Carolyn. Virginia hated when things deviated from the plan she'd made, and Carolyn knew it. Virginia chewed at her thumbnail anxiously as she waited impatiently for a nurse to appear. Why was Carolyn being so inconsiderate? Or had something gone seriously wrong?

"I haven't seen Dr. Matthews since early in the afternoon," one of the nurses informed her, "but I can have her paged for you."

Virginia stood by the desk and waited. Once she heard Carolyn's name announced over the loudspeaker system, she relaxed. However, after several repetitions of the page, Carolyn was nowhere in sight. Virginia began to worry in earnest and to feel hard done by at the same time.

The nurse who'd had Carolyn paged, returned and stated the obvious. "Dr. Matthews does not appear to be in the hospital. Perhaps she has left for the day."

Virginia literally had to bite her tongue in order not to tell the nurse that was ridiculous. Returning to Henry's room she fidgeted and coughed and tapped her fingers on the window in the hope that he would awaken so she could interrogate him. But Henry slept on. Finally she gave up and went down to the parking lot where she hastily looked around for their rental car. She didn't see it, so she climbed into Henry's ancient vehicle and drove home, expecting to find Carolyn there with an explanation or an apology for the mix-up. But the house was empty.

***

Carolyn really had intended to meet Virginia in the hospital. However, the early arrival of Henry's test results meant that she was finished meeting with Leonora by two-thirty. Carolyn was satisfied with their decision to add the anti-clotting agent Dipyridamole to Henry's medications. She wasn't convinced that the new drug would have any direct impact on Henry's current symptoms, but she agreed with Leonora that it would postpone the inevitable.

So Carolyn was in a good mood when she went to check on Henry in the afternoon. He was awake and cheerful, though exhausted. He had just returned from physical therapy and was extraordinarily pleased with himself. He was making the kind of progress, so he claimed his therapist had said, that could be expected from a man half his age. He and Carolyn joked for a while, and then she, groaning at the last of his feeble witticisms, left the hospital. She knew Henry was still grinning at his own cleverness while she was shifting into drive and leaving the parking lot. His cheerfulness pleased her. She smiled as she glanced at her watch. She had plenty of time to gas up the car and go to the bank for more money before it was time to meet Virginia back at the hospital.

The line of cars at the town's only service station was surprisingly long, so Carolyn made a quick turn out of the entrance and drove up the town's main street towards the bank. Though she found a parking space only a few doors down, the bank was busy too, so she stood in line for a long time. At first she simply looked around at the people, but soon she found herself making dinner plans in her head. Something quiet and elegant, she thought. After all, they would soon be leaving for the other side of the country, and a pleasant evening would be a nice memory to take from the stress-filled excuse for a vacation that was their time in Grant's Hill.

206

When her turn came, Carolyn cashed her traveler's checks and then drove back to the gas station. The line had diminished a little, but she still had to wait. The day was sunny, and she felt a little thirsty, so she got out of the car and walked over to the soda machine.

A thin woman with frosted hair stood by the machine. She wore red high heels, a tight black skirt, and a red sweater with racing cars appliquéd onto the front. The racing cars were covered in sequins, and Carolyn thought she hadn't seen anything so ugly in a long time. She averted her eyes and found herself staring at the woman's face. The profile looked familiar, and though she considered saying something, the woman's haughty grimace was so unpleasant that Carolyn thought better of it. This woman did not look anything like the friendly local people who delighted in small talk about the weather. Her face was hard and so heavily made up that Carolyn couldn't tell how old she was. Her eyes set off warning bells in Carolyn's head.

At the very instant when Carolyn realized she was staring, the woman caught her eye. "Excuse me, but do I know you?" a harsh yet cultured voice rasped.

"No, I don't think so," Carolyn replied.

"Well, then," the woman continued, "What the hell are you staring at?"

So much, Carolyn thought ruefully, for the refinement of the upper classes. "I do most humbly beg your pardon," Carolyn replied sarcastically. "You looked familiar for a moment, but I'm sure I don't know anyone with such lovely manners."

The woman scowled at her without a trace of embarrassment. "You're a fine one to talk about manners, staring at me that way. Where were you brought up, on a pig farm?"

Carolyn was tempted to respond in kind until she remembered how irritating it was when anyone responded with cheerful cordiality when she expressed annoyance. So she smiled brightly at the scowling woman. "Do you live around here?" she asked, pretending very hard that she really wanted to know.

The woman's lip curled as she gave one last look of repulsion at Carolyn before turning her head away.

"Hey, can I buy you a Coke?" Carolyn offered loudly. "Or would you rather have a Dr. Pepper?" She took a step towards the woman, who began to walk quickly towards the side of the service station. She stopped next to a car that looked vaguely familiar. It took Carolyn a few seconds to place the car, and during those few seconds Leticia stepped out from beside a gas pump.

"Mother, are you ready?" she asked with barely mastered irritation in her voice.

The woman stepped slowly to the passenger door and opened it just as Leticia spotted Carolyn. A smile spread slowly across Leticia's face, chasing away all traces of irritation. She moved quickly towards Carolyn. "Dr. Matthews, I'm so glad to see you! I've been hoping we'd run into each other sometime before your departure since Virginia hasn't succeeded in persuading you to accompany her to my home."

Carolyn opened her mouth, but no sound came out. Leticia didn't seem to notice.

"I've just come from the airport. My mother is here on her semi-annual visit." The irritation that had faded from her voice at the sight of Carolyn returned and then disappeared again. "She insisted that I stop for gas even though the tank was half full. I hope that's not going to set the tone for the entire visit."

Carolyn nodded, trying to recall what, if anything, Virginia had ever told her about Leticia's mother, but her mind was blank.

Ignoring Carolyn's confusion, Leticia continued. "Why don't you join us for coffee? Are you on your way home?"

Carolyn shook her head and cleared her throat, annoyed that she was having such a hard time getting her words out. "No, I have to head back to the hospital soon to meet Virginia."

"Well then," Leticia persevered, "we'll just get a quick cup right here in town. I won't take no for an answer, and I'm very stubborn. Just ask Virginia!" She flashed a brilliant smile at Carolyn, who thought for a moment that Leticia was coming on to her.

"Just follow us!" Leticia commanded, and Carolyn obeyed, finding it gratifying that someone besides Henry wanted her company so much.

CHAPTER 34
NEW INFORMATION
1980
❖

By the time Carolyn pulled into a parking space, Leticia was on her way into the café. Her mother walked slowly behind her, a disdainful expression on her face. Carolyn approached their table with some misgivings and waited to be introduced to the older woman. After a brief, uncomfortable silence, she nodded stiffly and announced her name.

"Oh, how rude of me!" Leticia exclaimed, blushing. "Mother, this is Dr. Matthews. Dr. Matthews, my mother, Lucille Barnes."

Lucille barely acknowledged the introduction. She stared out the window and yawned.

"My mother is tired, Dr. Matthews," Leticia explained, looking tired herself. "She arrived from Florida today and her flight was not a pleasant one."

"I'm sorry to hear that," Carolyn said, not meaning a word of it. She was sure the flight had been a lot more unpleasant for the attendants and other passengers than for the woman studiously ignoring her.

Lucille cleared her throat and fixed Carolyn with a baleful look. "And just what do you do, Dr. Matthews?" she inquired scornfully, placing emphasis on the word "do."

Carolyn's mouth dropped open, and Leticia answered for her. "Why, Mother, she practices medicine, of course."

"Well, she can't have much of a practice if she practices in this little dump of a town," Lucille snapped at her daughter. "That old fool Henry Carr has been the town doctor for years, ever since he gave up his practice in Baltimore." She sniffed. "It's one thing to spend one's summer's here, but to live and work in this place all year round is a sign of stupidity."

"I don't practice here," Carolyn replied, striving to sound more patient than she felt. She was slightly embarrassed that Lucille and she held the same opinion of Grant's Hill, and her distaste for the woman was strong enough to make her reconsider her judgment of the little town. "I practice in San Francisco. I'm a neurologist at the University of California Hospital."

Lucille appraised her shrewdly. "Well then, what in the name of hell are you doing here?"

"Mother!" Leticia interjected.

"Don't sound so shocked, Lettie! You've surely heard the word 'hell' before. This woman was harassing me at the service station, and I need to know how much I can sue her for before I decide whether it's worth the trouble."

This time Leticia's mouth flew open. Carolyn started to laugh. "What am I doing here? That, Mrs. Barnes, is a very astute question. Officially I am on vacation, but actually I am looking after that old fool Henry Carr, as you call him. He's very ill, and I am a close friend of his daughter. We're here together."

"Close friend, my ass," Lucille chimed in, calling forth another shocked exclamation from Leticia, which she ignored. "I know that Carr girl from way back. Don't think I don't know about her!"

Leticia buried her face in her arms and laid her head on the table.

"Don't take on so, Lettie! It's tiresome," Lucille said peremptorily. "I've nothing against it. I've heard that women are better lovers than men. If your father was any measure of men, women could hardly be worse." She turned to Carolyn. "Give me a cigarette, would you, Doctor?"

"Sorry, I don't smoke," Carolyn replied, wondering what Lucille might come out with next. She didn't trust the woman's professed tolerance for lesbianism, but she certainly preferred it to outright hostility.

When the waitress came to take their orders, Lucille asked her for cigarettes. The waitress pointed to a machine near the restrooms and the pay phone. After ordering coffee, Lucille excused herself.

Leticia, who lifted her head from the table only after her mother walked off, smiled apologetically at Carolyn. "Will the smoke bother you? She's down to a pack a day. I know it's not good for her, but it's better than popping Valium like a vitamin supplement."

Carolyn smiled weakly. She hated the smell of smoke. But even more than the smell she hated being unable to focus on anything but the smoke. It took away her mental sharpness and left her with a blurry feeling. She hoped that Lucille would ask permission before lighting up, but she knew, based on her brief experience with the woman, that was unlikely to happen.

When Lucille returned, she already held a lit cigarette to her mouth and sucked on it happily. Exhaling a perfect smoke ring, she seated herself and smiled. "And some people claim these aren't addictive!" she chuckled agreeably.

Carolyn fanned the smoke away from her face and coughed meaningfully, but Lucille ignored her reaction. "Well now, where was I? Ah yes, on the uselessness in bed of husbands and men in general. Except for Alex, of course."

"Alex," Leticia explained quickly, "is a race car driver my mother met in Florida. He's..."

Lucille cut her off. "Do be still, Lettie!" She turned to Carolyn. "Alex is thirty-three and my lover. Lettie finds it quite shocking, I fear. But she's not erotically very daring. Never was. Except... well, you know."

Lucille's garrulousness fascinated Carolyn. The woman seemed to have no personal boundaries.

"As I was saying," Lucille continued, "my late husband was terrible in bed and not much of a companion either. Business always came first. And Lettie, of course." She smiled a bit viciously at her daughter. "He just doted on Lettie and let her get away with entirely too much. Only the best private school for Lettie, even though her grades were mediocre. He had that young cop fired for trying to make her behave, and then he put up with her dalliance with that Carr girl. That didn't seem to bother him at all; so long as it wasn't a man with a bigger dick than his, he didn't mind."

Carolyn glanced at Leticia, who was staring into space, seemingly unperturbed by her mother's words. Carolyn wondered if she had heard it all so many times that she no longer took it in. Within seconds Lucille's piercing voice brought Carolyn's attention back to her monologue.

"Cal didn't want her to marry that nice Runcible fellow either. I told him not to be ridiculous. She'd have to marry someone sometime. It's not as though she had the brains and the ambition to be a doctor like that Carr girl. What an odd child that one was! Grant's Hill's own little saint!" Lucille didn't seem to be aware that she was talking about Carolyn's partner, or maybe she simply didn't care. She turned to her daughter. "Lettie, remember that Latin American Indian woman she helped? Malooza? Mandanga? What the hell was her name? Mendoza, I think." She turned back to Carolyn. "She used to cook and clean for us, you see. And she kept a large disorderly garden behind the house, all full of weeds. She called them vegetables and herbs, but then of course she would. Some of those weeds were quite poisonous too. She

211

taught Lettie all about them, didn't she, dear?" she asked in a saccharine voice, turning once again to Leticia.

Without appearing to shift her attention from Lucille, Carolyn watched Leticia out of the corner of her eye. She was more than curious about Leticia's reaction to Lucille's latest remark. Would she show fear and guilt or simply continue to nod blankly?

A look passed across Leticia's face momentarily, but long enough for Carolyn to ascertain that she was startled rather than fearful. There wasn't a trace of guilt. That meant she was either a complete sociopath or else innocent of her husband's death. The startled look yielded to something that Carolyn could not identify right away. Worry or concern perhaps? Anxiety?

Of course, Carolyn told herself, Leticia knows full well that Virginia must have told me of her expertise with herbs, including poisons. So the revelation of that couldn't be the cause of her reaction. For a second Carolyn let her mind wander. Then as if sudden enlightenment had come upon her, she smiled knowingly and turned her attention back to Lucille, who had barely paused for breath.

"What Lettie doesn't know about herbs and poisons wouldn't even fill a thimble. Why, when Henry Carr first took ill, she even treated some of his patients. He was absolutely furious, but their health did improve. He'd have an absolute fit if she offered to help him with her herbs, but maybe she should anyway. Sometimes I wonder, Dr. Matthews, if those primitives don't know more about healing than you doctors."

Carolyn didn't reply. Her mind was barely processing Lucille's string of verbiage. If Leticia were worried but not guilty and fearful, what could that mean? Did she know something? Obviously she'd suspected foul play or she wouldn't have insisted on the tox screens.

"Dr. Matthews, are you listening to me?" The sound of her name brought Carolyn out of her reverie. "I asked if you thought Dr. Carr would return to work. This town certainly needs a doctor, though I must say, I can't imagine what would ever prompt someone to set up a practice in such a dull place. Oh, it was all right during the summers in the good old days, I suppose, though I was bored out of my mind when Cal dragged us here."

Carolyn looked over at Leticia, who smiled grimly at her. Her face was blank again, and Carolyn wondered what she was thinking.

212

Lucille paused to drag on her cigarette. She glared at Leticia with narrowed eyes and then started in again.

"You know, Dr. Matthews, almost no one except Alex really listens to me. You are a rare person, if I may say so, truly extraordinary."

Leticia's blankness yielded to a look of intense embarrassment. Carolyn smiled faintly, while her clinical faculties kicked into high gear. Lucille, she noted, seemed to be getting drunk on her own words. Was there a psychiatric term for verbal intoxication? She didn't know of one, but she'd have to look it up.

"I don't know how an educated man like Henry Carr has endured this place all these years, and I don't know how my own daughter stands it. She came here right after her poor husband's shocking demise, you know, and she hasn't left since. I keep begging her to move to Florida. There are many attractive, eligible men in Florida. Of course, few men are as handsome as Paul was, but one can't go on mourning one's whole life."

Leticia, Carolyn was happy to note, had had enough. "Mother, can you please let someone else get a word in edgewise?" she snapped.

"You see, Dr. Matthews, it's exactly as I said. No one listens to me. Even my own daughter tries to silence me." Lucille's face took on an injured expression and Carolyn resisted the impulse to laugh. The woman really was something else. Just as Lucille was about to launch into another monologue, the waitress brought their coffee, and Leticia breathed an audible sigh of relief.

"Let's not fight, Mother," she said soothingly. "Put out your cigarette and drink your coffee, and then we'll go home. I'm sure you're tired after your flight."

"Of course I'm tired," Lucille grumbled, "but did you take that into consideration when you invited Dr. Matthews to coffee? You didn't think of my feelings at all. Really, Leticia, you could at least have consulted me before subjecting me to endless socializing. Not," she added with a savage smile at Carolyn, "that I haven't enjoyed this social hour immensely."

Carolyn smiled back, hoping Lucille would take Leticia's advice and put out the cigarette. She felt as if the smoke were blinding her to something that should have been obvious. Besides, she liked the idea of drinking her coffee without choking.

But Lucille lit up another cigarette without putting out the one smoldering in the ash tray. She began puffing away between sips of

213

scalding, bitter coffee. Carolyn's face must have registered her distress, for Leticia smiled weakly at her once again and rubbed her forehead with a mix of resignation and exasperation.

Lucille's torrent of words had run out. She sat looking old and a bit rumpled from her hours in the air. Carolyn wondered how she'd ever managed to raise a daughter who seemed as normal as Leticia. "Seemed" was the operative word, of course. Carolyn liked Leticia and hoped the woman had not killed her husband. But she was the one with means and opportunity, if he had been killed at all. Carolyn took a deep breath and immediately regretted it. The lungful of smoke made her dizzy. Leticia might be a sociopath. Her mother certainly was, Carolyn thought. She shook her head slightly. The pieces just didn't fit. The girl that Virginia had described seemed a much more likely murderer than the woman sitting across the table from her. She could imagine that girl as Lucille's daughter, but... Lucille Barnes was talking again.

"Dr. Matthews, is it true that you are planning to leave for the west coast any day now?"

"Yes." Carolyn nodded for emphasis. "At the end of this week."

"So Henry Carr is recovering?"

Carolyn knew that Lucille couldn't have cared less about Henry's recovery. She wondered what the woman was after.

"Slowly," she hedged. "We're leaving him in good hands. Dr. Epstein, a neurologist at Hopkins, has taken over his treatment. She lives locally and will either continue to work with him here or in Baltimore."

Lucille looked bored. Carolyn had given her more information than she wanted. She yawned. "How nice for him!" she said inconsequentially, then added, "I hope I'll get to see you again before you leave. She smiled in what she intended to be an inviting manner. "I've enjoyed our conversation more than I can say."

Carolyn looked inquiringly over at Leticia, who just shrugged.

"Please come to dinner tomorrow evening," Lucille offered.

Carolyn hesitated, and Lucille didn't wait for her reply. "If you have other plans, cancel them!"

Carolyn heard a choking noise. She didn't have to look at Leticia to know it came from her.

"Is something wrong, Lettie?" Lucille asked sharply. "You shouldn't try to speak with your mouth full of coffee."

Carolyn felt a stab of pity for Leticia. "I have to check with Virginia," she said firmly, wanting to be sure the dinner invitation was for two.

Lucille looked disoriented. "Virginia? Oh, you mean the Carr girl! I quite forgot. You can certainly bring her along. The more the merrier, as they say! I've never met her, you know, and I am curious. After all, she and Lettie were quite intimate at one time." She smiled sourly.

Virginia observed Leticia out of the corner of her eye and caught her blushing ferociously.

"I'm sure Virginia would be pleased to meet you, Mrs. Barnes," Carolyn lied. "I'll phone you tomorrow to let you know for sure."

The mention of Virginia reminded Carolyn to pay attention to the time; she looked at her watch. "Oh my God," she whispered. It was after six. "I was supposed to meet Virginia at six," she announced, rising from her chair, "and I'm late. I'd better phone the hospital to see if she's still there." She raced to the rear of the restaurant.

Leticia observed Carolyn intently, while Lucille observed her in turn. "Don't get any ideas, Lettie," Lucille warned. "She's taken, and you put that childishness behind you when you married Paul."

Leticia glared at her mother for a second, then forced a smile to her lips. "I like Carolyn, er, Dr. Matthews, Mother. That's all. She's an interesting woman."

Lucille snorted. "And you claim you aren't lonely here!"

Carolyn, looking chastened, returned to the table before Leticia had a chance to reply. "She's home, and that's where I should be if I don't want to spend the next month in the doghouse."

"Woof, woof," Lucille called out, with a malevolent glint in her eye. "Go home, girl! Good girl!"

Carolyn heard Leticia sigh, as Lucille cackled, overcome with her own humor.

"It's been a rare pleasure. Actually medium rare." Lucille grinned ghoulishly, showing all of her teeth. Carolyn said farewell to Lucille, who was lighting yet another cigarette. With a look of sympathy aimed at Leticia, Carolyn left the restaurant.

CHAPTER 35
AN ADULT CONVERSATION
1980
❖

"Woof, woof?" Virginia looked up and hooted. Her head rested comfortably in her Carolyn's lap some two hours after her partner's return from coffee with Leticia and Lucille. "You're making up the details to take my mind off your misdeeds," she accused Carolyn playfully. Virginia absentmindedly scratched at her ankle. When Carolyn denied that she was inventing the story, Virginia began to tickle her.

Carolyn twisted away from her fingers and caught her hand. "Don't! I'm ticklish!" she complained.

"Of course, you're ticklish," Virginia retorted. "Otherwise what would be the point of tickling you?"

"If you can't have an adult conversation with your head in my lap, off you go!" The two of them tussled for a moment before Carolyn rolled Virginia onto the floor and pinned her down. Once Carolyn was firmly on top of Virginia, she kissed her nose and mouth. "Oh no," Virginia squawked, "not my nose!"

Carolyn giggled and helped her up. Once Virginia had her head in her lover's lap again, she folded her hands across on her abdomen. "See, no hands, no tickling. What did you want to have an adult conversation about, and how adult do you want it to be?"

Carolyn ruffled Virginia's hair. "Your relationship with Leticia," she said. "If we go to her house, there's no telling what we'll hear. You may be happier not knowing some of it." Carolyn shifted to find a more comfortable position.

"Such as?" Virginia challenged. "The last time we talked you didn't think Leticia had killed her husband."

"It is possible though," Carolyn replied. "But I was thinking more about your history with Leticia. What if she tells you that you turned her off women? Or maybe she had a bunch of relationships with other women after you. Or maybe, just maybe, she simply pushed you and your relationship out of her memory. How would any of that make you feel?"

Virginia took a deep breath and shrugged. "I don't know, but none of it seems as important as whether she killed Paul. I don't want to have to wonder for the rest of my life." Virginia sat up and scratched some more.

Carolyn stood up and started to pace. "I thought you might feel that way." She smiled sadly at Virginia. "She had access to all those herbs, poisonous and otherwise. She wouldn't even have had to buy poison to kill him. She could do it without leaving a trail."

Virginia stood up and walked to the window. "So what do we do now?"

Carolyn kept pacing. "I don't know. We could do nothing. Or we could try to push some buttons tomorrow at dinner, if we go."

"Of course we're going!"

"I know that Johnson had records from the autopsy," Carolyn said, "but I wanted more than records, so I phoned the office of the medical examiner in Wyoming late this afternoon. The guy who did the post-mortem on Runcible is still there."

"And he remembered the case?" Virginia asked with raised eyebrows.

"Actually he remembered Leticia. He said she was very forceful in her insistence that her husband did not die of natural causes. She repeatedly phoned and pressured him until he agreed to test for the most common poisons. Until he actually met her in the flesh, he thought she was a grieving, nearly hysterical widow."

"And then?" Virginia queried.

"Then he got nervous because she seemed as interested in poisons as she was in the cause of death. He said he found her attractive," she added with a sidelong glance at Virginia, "but she gave him the creeps."

"Well," Virginia said with a small, strangled laugh, "attractive and creepy. Sounds like the heroine of a horror movie. Leticia doesn't have a split personality, does she?"

Carolyn shrugged. "They call it multiple personality disorder nowadays, and you'd know better than I if the diagnosis fits Leticia."

Virginia refused to let that comment pass. "That's not true. You just spent almost as much time with her today as I have the whole time we've been here."

"But you knew her back when..." Carolyn began, but Virginia interrupted her.

"She's not the same. Not the same at all."

"She seems sane enough," Carolyn mused, "but some seemingly very normal people are getting diagnosed as multiples."

Virginia snorted. "No" she said, "it doesn't fit. None of it does. I'm starting to doubt that there was a murder. The man probably just died."

Carolyn looked skeptical. "A young man in great condition with no history of coronary or pulmonary distress who had recently had a complete physical drops dead. I don't know. It could happen, but is it likely?"

Virginia thought about arguing, but she decided against it. Carolyn had a look on her face that she knew too well. It meant that there was something more. She sighed. "What else, Carrie?"

Carolyn stopped pacing and looked down at her feet. "The medical examiner said Leticia didn't come alone. She had another woman with her. The woman wore an air force uniform. They seemed to be very close friends. At least that's how he put it."

"A close friend," Virginia echoed. "Makes you wonder how close, doesn't it?"

Carolyn nodded. "They could have been more than friends. Maybe Paul found out. Maybe he was just in the way."

Virginia sat back down. "That puts a whole different cast on things, doesn't it?"

Carolyn resumed her pacing. "The medical examiner thought the other woman was as distressed as Leticia, if not more so."

"She could have done it as easily as Leticia," Virginia chimed in. "Or maybe they were both in it together."

"Do you still want to go to dinner at Leticia's tomorrow? Things could get ugly if we push her."

"They're already ugly," Virginia said firmly. She gestured to Carolyn to sit down next to her. She was tired of speculating about Leticia and the death of Paul Runcible. She wanted to let the matter rest for the night and she had Henry's stash of letters on her mind.

"You won't believe what I found in Henry's room today," Virginia began, putting her hand on Carolyn's knee. Carolyn listened attentively as Virginia recounted her discovery.

"I'm amazed," Carolyn said when Virginia had finished, "that you could keep from reading the letters."

Virginia hesitated, not certain how to explain her reticence. Finally she made the attempt: "Henry didn't nose around in my diary when I was younger. He didn't force friends on me or try to mold me into someone I wasn't. So I figure I owe him the same respect for his privacy now that our roles are reversed."

"Makes sense to me."

Virginia thought for a moment. "Henry was always so decent to me when I was a kid."

Carolyn grimaced. "But he may be doing now what he didn't do then," she observed softly.

"What do you mean?" Virginia looked perplexed.

"Henry may be responsible for involving you in this whole mess with Leticia," Carolyn explained. "Wasn't it awfully coincidental that Eric Johnson happened to run into us in Wyoming?"

Virginia shrugged. "I think you're being a bit paranoid, Carrie. He does live there after all."

Carolyn flashed an apologetic smile before continuing. "True, but we don't. Johnson has his vendetta, but why now, of all times, does he suddenly decide to follow up on a long-standing suspicion? What if your father's interest in having you come here motivated him to unleash Johnson on us?"

Virginia rolled her eyes. "Really, Carrie! You make Henry sound so sinister. He's a sick old man."

Speaking as much to herself as to Virginia, Carolyn went on, "Who really lured us here?" She caught herself and smiled at Virginia. "How did you happen to choose the Tetons for our vacation? Why Wyoming?"

Virginia looked exasperated. "Sounds like the title of a bad country song!"

Carolyn raised her eyebrows. "Come on, answer the question."

Virginia sighed. "Let me think." She stood up and paced for a few minutes. "A flyer," she said finally. "I saw a flyer at the hospital. No, that's not right. Not at the hospital. I got it in the mail. Wait a minute!"

Virginia flew into the bedroom. Then Carolyn heard the closet door open and shut and the sound of the suitcase lock clicking. In less than two minutes Virginia emerged with the flyer in hand. "Found it!" she sang out. She sat down on the sofa and switched on the lamp. Then she began to read aloud.

She didn't get far before Carolyn interrupted. "I don't need to hear the sales pitch. Just look and see who sent it, please!"

"Right," Virginia grumbled and turned over the piece of paper. "There's no return address. Wait a sec, there is something here at the bottom. The print is really small." She drew the paper to within two inches of her nose.

"You ought to get your eyes checked," Carolyn suggested.

"Thanks for the free medical advice, Doctor," Virginia retorted. "It was free, wasn't it?" She waved the flyer. "Now do you want to hear this or not?"

Carolyn nodded. "Go ahead."

Virginia squinted at the small print. "There aren't too many words. Just Globe Travel and…". She put the flyer down and looked helplessly at Carolyn.

"And what?"

"Baltimore, Maryland. Carrie, I've heard of it because they've always advertised a lot in the area.

Carolyn shook her head. "Of course there may other explanations, but it seems likely that Henry had Globe Travel send this to you, knowing where Eric Johnson was. He may also have tipped off Johnson that we were coming."

Virginia sighed. "I'd rather not believe it, but you may be right. I guess we can ask Henry tomorrow and hope he gives us a straight answer."

Carolyn put an arm around her. "I'm sorry, sweetheart. Tonight seems to be my night for bringing you down."

Virginia smiled at her. "Well, you could make up for it, you know," she said.

Carolyn's face flushed. "Just what did you have in mind?"

Virginia laughed and lifted Carolyn's shirt. "Do you really have to ask?"

***

Henry was in high spirits when Carolyn and Virginia entered his room the next morning. He greeted them with a series of very bad jokes, eliciting groans from Carolyn but no reaction at all from Virginia.

"Why so grim, daughter of mine?" Henry asked her. "Sorry you won't be collecting your inheritance any time soon?"

Virginia grimaced. She started to pace.

"Stop that pacing!" Henry ordered, and Virginia sat down, glaring at him.

"Now what's going on?" he demanded. "You look like you swallowed a cockroach."

"Your bedside table is a lot cleaner, isn't it?" Virginia ventured.

Henry raised his eyebrows. "All the pacing and glaring because I didn't say thank you?"

Virginia's glare intensified. "You were asleep when I last came by, so I cleaned up. When I put some socks in your suitcase, I found a bundle of letters from Eric Johnson. He used to be the policeman..."

"I know who he is," Henry interjected peevishly. "I believe I've told you that he and I are in contact. We're old friends." He jutted out his chin belligerently. "So of course I have letters. So what?"

Virginia exhaled angrily. "He managed to find us in Wyoming when we were on vacation. Did you tell him we'd be there?"

Henry sniffed but didn't respond to her question.

"Carrie just asked me why I chose to vacation in Wyoming. There was a flyer that came in the mail." She narrowed her eyes. "From a travel agency in Baltimore."

Henry shrugged. "You used to live in Baltimore, remember?"

Virginia nodded. "Yes. That was over ten years ago."

Henry smiled grimly. "So now you have a conspiracy theory?"

Virginia felt a wave of fury wash over her. She didn't want to yell at Henry. She wanted to strangle him. But she just stared at the wall above his head. How deluded she was, she thought, to have expected a straight answer. Carolyn watched her for a few moments, then reached for her hand, murmuring, "It's okay, Sweetpea." But it wasn't okay and she knew it.

Virginia forced herself to make eye contact with her father. That was when she realized that Henry was enjoying himself. She struggled to keep her voice steady. "The coincidences are kind of overwhelming, wouldn't you agree?"

"Coincidences do occur," Henry said factually, "even to high-powered specialists from California."

Virginia registered the taunt but found she could ignore it. "Do you mind if I look at the letters?"

"I most certainly do mind," Henry retorted. "My correspondence is private and I intend to keep it that way."

"I'm not interested in invading your privacy," Virginia said. "I just wondered if the letters contained anything about the Runcibles."

Henry smirked. "Say what you mean, dear! You want to know if Eric told me he was sure that woman had murdered her husband. Well he did! Satisfied?"

"No," Virginia snapped. "Not by a long shot."

Henry yawned pointedly. "You've tired me out with your questions and accusations," he complained. "I don't want to talk anymore."

"We were about to leave, Henry," Carolyn interjected before Virginia had time to object. "Take it easy, but do your exercises. I'll check in again later this afternoon."

With that Carolyn pushed Virginia out the door and pulled her in the direction of the nurses' station. She gently pressed Virginia into one of the padded chairs in the tiny waiting area and seated herself in another.

"That was a total farce!" Virginia spat out the words.

Carolyn shrugged. "He's ill. It's not a good idea to pressure him."

Virginia picked at a hangnail. "Well, I have no more sympathy for him. I don't care if he loses his practice. There's no way whatsoever I could live in the same town with him, let alone take over as his medical proxy. He lured us here with lies, and I resent it!"

Carolyn's face was a study in dismay. "You weren't really thinking of moving here. Were you, Sweetpea?"

Virginia stopped picking and looked up. "Not thinking really. Just fantasizing. You know, Carrie. What if I came back and took over Henry's practice and you took a position at Hopkins? We could live in his house and keep an eye on him. But now…" She burst into tears.

As Carolyn made a concerted effort to overcome her shock, she reached out and rubbed Virginia's shoulder. "He didn't exactly lure us here with lies, though he may have tried. His illness is real enough. But moving here isn't the answer."

"I know that," Virginia sniffled, trying to let go of her sense of betrayal. "I just feel so foolish for trusting my father. It's awful. He used to be the only one I could trust."

Carolyn gave her shoulder a last squeeze. "I'm going to hunt down Leonora. Care to come along?"

"Might as well," Virginia grumbled, wiping her eyes on her sleeve. "There's nothing else to do here."

They found Leonora in the doctors' lounge. She seemed genuinely glad to see them. After telling them that she was satisfied that the new combination of medicines was working well, she turned to Virginia with a smile and quipped, "Did your father live on French fries and butter? His arteries are unbelievable."

Virginia expected to feel the now familiar flush that afflicted her whenever Leonora spoke to her, but it was missing. "No," she replied with a smile. "Onion rings and mayo. With a helping of sprouts to make it all good for him."

Leonora laughed and then became serious. "Do you think he could follow a healthy diet if the nutritionist came up with one for him? Or will he eat whatever he wants the way he does everything else he wants?"

"He could, but I'm not sure he would," Virginia observed ruefully.

Carolyn had noticed Leonora's resigned tone but chose to ignore it. "He'll do what he wants unless there is someone around who can persuade him to do what he ought to do. That leads right to the reason we wanted to talk with you. What arrangements do we need to make for Henry's further treatment before we go back home? Will you continue as his physician?"

Leonora nodded. "Of course, unless you can come up with someone he'd prefer."

Carolyn shrugged. "He is getting used to you. I've noticed a distinct lessening of hostility."

Leonora rolled her eyes. "Right. He hasn't sworn or thrown anything at me in twelve hours. I guess that is an improvement."

"We have confidence in you," Virginia chimed in.

"Thanks." Leonora winked at her. "I wish confidence were contagious."

Carolyn cleared her throat. "Does he need to be moved to Baltimore?" she asked, wondering why Virginia was suddenly so comfortable with Leonora when she had been so awkward before.

"I don't think he'll need hospitalization after this week, but I am worried about follow-up treatment. He absolutely must not drive unless his coordination improves and the tremors decrease radically. How he can get to his appointments is the issue. My regular practice is at Hopkins, and I don't make house calls."

"I take it you don't want to see him here," Carolyn observed, hoping Virginia would say something helpful. Virginia's face, however, was blank as she scratched at her ankle.

Leonora shook her head. "He'll need ongoing tests and physical therapy. Both are more easily available there. This hospital, well, it's not terrible, but I wouldn't call it first class."

Carolyn sighed. "So I guess we'd better find someone to drive him to Baltimore."

"It's more complicated than that!" Virginia suddenly exclaimed, ready to be part of the conversation again. "He'll have to be convinced that he needs to go to Hopkins. Knowing my father, I'm willing to bet that he'll decide to treat himself once he's well enough to function on his own."

Leonora looked so shocked by that idea that Carolyn felt she had to say something. "Henry is stubborn, but he's not stupid. He's a physician and has a good idea what Parkinson's Disease is like."

Virginia chuckled mirthlessly. "I never said he'd stop treatment, Carrie. He'll just try to take things into his own hands, the way he always does."

"Well, he can't be hospitalized forever," Leonora said firmly, "and he's used to Grant's Hill. I'm not sure he can continue to live alone without some kind of assistance, but moving him to Baltimore would be harder on him than finding him an aide here."

Carolyn nodded. "You're right. He'll need a caretaker, someone with a car and valid driver's license."

"You might as well add a black belt in martial arts," Virginia added, "so he can load Henry into the car when it's time to drive him to the city."

Carolyn shook her head in astonishment. "He? Do you think Henry would put up with another man in his house?"

"Come on, Carrie! You don't seriously believe that any woman would be able to handle him, do you?"

Leonora stood up. "I hate to interrupt, but I need to get on the road. I have patients to see in Baltimore." She ushered them out of the doctors' lounge. "I'm sure that you'll find someone to look after him. I trust your judgment. Let me know what you decide," she concluded with a smile and headed down the hallway.

Virginia and Carolyn took their discussion to the hospital cafeteria. "I don't know, sweetheart," Carolyn said, stirring her muddy coffee with a plastic stirrer. "Henry might do better with a helper he liked. That way trips to the city would be more like excursions than just visits to the doctor. He needs more than a chauffeur."

Virginia sighed. "This coffee really isn't drinkable," she complained, taking another sip and making a face. "I agree. He needs someone he'd listen to voluntarily. But no such person exists, except maybe you."

Carolyn grunted. "We're not moving to Grant's Hill to look after your father."

"I didn't say we were," Virginia protested.

"How about that woman who runs his office? She's pretty bossy, but he must like her if he keeps her around. What was her name again?"

"Toni?" Virginia ventured. "Toni doesn't drive anymore. For God's sake, Carolyn, the woman is almost eighty. And Henry doesn't listen to her. She adores him and spoils him."

Carolyn raised her eyebrows. "She doesn't seem like that sort."

"Well, she is when it comes to Henry." Virginia shook her head. "I was only kidding about hiring someone with a black belt. Even though I'm still angry at Henry, the idea of someone pushing him around is unsettling."

Carolyn nodded her agreement. "Maybe we need two people, someone to help in the house and someone to entertain him and drive him to Baltimore." She stood up. "Think about it while I go look in on him again."

"Do you really need to do that?" Virginia grumbled.

"I promised. Though he's starting to trust Leonora's judgment, he still feels more secure if I check up on him." She laughed. "I don't think he's forgiven her yet for being straight. Thou shalt have no other men before me, saith Henry."

Virginia laughed appreciatively as Carolyn leaned over to kiss her cheek. "I'll be back in half an hour. Forty-five minutes if he has another joke attack."

Virginia watched Carolyn's retreating back until it was no longer visible. Then she went up to the cashier and bought herself a candy bar. Perhaps chocolate would help her come up with someone to drive Henry to Baltimore. She wasn't sure about needing two people. Maybe Henry would be able to look after himself at home for now. As for later, who knew what would happen?

She picked at a corner of the wrapper, aiming to peel it off in one piece. She didn't want to think about Henry's long-term prognosis. Taking a bite of her chocolate she thought instead about how her nervous feelings around Leonora had evaporated, along with the attraction she'd felt. She smiled as she remembered Leonora's reply to her announcement that they had confidence in her. Yes, she liked Leonora and the woman inspired confidence, but no more so than Carrie. Who'd have expected Henry's illness to be hard on her relationship when her father doted on Carolyn and she was devoted to his care?

"It isn't over yet," she heard a voice say so clearly that she looked around to see who was speaking. Then she realized the voice was in her head. Yes, there was still Leticia to deal with. The approaching visit with Leticia and her mother loomed large, though she wasn't particularly worried about meeting Lucille. Carrie had coped and so could she. Leticia, however, was another matter. They still couldn't talk without fighting, and she wasn't sure they ever would. On top of that, she still suspected Leticia of manslaughter if not first degree homicide. Carrie didn't seem to think it likely, but then Carrie had never known Leticia at her arrogant, selfish worst.

Virginia sighed and rolled her shoulders to release the tension. At least she wasn't going to face the Barneses alone. With that happy thought in mind, she got up to buy another candy bar.

Chapter 36
Dressing for Dinner
1980
❖

"Have you given any further thought to finding someone to drive Henry to Baltimore for his follow-up treatments?" Virginia called through the open bedroom door. When she got no response, she walked into the living room where Carolyn had her nose buried in a book. "For heaven's sake, Carrie, we have to leave for Leticia's in fifteen minutes, and you haven't even started getting dressed."

Carolyn placed the thick volume on the table and followed Virginia into the bedroom. "I don't know," she said.

"You don't know what?" Virginia asked, critically eyeing two shirts hung on the back of the closet door.

"I don't know who could drive Henry to Baltimore. He probably won't even want to go. Knowing him, he'll manage his own treatment as soon as he's back on his feet."

"We can't let him do that," Virginia mumbled, trying on a bright blue shirt and then rejecting it.

"We really can't stop him if he has a mind to do it," Carolyn replied, then added, "I like that shirt. Don't toss it on the bed like an old rag! Why are you dressing up just to go over to the Barnes' place? It's not a formal dinner party. I had coffee with Leticia and her mother, and I was wearing my ordinary clothing."

"It's rude not to dress up a little when you're invited to dinner at someone's home, Carrie," Virginia replied a little primly. "And the blue shirt doesn't go with my brown pants."

"So wear your black pants."

"I already wore them," Virginia said irritably.

"You already wore the brown ones too."

"Yes, but not to visit Leticia."

Carolyn took a deep breath and counted to ten silently. She knew Virginia was nervous. "Look, sweetheart, we can cancel if going to Leticia's is going to make you uptight."

"Don't be ridiculous! We have to go," Virginia insisted. "And you have to get dressed."

"I am dressed."

"No, you're not."

Carolyn pulled off her shirt and chinos. "Okay, am I dressed now?" she demanded.

"Carolyn Matthews, you are impossible!" Virginia scolded. "You can't go in your underwear."

"Well, I'm certainly not going without my underwear."

"Damn!" Virginia swore loudly. "The button on these pants fell off."

"So wear the black ones. Or the navy. They both look great on you."

Virginia scowled at Carolyn and threw the brown pants onto the bed with the rejected shirt. Carolyn walked over and picked up the shirt. "Look," she said, reaching into the closet and pulling out a pair of navy pants, "a perfect match."

Virginia smiled apologetically. "Sorry I'm being such a pain, Carrie. I'm just nervous."

"I knew that," Carolyn replied quickly, smiling back at her lover. "Now that I've picked your clothes for the evening, it's your turn to pick mine."

Virginia looked delighted. "Great!" She dug around in the closet for a few moments until she triumphantly extracted exactly what she was looking for. "Maybe I can't wear my brown pants, but you can wear yours. They'll look terrific with this burnt orange shirt. Remember how I found that at the street fair in January while you were at the convention listening to a talk on neurotransmitters?"

Carolyn made a long face. "But we won't match," she protested, accepting the clothes from Virginia. "I wanted us to pass for twins."

Virginia laughed. "Your shirt will match my eyes."

Carolyn shrugged. "And my pants will match your hair. Too bad I don't have navy hair and blue eyes."

Virginia snorted. "You are too silly for words, Carolyn Matthews."

"Of course I am. That's why you love me."

Virginia smirked and ordered Carolyn to hurry, but she had to admit to herself that Carrie was at least partially right. As long as Carolyn was acting like a mad child, Virginia felt that nothing too terrible could happen. That was reassuring.

She looked over at Carolyn, who was slowly selecting accessories. Carolyn caught her eye. "How about purple earrings?" she asked.

Virginia giggled. "Don't forget the bright mauve nose ring to go with them." She pulled a tube of concealer out of her bag and applied it to a blemish on her chin. "How long," she mumbled, "am I going to keep breaking out like an adolescent?"

Her murmur attracted Carolyn's attention. "What are you…" Carolyn began. When she recognized the make-up stick, she reached out her long arm and grabbed it. "My turn," she said, applying a layer of the waxy stuff to a scratch on her cheek.

"Hey!" Virginia yelled, grabbing the concealer back out of Carolyn's hand. "Is that an open cut? You don't want those chemicals in your bloodstream, do you?" She capped the tube and returned it to her bag. Carolyn rolled her eyes. "It's closed over. Anyway, it's not as if someone slashed me with a razor, sweetheart," she complained. "Don't make a fuss."

Virginia smiled condescendingly and patted the bag that hung from her shoulder. "I'll see you in the car if you ever finish your toilette," she said in a fond voice and left the bedroom. She was glad that they were teasing each other. Despite her nervousness about the impending visit to Leticia, she felt as if Carolyn and she had regained their closeness. She'd noticed yesterday when, for once, talking with Leonora hadn't reduced her to a blushing, stammering fool. When things were going well between Carolyn and herself, everything else slipped into place. As she passed through the living room, Virginia's eye fell on the thick tome that Carolyn had been reading. It lay open on the sofa, its spine nearly broken. She picked it up and looked at the title, *Forensic Toxicology*. With a sigh she strolled to the phone and pulled a sheet of paper off the message pad. She inserted it into the book as bookmark and returned the heavy volume to the sofa. Then she went out to the car, where Carolyn soon joined her.

"You're a little pale, honey," Carolyn said. "Let me drive."

Virginia handed over the keys and moved to the passenger's seat. "I noticed your latest reading material on the way out," she said, once she was settled. "Not exactly light vacation reading."

Carolyn started the car. After a moment's silence, she said so softly that Virginia could barely make out the words, "I borrowed it from the hospital."

"You're not reading up on neurotoxins either, are you?" Virginia said in what she hoped was a light tone.

Carolyn wasn't deceived for a second. "No," she said quietly, "I'm not."

Virginia sat in silence until they came to the first traffic signal. Then she twisted slightly in her seat to face Carolyn. "Have you found out anything?" she asked earnestly.

"Just a few confirmations of my suspicions," Carolyn replied, her foot descending on the gas pedal just as the light changed. "There are an amazing number of substances that can stop a human circulatory system, aren't there? Mostly we think of chemicals under the sink or tainted foods when we hear the word 'poison.' Any toxin that goes through the stomach takes its toll by burning and bleeding. But then there are those agents that enter the skin or the bloodstream. They're different in their effects."

Virginia was listening, but at the same time she was admiring her partner's style. Carolyn could make anything understandable, and she never sounded pompous. "It all fits with what I was saying yesterday," Carolyn continued. "No small-town M.E. in Wyoming could have the resources needed to trace all the possibilities. No other suspicious deaths occurred, so the M.E. had no other data points, no way to see a pattern, nothing else to go on." She reached over to rub Virginia's knee. Virginia recoiled and let out a scream, "Don't!"

Carolyn withdrew her hand. Even making allowances for stress, she felt Virginia was way out of line. She was about to say something when she noticed that Virginia was rolling up her pants leg.

"I knew it," Virginia announced bitterly. "I knew it, but I was hoping I was wrong. Shit! Shit! Shit! I have poison ivy."

Carolyn held her peace.

CHAPTER 37
DINNER AT LETICIA'S
1980
❖

Virginia shook hands with Leticia, who held her hand just a second longer than was necessary and flashed her conspiratorial smile. She could only imagine that after a few days with her mother Leticia would have greeted Count Dracula warmly. Carolyn looked pleased rather than perturbed by the warm greeting, so Virginia let out the breath she was holding and followed Leticia into the house, trying very hard not to scratch the new blisters that had formed on the back of her thigh.

Lucille sat in the living room. She wore a bright coral jumpsuit and had dyed her hair to match it. Virginia could only stare in consternation. She looked over at Leticia, whose face mirrored her own shock. Since Carolyn was unshockable, she did the honors. "Mrs. Barnes, I'd like to introduce my partner, Virginia Carr. Virginia, please meet Leticia's mother, Lucille Barnes."

Virginia stepped forward, uncertain as to protocol. Should she extend her hand or curtsy to the majestic, but unlikely looking figure before her. Lucille rose and offered Virginia a shark-like smile and a few words of greeting in condescending tones. Assuming the role of hostess, Lucille then walked purposefully though unsteadily to the sideboard and poured herself a tall glass of scotch. She added two ice cubes and a few drops of water. "Ladies, may I serve you or would you rather help yourselves?" she boomed. "If you wait for my daughter, all you'll get to drink is warm milk, carrot juice, or a cup of abominable herb tea." Virginia took a glass of white wine, and Carolyn joined Mrs. Barnes with a much smaller quantity of scotch and a lot more water.

"Don't water your drink down, Doctor," Lucille reprimanded her. "You want to feel it as well as taste it."

Leticia raised an eyebrow, but kept her thoughts to herself. She turned toward the kitchen. As she walked off, Virginia followed her, relieved to have a chance to speak to her alone. "Fred," she blurted out, "I've got a bad case of poison ivy, and it itches like hell. Carolyn can drive me to the drugstore unless you have something on hand." Virginia had spoken all the words in one breath. She hoped they didn't sound as stupid to Leticia as they did to her.

Leticia nodded. "Soaking in a baking soda bath helps sometimes. I have tea tree oil and calomel too, though I don't think they'll do much good." She eyed Virginia speculatively. "If those don't work, I know something else that works for itching. It's a disgusting mixture of red clay and crushed beetles. They use it in the Amazon."

Virginia made a face. "I don't have to eat it, do I?"

Leticia chuckled. "No, it's a salve."

"And you just happen to have the ingredients in your medicine cabinet."

The speculative look returned to Leticia's face. "You'd be surprised at the ingredients I have."

I just bet I would, Virginia thought, but she refrained from comment.

Leticia turned down the dials on the oven and stove top and reached into an upper cabinet to extract something. Virginia wondered what it was, but before she could ask, Leticia said, "Follow me!"

As they climbed the stairs, Virginia could hear Lucille's strident voice rising and falling with the rhythm of her intermittent gulps of scotch. Carolyn's responses were monosyllabic, but the older woman didn't seem to notice. Pausing briefly at a linen closet, Leticia grabbed a towel. She pushed open the bathroom door and had actually begun to fill the tub before Virginia had a chance to express her misgivings. "I don't really think I can take a bath now."

Leticia made her face a question mark, challenging Virginia to explain herself.

"It's kind of you to offer," Virginia began hesitantly, "but I should probably try tea tree oil or calomel first." Her voice trailed off, as she looked around the room so as not to have to make eye contact with Leticia. The bathroom would have showed signs of Lucille's dye job if it were the guest bathroom so she assumed it was the one Leticia regularly used. It was spartan, almost to the point of being bare. One bottle of shampoo and one bar of soap were all her eye could see. Not a sign of cosmetics, lotions or perfume. The bathroom could have belonged to a nun.

She gazed over at Leticia who was biting her lip. "You asked for relief. It's either the bath or the crushed beetles," she said firmly. "You've obviously been scratching, so the blisters have spread. You need to treat the affected area." She put her hands on her hips. "Christ!" she barked, sounding like the Leticia Virginia had known and loved, "why do I have to tell you this? You're the damned doctor!"

Virginia smiled at her. "Remember the time we went skinny dipping in the pond? It was after midnight, and the park was empty. Every time you heard a noise, you nearly jumped out of your skin."

Leticia smirked for a second, then composed her face. When she spoke again, it was with authority. "Get into the tub, Virginia. I'll call you when we're five minutes from eating. Don't make me waste the water."

Since when was Fred concerned about wasting water? Virginia shrugged. "Okay," she said huskily. She placed her wine glass on the sink and seated herself on the edge of the tub to remove her sandals. "How have you been holding up, Fred?" she asked casually, squinting up at Leticia.

"I was managing pretty well until the new hair color," Leticia replied wryly. "It's almost as orange as your eye color."

Virginia kicked off one sandal. "I don't get my eye color out of a bottle."

Leticia smiled a bit sadly. "I wish the hair dye were all she got out of a bottle. But at least she's still able to stand, and she isn't combining her daily quota of booze with pills the way she used to."

"Glad to hear it," Virginia said, kicking off the other sandal. "I didn't bring a stomach pump with me."

Virginia changed the subject smoothly. "I noticed that you're not drinking."

Leticia shrugged. "I drink, but not when I'm cooking. Alcohol dulls the palate, and I like to be able to taste what I'm preparing."

Suddenly Virginia realized that she and Carolyn would be eating food prepared by someone who might be a poisoner. She paled visibly.

Leticia grinned. "Don't worry," she teased. "My cooking hasn't killed anyone yet."

"That's good to know," Virginia mumbled, still looking worried.

"I'm actually an excellent cook," Leticia went on. "I learned a great deal about spices in Turkey." Her face got a bit dreamy. "I knew some wonderful women in Turkey."

When she looked up at Virginia's face and saw the slightly frightened expression, her face lost its dreamy look. "You're thinking about Johnson's stupid accusation, aren't you?" she said.

Virginia shrugged. "I can't help it. How often does a healthy military officer drop dead of heart failure for no reason? It's not that I don't believe you, just..."

"That you don't believe me," Leticia retorted. "But I'm not asking you to believe me. I'm asking you to believe the medical examiner who did the postmortem work-up on Paul's body." She sighed. "You've been investigating, right? You've looked at all his medical records, and talked to all the people in his military unit or in the command staff who might have had professional or personal reasons to harm him, and you found no one to suspect but me?"

Virginia didn't reply. Carolyn was the one who'd done their little bit of investigating, and she knew it didn't include interviews with any of the man's military colleagues. She resented being put on the spot, so she coolly lied, "Right." She unzipped her pants and stepped out of them.

Leticia looked at Virginia for what felt like a long time without saying a word, but Virginia didn't flinch. Stripping off the rest of her clothes, she made eye contact with Leticia and stepped into the tub. "I still think this is a bad idea," she said loudly over the sound of the running water.

"It's the bath or the beetles," Leticia said, not cracking a smile. "I think you've made your choice."

Virginia didn't reply, and after a few seconds, Leticia said softly, "I had no reason to kill Paul. All things considered, our marriage was a happy one."

Virginia turned off the water. "What does that mean?"

"We loved each other," Leticia said firmly.

"I was asking about 'all things considered'." The blisters stung as the water washed over them, but Virginia realized that after the stinging eased, they felt somewhat less itchy.

"We didn't really know each other when we married. I had a fantasy of Paul as the perfect, gallant knight. He wanted access to my family's money and found my outspokenness and tomboy behavior endearing." She made a face. "At least initially anyway. But we adjusted to each other. I think the only real fight we had was about my clothing when we were stationed in Turkey. Paul insisted that I give up my Turkish skirts and shawls." She smiled. "I never did though. I just made sure I was never seen by anyone in the military, including my husband."

"You loved it there, didn't you?"

Leticia nodded. "I felt part of something despite my foreignness. It was only in Turkey that I realized how lonely I'd been my whole life."

"Even with me?" was what Virginia was tempted to ask, but she realized she didn't want an answer to that question. "Even with Paul?" she asked instead.

Leticia nodded. "Oh yes, especially with Paul. Maybe if our sex life had been better, I'd have felt truly connected." She giggled nervously.

Virginia was so startled that she sloshed water onto the floor. "Was he a lousy lover?" she asked clumsily, "or did you just not like sex with him?"

Leticia shook her head. "From what I've heard he was quite good. I was the problem. After our honeymoon I withdrew. Sex is not what it's cracked up to be, I think."

Virginia's eyes opened wide. "How can you say that? You were so passionate when we were together."

"Oh, that wasn't sex," Leticia replied airily. "Not the real thing. What we did was...well, it was different." She blushed. "I liked that."

Virginia nodded. "That's because you're a lesbian, you idiot!" she said forcefully. "Of all the stupid ideas, marrying that man was one of the stupidest."

"Shut up, Virginia Carr!" Leticia said sharply, her eyes blazing. "I am not a lesbian. I don't want to be one, and I'm not one. I loved my husband and..."

"Right!" Virginia yelled, standing up in the tub in her fury. You loved him and hated having sex with him. So what happened? Did he force you to have sex? Is that why you killed him?"

"What a presumptuous bitch you are!" Leticia said, struggling to keep her tone conversational. "You know nothing at all and think you know everything." She took a breath. "If you must know, Paul was wonderful, a much better, more understanding person than you'll ever be. As soon as he realized that I did not enjoy sex with him, he stopped trying to initiate it. I appreciated his kindness and told him that I wouldn't mind if he slept with other women as long as he was discreet." She handed Virginia a towel. "Dry yourself very gently so as not to irritate the blisters."

Virginia shook her head as she stepped out of the tub. "I don't understand you at all, Fred, but I guess I never did. Why the hell didn't you leave him?"

"I needed him. I needed a way to be a grown woman, out from under my mother's thumb. She'd been so passive when my father was alive, but once he was gone she turned into a tyrant. She was determined to

235

see me married. I think she was afraid I'd decide to stay with you after all. If I was going to marry someone it might as well have been Paul. I knew from the start that he was a good man, and I was right."

Virginia finished drying herself and started to put her clothing back on. "You were right, Fred."

Leticia looked startled. "Right? About what?"

Virginia smiled. "The bath. It helped."

Leticia sighed, suddenly very tired. "I'm going to see to the food. I'll leave you the calomel and tea tree oil. You can try them and see which feels better."

"How about the crushed beetles?"

Leticia shook her head. "There aren't any crushed beetles," she said, putting two small vials on the edge of the washstand. "I made that up." She turned to leave.

"Wait!" Virginia called out. "I need to know if your husband knew about you. About you and me, I mean."

Leticia stopped in her tracks. "He suspected that there had been someone, and I think he sensed it was a woman. He didn't say anything. He didn't mind. Many men would have, but he really didn't. Who knows? Perhaps he would have if it had been a man."

Virginia looked down. She doubted that Paul Runcible would have minded even if Leticia had had a relationship with Bigfoot. So long as he could keep his hands in the till he'd have been content. When she looked up, she saw Leticia staring at her. "Was there something else?"

Virginia nodded. "Did you, uh, find someone?"

Leticia smiled thinly. "Of course not. I told you I didn't want to be a lesbian. Besides, if it had come out, Paul's career would have suffered."

Virginia felt like crying. "Do you at least have friends?" she asked in a shaky voice.

"Don't you feel sorry for me, Virginia Carr!" Leticia snapped. "I thoroughly enjoyed being married to Paul. We traveled the world. I got to see places I'd never even dreamed of. He was stationed in Asia, the Middle East, even Africa for a few months. I learned so much, about plants, about food, about life in the rest of the world. Most people don't get to do that. I picked up stories, recipes, and herbal lore in every place we lived.

"When he was posted to Laramie, he told me he'd understand if I didn't want to live in Wyoming. I wanted to preserve our marriage and couldn't imagine doing that if we lived apart. Besides it would have looked bad. We had wonderful dinner parties for the air force brass. I catered them myself. Paul was impressed. He said I could have been a gourmet chef."

Virginia sighed. She was sure Leticia hadn't killed her husband, but that was all she was sure of. Leticia just didn't make sense to her. As she started dressing, the blisters began to itch again. She looked up to tell Leticia that the cure hadn't worked after all, but Leticia had already left. Virginia ran her fingers through her hair. She wanted to talk to Carolyn alone, but she knew that wasn't going to happen unless Carolyn came up to look for her. She stopped buttoning her shirt and listened for Carolyn's footsteps, but the only thing she heard was the sound of her own breathing. So she sighed once more and finished dressing. The room felt close and her head ached. She was hungry and there was nothing to do but go back downstairs and hope she could get through the meal without scratching herself bloody.

It wasn't until she was halfway to the stairs that she remembered the woman who'd gone with Leticia to the medical examiner. She wished she'd asked about her. Maybe she'd had something to do with Runcible's death. Rubbing her neck she descended the stairs and entered the living room, where she found Lucille Barnes glaring furiously at her daughter.

***

Lucille Barnes squinted as she glanced over at Carolyn, who gave no sign of distress at all. In fact, Carolyn smiled fondly as Virginia entered the room. Lucille wondered how Carolyn could be so casual when the sound of running water in the tub and two voices coming from the bathroom had made it clear that Leticia and Virginia were friendly again. Entirely too friendly in Lucille's opinion, and she expected Carolyn to feel the same way.

Virginia glanced at Carolyn's empty glass, and smiled as Carolyn raised one finger and looked significantly at Lucille's glass, which was full again. Leticia, who was the only one capable of interpreting her mother's offended silence correctly, knew she had to bite the bullet. "Mother, you look upset," she began, "I'm sorry we took so long."

"Upset?" Lucille parroted her daughter. "Why should I be upset when you take off for an hour with a lesbian?" She pronounced the last word very distinctly. "Not that I have anything against lesbians," she added, smiling thinly at Carolyn. "But she is another woman's lover after all."

Leticia glanced quickly at Virginia, who was struggling to keep a straight face, then at Carolyn, whose lips were twitching. Leticia wasn't sure why they found her mother's comments so funny. But then she found herself struggling not to laugh. Really, using the word lesbian to scare her was ridiculous. She didn't stop to wonder why it had succeeded so well for so long. "I don't think," she said softly, biting back a giggle, "that Dr. Matthews is afraid of my stealing Dr. Carr away, so you needn't worry."

"Of course, I worry, my dear," Lucille slurred, losing the battle with her drink. "There are appearances to keep up, you know."

Leticia shrugged and turned back to Carolyn. "May I freshen your drink, Dr. Matthews?" Carolyn shook her head.

"Come on, Dr. Matthews," Lucille urged, before Carolyn could verbally decline. "You won't be so unkind as to make me drink alone, will you?"

But Carolyn refused to be bullied. "You're not drinking alone, Mrs. Barnes. Dr. Carr and Mrs. Runcible have full glasses. I don't want another drink just now." Carolyn spoke very firmly, but before Lucille had a chance to sulk, she added, "I do want to hear more about those notebooks you've been describing."

Lucille hesitated for a moment. She had enjoyed talking about Lettie's notebooks to Carolyn. She felt important answering questions. She delighted in describing plant toxins with especially gruesome effects. However, Lucille was adamant about getting her way. She'd been pushed around by Cal for too long and had no intention of ever letting anyone get the better of her again. Give in once, and people think you're a pushover! If there was one thing Lucille Barnes was not about to be, it was a pushover. So she put aside her pleasure in feeling important. "Not another detail unless you have a drink with me. A real drink, not one of those juices or teas Lettie likes to concoct," she insisted, looking at Carolyn out of half-closed eyes.

"Dinner!" Leticia announced more forcefully than was strictly necessary. "It'll be ready as soon as I get the bread out of the oven."

Virginia glanced at Leticia, whose face was flushed. Her expression was worried, and Virginia wondered if the worry were only about the impression her mother was making. She followed Leticia into the kitchen, hoping to be able to pose a question while helping to serve.

"Get out of here, Virginia! You're in the way." Leticia winked to show that she wasn't angry, but she insisted that Virginia leave. "I can't stand people in my way when I'm trying to get a meal on the table."

"I want to help," Virginia insisted, but Leticia shooed her out. "I don't need you. Go give Carolyn a break from my mother."

Virginia had no choice but to comply. She encountered silence in the living room, so offered to pour wine for Lucille Barnes.

Lucille turned on her drunken smile. "I don't mind, Dr. Carr," she chirped.

***

Carolyn caught Virginia's eye and smiled weakly. Though her gaze never left Carolyn's face, Virginia could still see Lucille out of the corner of her eye as she reached for the wine bottle. She was astonished at how much and how quickly the woman drank. She could tell from Carolyn's rising eyebrows that she too was aware of Lucille's state.

"Do you think she…?" Virginia began.

Carolyn nodded slightly.

"Huh?" Lucille interjected. "Are you talking about me?"

Neither Carolyn nor Virginia met her eyes. "No, Mrs. Barnes," Carolyn said smoothly, "why would we do that?"

"Well, then, what were you talking about?"

"Our diagnostic techniques," Virginia replied.

Lucille grunted and reached for the wine bottle. "Doctors!" she grumbled, as she poured a third glass. "Talk shop all the time. What a bore!"

Before either had a chance to reply, Leticia summoned them to the table, where she set a tureen of steaming soup. Lucille followed the pair of them on surprisingly steady legs. She regarded the table with its woven placemats and dark, hand-thrown dishes disdainfully. She was convinced that Leticia had deliberately hidden the family's delicate china and antique lace tablecloths and napkins just to spite her. "It's summer, Lettie," she complained. "No one serves hot soup in the summer."

Leticia merely smiled at her mother and began to ladle the spicy soup into bowls for her guests. And then, except for the sound of spoons against pottery, there was silence.

***

Carolyn trotted into the kitchen after Leticia. She had offered to carry the empty soup bowls, and Virginia was a little offended that Leticia

239

had agreed. "I thought she couldn't stand people in her kitchen," she muttered. Lucille Barnes was staring at her. When they made eye contact, Lucille smiled grimly.

"Ah, I begin to understand. Dr. Matthews is not the jealous one; you are." Virginia rolled her eyes and hoped that Carrie and Fred wouldn't stay in the kitchen for too long. Otherwise it would be their fault if she strangled Mrs. Barnes.

In the kitchen, Carolyn's eyes were drawn to the largest spice rack she'd ever seen. The array of bottles of powdered spices and chopped herbs brought to mind an alchemist's workshop. When she looked up, she saw a wooden frame on a pair of ropes about a foot below the ceiling. Large bunches of herbs and dried flowers hung from the frame, almost obscuring it from view.

"How much of this stuff dates from Mrs. Mendoza Velasquez' time with your family?" Carolyn inquired, keeping her tone casual.

"Just about everything you see here is more recent, though we made the drying rack and hung it ourselves."

Carolyn smiled. "Virginia talks about her a lot. Of course, she was very fond of Mrs. Mendoza Velasquez, but I sense she was a little intimidated too."

Leticia nodded. "Oh, Ana was intimidating all right. She had an uncanny ability to read people, so she usually got them to do things her way. She could be charming and very persuasive. I hadn't the slightest interest in her herbs and tinctures when we first met, but she managed to draw me in." She laughed. "I wanted to spend time with her, but it was more than that. She claimed I'd do a great service to the world by learning what she had to teach." Leticia looked sideways at Carolyn. "At that time Virginia was very set on being of service to the world, and I wanted to impress her. So I started taking notes and trying to become a better observer."

Leticia ran her hand over her eyes for a second. "I thought I would become a healer, but actually I work with Cyrus Marshall, the ethnobotanist at Hopkins. We're putting together a catalogue of all I learned from Ana, with a volume dedicated to all the herbal lore I added to my notebooks on my travels. I've been trying to persuade him to include information on the dried herb collection from around here. I have a large assortment of local herbs that I've dried."

"So the stuff you have in here is all local?" Carolyn queried, but then didn't wait for a reply. "Of course. You can't find South American plants in Delaware. Silly question!"

It was Leticia's turn to smile. "Cyrus has students who spend years gathering plants all over the globe. They work in just about every country south of the border. And as for me, well, you'd be surprised how many potent herbs even laypeople can order from catalogues. Lately Chinese herbs are all the fashion." Leticia's smile faded. "Of course, your medical colleagues are appalled and horrified and all that." She looked up at Carolyn to gauge her reaction, but Carolyn's poker face didn't give her away. "I have an extensive collection, a mix of local and imported herbs," Leticia concluded.

"Did Mrs. Mendoza Velasquez give you any samples?" Carolyn asked.

Leticia gazed at her quizzically as she transferred vegetables and grilled meat onto serving dishes. "Yes, she did. They don't look much different from these, but I can show you both my notebooks and the samples, if you're interested."

"I'm interested," Carolyn replied quickly. "Very much so."

"Uh huh," Leticia murmured to herself. She handed Carolyn plates and a tray of food. "Let's eat first," she said decisively, placing an assortment of sauces and condiments on another tray and raising it from the counter. "I can show you after dinner."

CHAPTER 38
OTHER PEOPLE'S DREAMS
1980
❖

"You weren't exaggerating about your cooking at all!" Virginia announced with genuine admiration. "That's the best meal I've had since we left the Bay Area."

Carolyn added her appreciative and grateful comments, but Leticia was only listening with half an ear. Her attention was riveted on her mother, who swayed in her chair and seemed about to fall onto her empty wine glass at any second.

"Excuse me." Leticia rose from her seat. As she approached Lucille, she said gently, "Let's go upstairs, Mother."

Lucille raised her eyes and took in her daughter's face, then closed them again. Her head began to sink, and Leticia reached out and touched her shoulder.

Lucille's body shrank from her touch and she swore, "Get your fuckin' hands off me!" Her head snapped up and she glared furiously at Leticia. "I'll go upstairs whenever the hell I'm ready."

Leticia stepped back and struggled to preserve her composure. "You seem to be having difficulty staying awake," she said in the same gentle tone she'd just used.

"You're boring, that's why," Lucille complained. "You always have been about as exciting as a wet noodle, Lettie."

Leticia didn't reply to her mother's taunt. Instead she turned to Carolyn. "I'll go get the notebooks now."

As soon as she had gone, Carolyn jumped up and began to stack the dishes. Lucille hissed through her teeth and picked at the tablecloth. "Children!" she said loudly. "I wonder sometimes why I bothered to have Leticia."

Carolyn stopped what she was doing momentarily and made eye contact with Virginia, whose expression was a combination of fascination and repulsion. Carolyn started stacking dishes again.

"You wouldn't guess, would you, that Leticia is everything in the world to me," Lucille sighed. "I love my daughter and try to do my best for her, but she was always closer to Cal, daddy's girl. Of course, daddy's girl was a real tomboy. She wanted to be just like him, or maybe to give him the son he never had. Not that he ever complained about that. Far from it. He doted on his little girl and wouldn't see any of the signs that there was something very wrong with her."

"Wrong with her?" Virginia repeated the words, sounding bewildered.

"Yes, wrong with her! Lucille said adamantly. "I'm not talking about her little fling with you, Dr. Carr. Many adolescents are unsettled in their sexuality. But she obviously couldn't satisfy her husband."

Carolyn's eyebrows rose and she looked over at Virginia, who tried to indicate without words that she knew what Lucille was talking about. Carolyn shrugged and turned her attention back to Lucille's monologue.

"I've given up trying to understand why Lettie insists on living like a nun. She is still young, reasonably attractive when she dresses well and puts on make-up, which is once in a blue moon, and has money. She's certainly nothing like me. Once Cal kicked the bucket I found myself much sought after, let me tell you. And the men I had were certainly eager and willing to do more than make money. I satisfied them and they gave me what I wanted. And believe me, it wasn't just jewelry." She laughed, but the sound was more like a convulsive coughing fit.

Lucille quickly recovered. "Paul was awfully attractive and seemed gallant enough. I wouldn't have expected him to run around on Lettie. A woman shouldn't put up with that. I wouldn't. Men are many things, annoying and even odious, but there's a line, I tell you."

Carolyn and Virginia made eye contact, and Virginia mouthed, "Tell you later."

"A woman should never, never stay with a man who cheats on her. It's humiliating," Lucille mumbled. "I tried to talk with Lettie about it, but she just put me off, said I didn't understand. Oh, but I understood all too well. Someone had to do something, but she wasn't about to. Not Leticia Daddy's Girl Barnes Runcible. 'Mind your own business, mother!' Can you believe it? What a thing to say to me when I had her best interests at heart. If she'd listened to me and divorced him, her life would be different now. But she was happy, she told me. Happy! With a cheating rat of a husband! 'He's my best friend, Mother'. What a stupid thing to say! Someone needed to put a stop to it. Someone had to…" Lucille's head fell forward and she began to snore.

"Oh God." Virginia looked over at Carolyn, who seemed distracted. "Carrie, what are you thinking?" Virginia's voice had an urgency to it.

"I suspect we've been ignoring the obvious." Carolyn pointed her chin in the general direction of Lucille. "We'd better see if we can carry her over to the sofa."

They lifted Lucille quite easily and carried her to the sofa, where Carolyn covered her with the Navajo blanket that lay on a bench by the fireplace. Virginia backed away, eager to put distance between herself and the alcoholic fumes emanating from Lucille.

"I can't believe Leticia didn't tell her mother about the agreement she had with her husband," Virginia mused.

"What agreement?"

Virginia spoke slowly. "She didn't like sex with him and he was nice about it. So she told him to take up with other women. Discretion was their byword. I don't even know how her mother found out. Adultery is against the military code of justice. He could have gotten in trouble."

Carolyn snorted. "Right, and no one in the military cheats on his spouse of course."

"I didn't say that, but he was ambitious."

After Carolyn had draped the blanket over Lucille, she stood looking at the woman on the sofa, her mind still working. "It's not impossible," she said very softly. "She's had ample opportunity to study Leticia's notebooks on her visits. She was telling me some grisly stories earlier in the evening."

"What are you talking about?" Virginia demanded. "You don't think Mrs. Barnes…"

Carolyn put her fingers to her lips. "Shh. Don't say another word. We'll talk later, after we've seen the notebooks. What's taking Leticia so long?"

"But Carrie," Virginia protested, "she wasn't even there when he died."

Carolyn shook her head. "It doesn't matter. All she had to do was find a poison that was hard to detect and would last a long time without degrading. And of course, she had to apply it to something that Runcible was likely to use but Leticia wouldn't touch."

Virginia frowned. "Like his toothbrush?"

Carolyn shrugged. "Something like that, yes. But let's let the matter drop. Let's just enjoy Leticia's company."

Virginia smiled. "You like her then?"

Carolyn grinned back at her. "Leticia? Yes, very much."

"But not too much," Virginia said firmly, as worry lines started to form around her eyes.

"No, sweetheart," Carolyn shook her head fondly. "You have nothing to worry about."

Carolyn and Virginia carried the dishes into the kitchen.

***

By the time Virginia and Carolyn had finished drying the dishes and reentered the living room, Leticia was sitting next to the low table centered in front of the two rocking chairs. On the table lay a tall stack of notebooks. Next to it stood an old wooden box that looked as though it came from halfway around the world, if not another century. It was the size of a jewelry case with dark, intricate carvings of vines and leaves. Leticia smiled at Carolyn and Virginia, but her face was drawn and drained of color. "I see that my mother has passed out," she said tonelessly. "Did she make it to the sofa on her own or did the two of you have to assist her?"

Carolyn seated herself in the big wooden rocker across from Leticia. "We helped. Does she do this often?"

"More often than I like, but not all the time," Leticia admitted. "Whenever I suggest that she get help, she tells me I'm the one with the problem. Her boyfriend doesn't mind. Her friends I've met in Florida never say anything about her drinking. Maybe she only does it around me."

"I doubt that," Carolyn interjected quickly. "If her friends are heavy drinkers, no one would comment on her drinking."

The phone rang, but before Leticia could move to answer it, Virginia jumped up. "I can get that. You look all in."

"In the pantry," Leticia said with a sigh. "And thanks." She turned back to Carolyn. " I feel so sorry for her. In spite of what she says, it's been difficult since my father's death, no matter how many men she picks up and discards."

Carolyn looked intently at Leticia, but she couldn't read her facial expression. "You don't approve of your mother's love life?"

"Love?" Leticia repeated the word sardonically. "I don't think love has anything to do with it. Loneliness maybe and maybe..." She didn't finish her sentence.

"Libido?" Carolyn offered.

245

"I think she drinks too much to have much of a sex drive. I was going to say ego gratification or making up for lost time." Leticia shrugged. "Or maybe revenge."

"Revenge?"

"On my father. Sounds odd in a way, but she bears a grudge. Seems like resentment motivates her, though I don't exactly know why."

Carolyn looked thoughtful. "She's probably lonely, and loneliness is certainly enough reason for most people to couple up." Carolyn paused, then went on. "How about you? How do you deal with it?"

"Loneliness? Oh, I'm never lonely. Being alone is such a luxury." She smiled at Carolyn. "I'm an independent sort of girl, I guess."

"Woman," Carolyn corrected her automatically. "You're supposed to say woman nowadays. To call an adult woman a girl is demeaning. A couple of patients at the hospital got very upset at being called girls. It makes sense. I mean, calling someone a girl who's run a business for twenty years and raised six children is condescending, don't you think?"

Leticia shook her head. "Don't tell me you're a woman's libber, Dr. Matthews!"

Carolyn grinned at her. "Not actively, no. But as a professional, it's important to me that I'm not put at a disadvantage because I'm a woman."

"You're ambitious then?"

Carolyn nodded. "I want to do what I do well and I want recognition for that. Does that seem unfair to you or like cold-blooded ambition?"

Leticia laughed. "Not unfair, but maybe unfeminine. Self-sacrifice is a virtue for a woman."

Carolyn snorted derisively. "Not for this woman."

Leticia looked down at her hands. "You know, it's funny that I called myself a girl just now. I used to think I was a boy. At least partly anyway. As if one could be partly a boy!" She laughed nervously. "I made Virginia call me Fred when we were young. Did you know that?"

"Because you didn't like the name Leticia?"

"Well, I didn't, but that wasn't the real reason. I felt constrained, stifled really. I wanted the kind of freedom that boys had. You know, presto, I'm a boy! And then no one would be upset when I showed up filthy with scraped knees and my hair looking like a bird's nest." She looked up. "I was so deluded."

246

Carolyn stretched her long legs out in front of her. "I didn't envy the freedom that boys had. I was pretty much allowed to do anything I wanted. But when I hit adolescence I started to feel vulnerable, and I didn't like that one bit. I'm enjoying being not quite so young anymore. Now I'm in charge of my life. At least as far as anyone can be. That feels good to me."

Leticia continued as if Carolyn hadn't spoken. "I felt conflicted when I called myself Fred. I had my dreams and expected to live them. That was the boy in me. The girl needed to please other people."

Carolyn nodded. "So you buried part of yourself to live out other people's dreams." She wondered how much that observation fit Virginia as well.

Leticia wanted to object, but before she could say anything, Virginia came back into the room. She looked upset and a little frightened. "That was Leonora, Carrie. Henry signed himself out of the hospital."

"We can't do both at the same time, honey. The dispensary at the hospital closes in half an hour, and Henry left without getting any of his meds."

Virginia's jaw tightened, and Carolyn recognized the onset of a fit of stubbornness. "I called him at home," Virginia replied tersely, "and he didn't answer. Maybe he fell, maybe he's unconscious. We have to find him first." She took a deep breath to counteract the hysteria mounting in her chest.

Carolyn shook her head. "But he'll need his meds. Or we'll be right back where we started. Someone else can check in on him at home. Why don't you call what's her name...his office manager?"

"Toni," Virginia interjected impatiently. "She doesn't have a car. She lives near the clinic, not his house. It'd take her forever to get to him."

Leticia cleared her throat. "May I make a suggestion?"

Virginia glared at her, tempted to tell her to mind her own business. Carolyn, however, smiled and said, "Be my guest."

"I have a car. One of you could ride with me and the other could take your car."

Virginia felt guilty about her desire to snap at Leticia, who really was trying to help. She took another deep breath. "Thanks, Fred. That's really kind of you."

"And it's a good idea," Carolyn added. Turning to Virginia, she continued, "Do you want to drive or ride with Leticia?"

Virginia drew a blank, unable to make a decision. Leticia took her arm. "She'll come with me. We'll check out the house. But before we go, may I suggest a phone call to Toni to have her check his office. He may have decided to stop off there."

Virginia nodded and retreated to the pantry.

"Tell Virginia I'll see her back at the house after I get the meds," Carolyn said to Leticia, picking up her car key and heading out the door.

"Toni's worried that..." Virginia started to speak as she came out of the pantry. "Where did Carrie go?"

"To pick up the medications. She'll meet you back at the house."

Virginia nodded. "Okay then. We're off."

Leticia, Virginia noticed, drove a lot like Carolyn, very fast but with total control. She wondered if that similarity might tell her something about herself and started to smile, but then her worry about Henry hit her like a fist in the stomach and the smile died on her lips. "I don't know what he's thinking," she muttered. "To go off like that. He's a doctor. He ought to know better."

Leticia wasn't sure if Virginia was speaking to her or to herself. "He's probably feeling abandoned since the two of you are leaving," she ventured. "Surely you can understand that."

"Why?" Virginia snapped. "Because you abandoned me all those years ago? I didn't go acting out, did I?"

"Well," Leticia said softly, reaching out to put her hand on Virginia's arm, "actually you did. I mean, your performance the last time we saw each other was acting out, wasn't it?"

Virginia shrugged angrily. "Forget it." She shook off Leticia's hand. "My father is not a teenager dumped by his first love. He's an adult man, who should have the good sense to realize that his adult daughter has her own life to live."

Leticia made a small sound halfway between a grunt and a cough. "Emotional reactions rarely have anything to do with good sense."

Virginia looked over at her for the first time. "I'm sorry," she said. "I'm not being very nice to you, but I'm just so worried about him."

"I know," Leticia said gently. She pulled up to Henry's house. "Look, his car is here."

Virginia sat frozen in place. She realized she was terrified of what she'd find in the house. "Fred, would you be willing to do me a huge favor and come in with me?"

Leticia killed the motor and opened her door. "Of course."

**

Carolyn shifted from one foot to the other. She wished the pharmacist's assistant would move a little more quickly. The young woman seemed to have lead in her feet.

"What did you say the name of his doctor was?"

Carolyn sighed. "Epstein, Leonora Epstein."

"Right, I remember that she called, but I can't find the prescriptions. It'll just take another couple of minutes."

Carolyn suppressed a sigh, afraid that any sign of impatience would slow the process down even more.

"Got it! Now who did you say you were?"

"Carolyn Matthews."

The assistant frowned. It says here to release the meds to Virginia Carr."

"Virginia Carr is my...partner. She sent me to get the medications while she went to look after her father."

"I don't know." The young woman frowned again. "I can't just give anyone meds.

"Call Dr. Epstein!" Carolyn ordered. "Or better yet, hand me the phone and I'll call her."

"I'm sorry, but I can't give you her home phone number."

"Oh, for heaven's sake! I know her home phone number. Give me the phone."

Just as Carolyn had feared, her impatience made things worse. The young woman raised herself to her full height and snapped, "I can't let you use the hospital phone without authorization." She picked up the package of medications and disappeared from the dispensary window.

Carolyn waited only until the door slammed. Then she reached across the barrier and grabbed the phone. Leonora answered on the first ring.

"You didn't tell me you were a doctor," the young woman said reproachfully less than two minutes after Carolyn had hung up. "Dr. Epstein just phoned my supervisor." She stared suspiciously at Carolyn. "I wonder how she knew you were here."

Carolyn shrugged noncommittally and reached out to take the package of medicines, but the young woman drew back. "How are you going to pay for these?" she demanded, trying to reassert a measure of her tattered authority.

Carolyn beamed at her. "Will you accept cash?"

Grudgingly the woman smiled back. "Sorry," she said. "It's been a long evening."

Carolyn nodded, paid, and set off with the medications before anything else could slow her down.

***

"He can't just have disappeared into thin air," Leticia said in as comforting a voice as she could manage. She seated herself on the sofa and started to put her purse on the coffee table. To do so, she had to shove aside the massive tome lying there. Its title caught her eye, Forensic Toxicology. She had to make an effort not to pitch it to the floor.

Virginia kept wringing her hands and walking between the front door and the kitchen window, as if she had to be on guard in case Henry appeared. Her constant motion was making Leticia sorry she'd come into the house.

"Sit down, Virginia! Pacing back and forth isn't going to make your father show up any sooner."

Virginia stopped moving and glared at her. Then she sat down on the chair closest to the door so she could keep an eye on the driveway. "I can't believe he's not here. Toni said he wasn't in the office either, though he might have been earlier since his medical bag was missing. I wish Carolyn were here. What can be taking her so damned long? All she has to do is pick up some meds, for God's sake."

"Sometimes hospital red tape can make a simple task complicated," Leticia said without thinking. Then she shook her head. "But of course, you know that since you're a doctor."

Virginia sighed. "I wish to hell Henry would just go back to the hospital until Dr. Epstein discharges him. This hide and seek can't be good for him." She turned her head to the side as if considering something. "You don't think he did go back there, do you? I mean, he could have and we wouldn't know."

Leticia replied thoughtfully. "You know him better than I do, but I doubt it. Besides if he'd gone back, someone would have called to let you know, don't you think?"

Virginia shrugged and fell silent. Her head ached and she wished she hadn't asked Leticia to come in with her. She'd been anxious, but having her in the house wasn't helping. "If you want to go home, you can," she said sullenly. "I was just afraid I might find him unconscious or dead."

Leticia tapped her fingers on the top of the coffee table. She was tempted to take Virginia up on her offer. Idly she wondered if Lucille was awake.

"That's Carrie!" Virginia announced, jumping to her feet. "I hear the car." She raced to the door and opened it, peering out into the darkness. The noise disappeared in the distance. "Humph, guess it was someone else." She returned to her seat and stared at Leticia. "So tell me something to help me keep my mind off my father," she demanded.

Leticia stared at her. "What?"

"Tell me something about you that I don't know. What's it like being a rich heiress?"

251

Leticia stared at Virginia. "Whoa, wait a minute. I'm not a rich heiress."

"Oh come on, of course you are. Your father's money came to you after your husband died, didn't it?"

Leticia rolled her eyes. "It came and it went. Anyway a lot of his money went straight to my mother."

"But I thought your husband married you because you were a rich heiress."

"Well, you thought wrong."

Virginia fell silent. "This isn't helping, you know."

Leticia laughed without mirth. "I'm surprised. I thought picking fights with me was ..." She chose not to complete her sentence.

Virginia shook her head. "Sorry, Fred. It's just..."

"I know, I know. You're worried about your father."

Virginia stared out the window. "We're not going to be able to leave tomorrow unless he shows up. Carrie will be really disappointed. She was looking forward to getting back home. This really wasn't the vacation she was hoping for."

"I can imagine."

Virginia stiffened. "We haven't had a vacation in two years," she grumbled. "We can't just take off whenever we want to. This was carefully planned."

Leticia snorted. "You planned to come here and harass me about my husband's death for your vacation? I had no idea."

Virginia took a deep breath. "No," she said very distinctly, "we planned a peaceful stay in the mountains. Then my father got sick."

Leticia laughed, recognizing that slow, distinct way of speaking from Virginia's adolescence. She only talked that way when she was furious. "I know, investigating me was just an afterthought."

"This is stupid!" Virginia got up and walked back to the kitchen window. "I wish Carrie would get back."

"So do I," Leticia said, getting to her feet. "Since this conversation is just irritating both of us, I'll head home and check up on my mother."

"Wait!" Virginia ordered. "I wanted to ask you something."

Leticia stood still.

"What did you mean when you said your money came and went?"

Exasperated, Leticia walked to the door. "I gave it away. To people who needed it more than I did. Flood victims, earthquake victims, people with medical needs that couldn't be met in their home country.

You figure it out, Dr. Carr. You're the one who wanted to be a humanitarian." Leticia closed the screen door gently behind her.

Virginia stopped pacing and took a breath. Leticia, the spoiled brat, had given her money to a bunch of needy people? Virginia could hardly believe it. She curled into herself on the sofa and waited quietly for Carolyn.

CHAPTER 40
POTENCY
1980
❖

When Carolyn came through the door, Virginia sat on the sofa chewing her fingernail. She gave no sign of pleasure or relief at the arrival of her lover.

Uh, oh, Carolyn thought, when she observed Virginia's withdrawn look. She began to speak, hoping that she might utter a phrase that would dispel the fog. "Sorry I'm so late, but I had to wait for the meds, and then the night nurse stopped me on my way out and told me Henry had left his stuff in his room and they'd throw it all out in the morning, so I..."

Virginia wasn't listening to Carolyn's excuses. She scolded Carolyn as if she had orchestrated the evening's events. "Henry isn't here. The house was empty when we came in. Leticia went home. I've been alone and worried stiff."

"I understand, Sweetheart, but there's nothing I can do about it. Henry will show up." She tried to project a certainty she didn't feel.

"You'll have to cancel our flight reservations."

Carolyn could see that Virginia was shaken and therefore inclined to be stubborn. "I'll do it in the morning if he hasn't shown up by then."

"It will be too late in the morning."

"No, it won't. Trust me."

Virginia sniffed but said nothing more. If Carolyn wanted to pretend she was being reasonable, that was all well and good. It wasn't her father who was missing.

"I'll make us a cup of tea," Carolyn ventured. "It's going to be a long night."

"I thought you cared about Henry," Virginia said abruptly, "but I'm the only one."

"Of course, I care about Henry. And so does Toni. Have you spoken to her since you got here?"

Virginia's lip curled. "He's not at the office, if that's what you're hoping. He's disappeared off the face of the earth, and you want to make us a cup of tea!" The scorn in her voice was unmistakable, but Carolyn didn't want to fight.

"Henry is a resourceful man."

"He's a sick man, Carrie. I doubt that he's thinking clearly."

Carolyn couldn't suppress her chuckle. "Oh, he's thinking clearly all right. Probably having the time of his life."

"How can you be so unfeeling? He could be off in a ditch somewhere, dead or unconscious. What if his medications are off again?"

Carolyn shook her head. "I doubt that very much, but if you like, we can drive around and inspect all the ditches in Grant's Hill."

Virginia glared at her. "Can't you be serious for once?"

"I am serious. But if we go off searching for him, we won't be here when he arrives."

"If he arrives," Virginia moaned.

Just as Carolyn threw her hands up in despair, the phone rang. Virginia froze, so Carolyn picked up the receiver.

"Okay," Virginia heard her say, "we'll be right over."

Before Virginia had a chance to inquire or comment, Carolyn took her arm and pulled her through the door. They were in the car and Carolyn had started to drive away from the house before Virginia gathered her wits enough to ask, "Who was that and where are we going?"

"Leticia. To her house."

Virginia exhaled angrily. "Didn't you just say we had to stay until Henry got home? I don't have any interest in seeing that woman again. Not now. Not ever."

Carolyn stared straight ahead. "Henry's at Leticia's house. She found him there when she got in and phoned to tell you."

"Well, why didn't you say so?" Virginia grumbled. "She must have gotten home at least fifteen minutes ago, so what took her so long?"

***

When they reached the Barnes' house, Virginia and Carolyn were surprised to find the front door wide open. "No need to knock and don't just stand out there gawking," Henry said loudly when he caught sight of them. "Now the party can get going."

Carolyn stepped into the living room. "Well, Mrs. Barnes," she said to Lucille, who sat upright on the sofa sipping a scotch, "it seems you've recovered. A little hair of the dog that bit you?"

Lucille laughed shrilly. "As a matter of fact, Dr. Matthews, if you were as good at medicine as my dear friend Dr. Carr here, you'd have known what to give me." She held up a bottle of high potency B vitamins. "Much better than the hair of the dog."

"I brought my medical bag with me," Henry announced, looking pleased with himself. "I don't usually make house calls, but in this case, I've made an exception."

Carolyn laughed. Virginia nudged her hard with her elbow. "It's really not funny," she complained.

"You, my dear girl," Lucille interjected, "have as little sense of humor as my daughter, who took herself off to the kitchen. She is a total party pooper, and I'd guess that you are too." Lucille enunciated each syllable, carefully counteracting the tendency to slur her words.

"Where are you going?" Henry demanded. "The party has barely begun."

Virginia shot a hostile look at her father. "I need to thank Leticia for letting me know your whereabouts. She had the decency to call. You ought to be ashamed of yourself..." She took a deep breath and walked forcefully out of the room.

"How sharper than a serpent's tooth, eh, Mrs. Barnes?" Henry intoned. "We are both cursed with ungrateful children. But you at least were invited to the farewell party, whereas I was left to molder in a lonely hospital room."

"I was hardly invited, Dr. Carr. That is too weak a word. Rather say that my peace and quiet was imposed on. I came to visit my one and only child and have hardly been allowed any time alone with her." She sniveled pathetically. "One might think I were an evil stepmother, the way she avoids me. This party was inflicted on me, let me assure you. But still, I am pleased to have the chance to see you looking so well. You certainly don't seem to me to belong in the hospital."

"That reminds me, Henry," Carolyn interrupted them, "I picked up your meds and left them at your house. You're due for another dose in three hours and fifteen minutes, so we'd better be sure the party is over by then."

Henry appraised her carefully. "Thank you, Carolyn," he said, deciding that Carolyn was simply stating a fact rather than taunting or scolding him.

Carolyn smiled at him. "You're welcome, sir. Dr. Epstein said she'd send you your prescriptions in the morning."

Henry just grunted at the mention of the neurologist. Then he stood up and poured himself a glass of club soda. "I'm not mixing alcohol with my medications, you see," he observed with a sideways glance at Carolyn. "I am in my right mind."

"I never doubted it," Carolyn said honestly. "How did you get here anyway? Your car is still in the driveway at your house."

"As I said, I am in my right mind. I had no intention of driving unless I knew for sure that I was no risk to myself or others. I took a taxi."

Carolyn nodded, wishing Virginia would come back from the kitchen and talk to her father.

"And in case you've forgotten," Henry added in a superior tone, "I knew you were here because you told me you would be when you came to see me earlier today."

"Would you like a drink, Dr. Matthews?" Lucille asked pointedly. She'd had enough of the exchange between Carolyn and Henry.

"No, thank you, Mrs. Barnes. It's getting late. Virginia and I should be heading back. We have a flight to catch tomorrow morning."

Mrs. Barnes nodded. "Well, don't let me keep you. Dr. Carr and I have a lot to discuss."

"You're not keeping me, Mrs. Barnes. Virginia is," Carolyn replied with just a touch of impatience. "I wonder what she's up to."

"I'd rather not know," Lucille replied, taking a long sip of her scotch.

***

When Virginia walked into the kitchen, Leticia looked up from the large pot she was scrubbing and smiled tentatively. "I came in and found the two of them jawing away, complaining about the ungratefulness of their offspring and the general unreliability of the younger generation." She shrugged. "As if we were still the younger generation and not approaching middle age. Anyway, your father ordered me to call you and demand that you appear here at once. But when I reached for the phone, he took it out of my hand and told me he'd changed his mind. Then he launched into a diatribe about broken promises."

Virginia stood silently, so Leticia finished with a brief laugh. "I told him I had to go to the bathroom and ran upstairs where I have another phone. I'm sorry it took me so long to notify you. I know you were worried."

Virginia didn't say a word. She just walked up to Leticia and put her arms around her. "Thank you for calling," she finally managed to whisper. "He's an impossible man, but he is my father, and I love him."

Leticia's shoulders tensed and she extricated herself gently from Virginia's embrace. "Well, he seems to be doing very well," she said, absentmindedly reaching for the big pot again.

257

Virginia smiled at her. "I think that's clean," she said. "I'm sorry if I upset you."

Leticia shrugged. "I'm not upset, but I am confused. One minute you treat me as if I'm public enemy number one and then you hug me. What am I supposed to think? At least with Susan I know where I am." She blushed and covered her mouth with her hand.

Virginia looked perplexed. "Who is Susan?"

"Oh, come on! I know I've mentioned Susan to you. She's a friend. Well, actually she was Paul's friend and over time we've become close friends. In fact, if my mother weren't here, Susan would be visiting right now."

Virginia looked offended. "You certainly have not mentioned her to me! Is she the one who went with you to the medical examiner? He remembered that there were two women."

Leticia rolled her eyes.

"So are you and Susan, well, you know…interested in each other?"

Leticia blew air out her nose like an irritated horse. "You have a one-track mind, Virginia Carr. Susan is US Air Force JAG."

"What the hell does that mean? And what does it have to do with your being interested in each other?"

"Susan is a military lawyer, and our being interested in each other, as you so quaintly put it, is against regulations."

"Oh, for heaven's sake! You can't seriously expect me to believe that there are no lesbians in the military. Surely even you don't think that."

Leticia smiled tightly. "Susan follows the rules to the letter. That's just how she is."

"Sounds lovely," Virginia said acerbically. "Just the kind of person I'd love never to meet."

"Don't worry. You're not likely to meet her. I'll certainly never introduce you."

Virginia ignored the barb. "You are unbelievably secretive, Fred. Carrie and I have wondered who the other woman at the medical examiner's was since we first found out about her. We thought maybe you and she were co-conspirators."

"I'm not secretive. You're just nosy. Don't the two of you have anything better to do than indulge your overactive imaginations about me? I thought doctors had to work."

"Don't try to turn the tables, Fred. This Susan could very well have had reason to kill your husband. Maybe she had an affair with him and he dumped her."

Leticia laughed sharply. "Oh good grief, you are dense, Virginia Carr. She cared very much for Paul, but she would never have had an affair with him."

"Because she's a lesbian?"

Leticia suppressed a scream. "No. Because adultery is against regulations."

Virginia groaned. "You're nuts! Anyway, technically she wouldn't have been committing adultery. Only he would."

Leticia sighed. "You are clueless!"

Virginia took a deep breath. "So this woman avoids trouble at all costs?"

"Not exactly. She follows the rules unless the greater good requires that she break or bend them. Having an affair with a married man or with his wife doesn't count as the greater good."

"What would then?" Virginia challenged her.

Leticia remembered that confrontational stare from the old days. A wave of nostalgia hit her, so she stalled. "What would what?"

"Count as the greater good?" Virginia replied patiently.

Leticia could tell Virginia actually was interested, but she shot her a suspicious look anyway, just for old time's sake.

"No, I really want to know. This woman is starting to fascinate me."

"Uncovering corruption or preventing a coup d'état, maybe saving a lot of lives by revealing a terrorist plot."

"Something that would never happen, you mean?"

Leticia stopped playing and let sadness come into her eyes. "Corruption happens all the time. In fact, Susan was convinced for a while that Paul's death had to do with something he'd found out about his superiors."

"Maybe it did," Virginia speculated. "We never thought of that."

"No, she just wanted him to be as uncompromising as she is. He wasn't a whistleblower though. Too ambitious. He knew how to turn a blind eye if necessary. Because Susan cared so much for him, she wanted to believe he was an idealist."

"I take back what I said about her at first," Virginia said with a small smile. "I'd love to meet this woman. She sounds too good to be true."

"She is good," Leticia said softly.

"And you're in love with her, aren't you?"

Leticia's face flushed. "Don't be ridiculous!"

Virginia smiled at her triumphantly. "Deny it if you like but I can recognize the signs."

Leticia pointed at the door. "Don't you need to talk with your father?"

"Henry can wait. I think he deserves to sweat a little." Virginia knew that Leticia wanted to shoo her out or at least change the subject.

"I doubt that he's sweating. He and my mother were having too much fun criticizing us." Leticia hesitated for a second. "May I ask you a question?"

Virginia looked surprised. "Sure. I suppose it is only fair." She leaned against the wall, suddenly aware that her entire body felt tired and the poison ivy blisters had started to itch again. "Ask away."

Leticia put the big pot on the shelf and turned to face Virginia. "I've noticed that you tend to call your father Henry, never 'dad' or 'father'. I find that curious."

Virginia grinned at her. "That's not really a question, but I'll answer anyway. I've called him Henry, ever since I was quite young. When I began helping him in his practice we became colleagues, rather than parent and child. It was a game, but also a mark of the special intimacy we had. Fathers and daughters can and usually do grow apart eventually. Fellow healers, however..." She shrugged and made a move to scratch at a particularly itchy spot just above her knee.

"Don't!" Leticia ordered, taking her hand. "You'll just spread it."

Virginia smiled faintly and tugged her hand free. "Okay, I'll try not to." She hesitated, then shrugged again. "Anyway once you get used to calling your father Henry the whole time you're growing up, it's hard to revert to calling him 'dad.'"

Leticia looked serious. "Are you sure the pretense of being colleagues was a game to him?"

"Of course, it was a game to him. What else could it have been?"

"This evening when he was so upset, he made it sound like you'd promised to practice medicine with him and then let him down." She put up her hand to ward off Virginia's imminent protest. "I know. It's totally unrealistic of him to expect you to fulfill his fantasy, but I think he took your game more seriously than you did and now feels deeply betrayed."

Virginia shook her head. "I know that, Fred, but it's his problem. How can he expect me to uproot myself and desert the life that I've made…". She shook her head again. "It doesn't make sense. He was the parent who always encouraged me to follow my dreams, no matter what. My mom was the cautious, pragmatic one."

"As long as your dreams and his dreams were the same," Leticia said gently, "it wasn't too hard for him to encourage you."

"Now it feels like I was being brainwashed rather than supported, and I didn't even know it at the time," Virginia said bitterly. "He's not the only one who feels betrayed."

"I'm sorry," Leticia murmured. "I have to say this, though: the two of you need to clear the air. Maybe not right this minute and certainly not here with my mother and me as an audience, but sometime soon."

"I doubt there's any point in talking about it. Both of us will just get upset. He's a stubborn man and would never admit he's wrong."

Leticia smiled. "Just like his daughter," she started to say, but thought better of it. Instead she shrugged. "Well take what I said for what it's worth, which may not be all that much."

"Thank you, Dr. Fred," Virginia said in what she hoped was a light, joking tone. "I'm glad you don't charge for your professional advice."

"It's not professional advice, Virginia, just an observation from a friend, who's known you for a long time."

Virginia chuckled, but the tone was bitter. "You mean you knew me a long time ago. We're not exactly friends, Fred. But I appreciate your honesty."

Leticia sighed. "We'd better go join the others."

***

Carolyn was looking through Leticia's notebooks with Henry peering over her shoulder. He had one hand on the table and was leaning heavily on it for support. Carolyn pretended not to notice that he was shaky, but Virginia let out a small gasp each time he teetered, however slightly.

"I hope you don't mind, Mrs. Runcible," Carolyn said apologetically, when Leticia entered the room. "You were going to show them to me, so I took the liberty…"

Henry raised his head and glared at his daughter. "What the hell were you two doing in there for so long?"

Virginia met his eyes. "Talking. Mostly about certain people's irresponsible and obnoxious behavior."

261

Henry chortled and then had to pant to catch his breath. "I'm sure a murderess has a lot to say about obnoxious behavior."

At the word 'murderess', Lucille, who'd been silently sipping her drink, dropped the glass and spilled the contents on her outfit. "Damn it, man!" She jumped to her feet.

"I'm very sorry, Mrs. Barnes," Henry said, not sounding sorry at all. "I don't wish to upset you, but it's common knowledge that your daughter did away with her husband. Poisoned him. Probably used one of the poisons in that box," he added, pounding the top of the box of potions with his free hand.

"Don't be ridiculous. My daughter did not kill her husband. Much as he deserved killing, she didn't have the guts."

"Mother!" Leticia howled, "What are you saying?"

Virginia and Carolyn glanced at each other. Virginia started to walk toward the empty seat next to Carolyn. She thought she'd feel better if she sat down. The itchy blisters on her legs were making her dizzy. However, before she'd taken two steps, Henry sat down in the empty place, shaking his head. "Anyone can commit murder, Mrs. Barnes, if the motive is strong enough and the circumstances are right."

"Damn!" Virginia swore under her breath. She started to scratch her leg.

"Hogwash!" Lucille responded immediately and in a voice so loud that Virginia's hand stopped in mid-scratch. "The last courageous act Leticia ever performed was getting into your daughter's pants, Dr. Carr! As a mother I had to disapprove, of course, but it did show a bit of initiative. Since her father's death, however, she's been woefully lacking in gumption. That husband of hers ran around on her, and she knew it. It was obvious. But she did nothing, absolutely nothing."

"You've just provided an excellent motive for the crime, Mrs. Barnes," Henry said smugly.

"You don't know what you're talking about," Leticia said, but it wasn't clear if she meant Henry or her mother.

"She let that priss in uniform wrap her around her little finger, when anyone could see that the bitch was Paul's whore. When I showed up after his death, whom do I find holding my daughter's hand and crying her eyes out, but that slut Susan Russell."

"Shut up!" Leticia screamed, her face turning dark red and her whole body shaking. "Susan is my friend. She was Paul's friend."

"I'll just bet she was Paul's friend," Lucille hooted. "I can imagine exactly how friendly they were."

"Susan was not sleeping with Paul," Leticia insisted, her eyes shooting darts at her mother. "Yes, Paul had affairs with three women during our marriage. Susan was not one of them. When she found out, she was devastated by what she thought was his betrayal of me, so I had to explain it all to her."

Lucille frowned, not sure what Leticia meant by explaining, but it probably wasn't important anyway. "It doesn't matter." She waved her hand dismissively. "You knew and did nothing."

"You don't understand," Leticia said, trying to get her voice under control. "I told Paul to find other women. I didn't want to have sex with him."

Lucille sat down hard. "You what?"

"If you all have to know, Paul and I had sex on our honeymoon. It was awful, but he didn't seem to notice right away. Then when he finally did, he offered not to approach me again. I told him I had no objection to his finding a lover as long as he was discreet." She stared out the window into the darkness for a few seconds. "I met the women he was involved with. He told me that if I didn't like them, he would drop them. In fact, he did drop one because she was rude to me."

"Maybe she killed him," Virginia ventured. "In revenge."

"No, she left the area a full year before he died."

"Oh my God," Lucille moaned. "It was all for nothing then. Why didn't you tell me?"

"What was all for nothing?" Carolyn asked gently.

"Getting me married to Paul," Leticia interjected before Lucille could reply. She went over to Lucille and put her arm around her. For once Lucille didn't shake it off. "You never really gave me a chance to tell you, Mother. Besides I knew you'd be disappointed and you'd already been through enough."

Henry shoved the pile of the notebooks onto the floor and changed the subject abruptly. "So you're working with old Cyrus, are you, Mrs. Runcible? We were at Hopkins together. He always had a million young women following him around, but I'm the one who got Louise in the end. I don't think he ever married, did he?"

Leticia smiled at Henry. "He did, but his wife died years ago."

"Are you sure you didn't poison her too?"

Leticia's smile didn't fade. "Dr. Carr, I didn't poison my husband, and I certainly didn't poison Mrs. Marshall. She was dead long before I met Cyrus. I know you don't like me because I practiced herbal medicine for a while. But an herbalist is not, by definition, a poisoner."

Henry blushed. "Who says I don't like you? Eric Johnson doesn't like you, but I like you all right."

"Eric Johnson holds a grudge against me from my adolescence. If you write to him again, tell him I'm sorry he got fired and if I had it to do over, I wouldn't complain to my father. Will you do that for me?"

Henry chuckled. "I will, but he's still going to keep after you for killing your husband. You know that, don't you? Nothing I say will change his mind." Henry coughed several times and Virginia looked alarmed, afraid he was choking. He pulled himself together and smiled at Leticia. "To my mind, it's not at all clear that you killed your husband. But Eric is sure, and he's an expert after all."

Lucille snorted. "I remember that young man, and I doubt that he's an expert in anything. Police, Dr. Carr," she intoned, "are not experts the way doctors are. You studied long and hard to master your profession. He spent a few months shooting at paper targets."

Henry was pleased by the compliment but he wasn't ready to let Leticia completely off the hook. "Your daughter could easily have had something in that box of herbs and potions that the medical examiner couldn't detect. Those aboriginals knew about poisons. They hunted with poisoned darts, didn't they?"

"Come, come, Dr. Carr," Lucille said loudly. "You're letting your imagination run away with you. Surely modern science could detect anything a primitive could come up with."

"I'm convinced we'll find an empty space where the poison once was if we open this box," Henry said with a sly look at Leticia. "May I?" He didn't wait for an answer. "Good grief! There are at least four spaces in this box that look like they once held small vials." He continued, speaking to no one in particular. "I can see the imprints of the bottles in three of the spaces, but not the fourth. That one is a bit stained, as if someone had spilled a little of the contents, perhaps before pouring it into someone's drink or food," he mused. Henry peered at Leticia and noticed that she looked upset. Upset but not guilty. Could Johnson have gotten it wrong?

"What do you mean, four spaces? There was only one when I..." Leticia caught herself and bit her lip.

Henry turned to Lucille, who struggled visibly to manifest an expression of innocence. "Don't look at me," she announced. "I have nothing to do with any of this."

"Famous last words," Carolyn whispered, leaning into Virginia who had positioned herself so that her arm was lightly touching Carrie's.

"What was that, Dr. Matthews?" Lucille demanded peremptorily. "If you have something to say, say it out loud."

"I was just remarking that you might have accidentally knocked the box over while you were indisposed and forgotten about it. Maybe we should check the trash."

Lucille sneered at her. "Come to think of it, I do vaguely remember waking up and finding some broken glass on the floor. Perhaps I even cleaned it up. I can't really say."

"But you were unconscious when we left," Leticia said.

"And still out when I came in," Henry added. "I rang the doorbell half a dozen times and almost gave up before I thought to try the door. I was surprised to find it unlocked."

"I locked it when I left with Virginia," Leticia asserted. "I'm sure of that."

"Something I ate at dinner obviously didn't agree with me" Lucille snapped accusingly, "I'm sure that's why I passed out. I may have awakened and passed out again before your arrival, Dr. Carr. As I said, I don't remember."

When no one responded, she continued in a louder voice. "In any case, what difference does it make?"

"You could have killed Colonel Runcible and destroyed the evidence," Henry said. His voice wasn't at all agitated, and his face wore a look of mild curiosity.

"Nonsense! I wasn't even there when he died."

"Do you know," Carolyn asked Leticia, "what was in the vials that were destroyed today?"

"Everything's labeled," Leticia mumbled. She walked past Henry and leaned over to look in the box. "Valerian extract is the first one. Hawthorn is next. Foxglove tincture is the last."

"Foxglove?" Henry interjected. "Isn't that the source of digitalin?"

Leticia nodded. "Valerian is a sleep aid. Hawthorn supports circulatory function."

"An overdose of digitalin could be fatal," Henry said solemnly.

"True," Carolyn said, "but if Leticia is correct, that vial just got broken today."

"Still the contents might have been used before and replaced with water," Henry speculated. "The guilty party could easily have panicked at the possibility of discovery, Carolyn, knowing that you were about to examine the box of potions." Carolyn noticed that when Henry spoke of the guilty party, his eyes came to rest momentarily on Lucille rather than Leticia. He might be ill, but he certainly hadn't lost his sharpness.

"Possible, but unlikely," Carolyn replied, turning to Leticia. "What was in the vial that was missing before your mother's...uh, accident with the box this evening?"

"Oh, that was one of Ana's. A kind of hunting potion for tipping arrows."

"Curare," Carolyn spotted the label and read it out. "I've heard of it. It's supposedly undetectable after a few hours. After it shuts down the heart and circulatory system it has to dissipate quickly or the meat would be poisonous."

"Never heard of it," Henry said. "But if it dissipates quickly, that points the finger of guilt back at Mrs. Runcible, doesn't it, since she was the only one present at the time of her husband's death?"

"Not if it was combined with a preservative," Carolyn replied. She walked over to the photograph of Paul Runcible and picked it up. "Did your husband often cut himself shaving?" she asked Leticia.

Leticia nodded. "It was something everyone knew about him. He used a straight razor and was not all that good with it."

"Did he keep a supply of styptic pencils?" Carolyn continued.

Leticia shrugged. "I think so. I can't say for sure. He always had toilet paper hanging off his face. It didn't do anything for his image."

"Aluminum sulfate," Henry said. "You think that could have preserved the active ingredients in that whatever it was?"

"Curare," Carolyn replied. "We'll never know, will we?" She smiled at Henry and turned back to Leticia. "Do you still have his shaving stuff?"

Leticia replied immediately. "Of course not. Mother and I got rid of all of it. It was morbid to hold on to it." She smiled a little sadly. "Susan had asked for his shaving mirror as a memento, but Mother broke it and threw it away. I think that's one of the things Susan holds against her to this day."

Virginia looked from Carolyn to Leticia to Lucille and finally at her father, who seemed to be thriving as a would-be detective. Maybe he really wasn't ill. Maybe he was bored. She shook her head. Of course, he was ill. He had Parkinson's, but the medications seemed to have turned him back into his old self. She felt a small smile arise on her face at that thought.

"Henry," she said. "I think you and I need to talk."

Henry got a stubborn, wary look on his face. "Whenever I hear those words, I know you're looking to pick a fight with me." He frowned. "Talk about what?"

"About your future." Virginia put up her hand to stop Henry from launching into a tirade. "Just hear me out, please."

"I'm listening."

Virginia wondered as she spoke, if she ought to have checked with Carolyn about the plan that was taking form in her mind. She peered over at her as she invited Henry to move to California. The look on Carolyn's face was accepting, even satisfied. In fact, Virginia thought as she continued to set out a few options for Henry, Carolyn looked as pleased as she always did when Virginia had come around to her way of thinking. Maybe, Virginia thought, just maybe that's what's happened.

"I was sorry to hear about Mrs. Barnes," Carolyn said to Virginia as she pulled out of their garage and drove down from Parnassus Heights towards the heart of San Francisco. "I suppose it really wasn't unexpected, given how much she drank, but even though Leticia said the prognosis was poor, I didn't expect her to go downhill so fast."

"Were you really sorry?" Virginia asked, sounding surprised. "I'd have thought that, given what we know about her..."

Carolyn shrugged as she braked so as to avoid hitting a pedestrian with a camera around his neck. "I had a soft spot for her, even if she did knock off Paul Runcible. Of course, we don't really know that she did it, though it certainly seems likely."

Virginia wondered aloud, "Don't you feel the least bit disappointed that she was never arrested?"

"For killing the man? No, not really. I didn't know him, so I had no personal investment in seeing his killer caught. What good would it have done? None whatsoever! Besides, sweetheart, cirrhosis is worse than most punishments the criminal justice system can deliver.

Virginia sniffed. "I wanted to see that woman punished, I admit it, for ruining her daughter's life, if for nothing else."

"Don't let Leticia hear you say that her life was ruined. She'd certainly give you a piece of her mind."

"She always does that, Carrie. I swear, you and she can have nice long phone chats, but after five minutes on the phone, she and I always end up fighting."

Carolyn shrugged. "You two must still have unresolved issues."

Virginia snorted. "No, we just disagree about almost everything."

"She loved her mother, you know, despite everything, and in her sick way, Lucille loved Leticia as well."

"Ugh! Don't mention Lucille Barnes and love in the same breath!" Virginia yawned. "I'm looking forward to seeing Leticia though. Who'd have thought that she'd tack a trip to San Francisco onto the end of her visit with Susan?"

Carolyn smiled and turned into the driveway of a small apartment complex. "It will be nice to see her again, but I was hoping she'd bring Susan along. Now that Susan is leaving for Washington, it's unlikely we'll ever meet her." She gave a quick sideways glance at Virginia. "Unless we go back to Grant's Hill, that is."

Virginia smiled back at her. "No reason to do that, is there?" She got out of the car and started up the small hill.

"I'll park and join you," Carolyn called to her through the window and turned into the long, narrow parking lot.

As Virginia got to the top of the hill she could see him coming, chugging around the side of the building on what he called his "ridiculous contraption," a cross between a motorized wheelchair and an electric scooter. She smiled, remembering how insistent he'd been that she'd never get him to ride on such an absurd vehicle. Now he loved it and pretended he'd always loved it. Henry saw her and sped up. "Where's Carolyn?" he demanded. He began wheeling in circles around her. "I need to ask her advice."

"She'll be along as soon as she parks. Is there something I can help you with?"

Henry smiled mischievously. "Yes, my packing. But I need advice from Carolyn, not you. Romantic advice, Virginia. You're too much like me and not enough like Ada to have a clue about what I should do next."

Virginia shook her head. "You're moving into her building, onto the same floor, for heaven's sake. How much more do you need to do right now? If I were you, Henry, I'd take it slowly."

Henry braked. "I don't have time to take it slowly. I'm getting on and my disease is progressing." He chuckled madly. "You know, that's how my first encounter with Ada started, don't you? I joked about my progressive disease and she took me seriously. Didn't even know I was a doctor until after she'd given me a little lecture on progressive diseases."

Virginia had heard the story over and over again. "Well, she was a pharmacist before her MS put her out of work."

"A pharmacist is not a physician, as you well know. Anyway, Carolyn owes me advice. If she hadn't pushed me into that support group, Ada and I would never have met."

Carolyn could tell that Henry was haranguing Virginia about something, so she slowed her walk to a leisurely amble. Today they'd help Henry finish packing. Tomorrow the movers would come and put most of his belongings into storage for a month, until his new apartment at the assisted living complex was ready. In the meantime, he'd stay with them, just as he had five years earlier when he'd made the move to the west coast. She smiled and waved as Virginia caught sight of her. Henry kicked his contraption into gear and started towards her. She was ready for him.